BODY BY WEIMAR

BODY BY WEIMAR

Athletes, Gender, and German Modernity

Erik N. Jensen

OXFORD
UNIVERSITY PRESS

OXFORD
UNIVERSITY PRESS

Oxford University Press is a department of the University of Oxford.
It furthers the University's objective of excellence in research, scholarship,
and education by publishing worldwide.

Oxford   New York
Auckland   Cape Town   Dar es Salaam   Hong Kong   Karachi
Kuala Lumpur   Madrid   Melbourne   Mexico City   Nairobi
New Delhi   Shanghai   Taipei   Toronto

With offices in
Argentina   Austria   Brazil   Chile   Czech Republic   France   Greece
Guatemala   Hungary   Italy   Japan   Poland   Portugal   Singapore
South Korea   Switzerland   Thailand   Turkey   Ukraine   Vietnam

Oxford is a registered trade mark of Oxford University Press
in the UK and certain other countries.

Published in the United States of America by
Oxford University Press
198 Madison Avenue, New York, NY 10016

Library of Congress Cataloging-in-Publication Data
Jensen, Erik Norman
Body by Weimar: athletes, gender, and German modernity / Erik N. Jensen.
   p.   cm.
Includes bibliographical references and index.
ISBN 978-0-19-539564-8 (hardcover); 978-0-19-931124-8 (paperback)
1. Sports—Social aspects—Germany—History—20th century.
2. Athletes—Germany—Social conditions—20th century.   3. Athletes—
Germany—Public opinion—20th century.   4. Sports—Sex differences—
Germany—20th century.   5. Body image—Germany—History—20th century.
6. Sex role—Germany—History—20th century.   I. Title.
GV611.J46 2010
306.4'83094309042—dc22   2009053318

Printed in the United States of America
on acid-free paper

I dedicate this book to the archives, libraries, academies, foundations, and public agencies that continue to support and encourage scholarly inquiry. In the face of increasing skepticism as to the value of the humanities, I am both amazed and grateful that such institutions continue to exist.

Acknowledgments

In his 1905 *Reflections on History*, Jakob Burkhardt warns of the risks attendant with studying a single subject for an extended length of time. "The man who walks one road of limited interest too long may fall by the wayside," he advises, before adding this truly cautionary tale: "Buckle's study of the Scottish divines of the seventeenth century cost him paralysis of the brain." My project has not cost me paralysis of the brain...yet. I have been walking this one road for a very long time, though, and it is only thanks to the advice, encouragement, timely pressure, and tremendous help of a great number of people that I have managed to near its end without having gone the way of Buckle.

First of all, a number of institutions and individuals granted financial, logistical, and intellectual support for my foray into the history of sports in the Weimar Republic, and without them I could not have even begun this project. Two Fulbright Fellowships, an initial award for the academic year 1997–98 and a renewal for 1998–99, enabled me to live, study, and conduct my initial primary research in Berlin. In 2006, the American Council on Germany supported me with a Richard M. Hunt Fellowship so that I could return to Berlin for some critical follow-up trips to the archives. During my initial stay in Berlin and on subsequent trips, the directors and staff of the *Sportmuseum* granted me unfettered access to their collection of sports magazines and other documents from the 1920s, and they assisted me throughout my searches with friendliness and professionalism. The *Staatsbibliothek* in Berlin proved an invaluable resource as well, and its staff managed to ferret out some real gems for me from the library's vast holdings. The *Zentralbibliothek der Sportwissenschaften der Deutschen Sporthochschule Köln* has proven remarkably speedy, efficient, and professional—just like a Weimar body—in providing me with several of the images that I used for this project, and I particularly wish to thank

Elvira Friedrich for her seemingly limitless courtesy and patience in the face of my various requests.

While in Berlin, Professor Gertrud Pfister generously shared with me her vast knowledge of the history of physical culture as well as the holdings of her personal library. Alfons Arenhövel, a one-man archive of Weimar German sports documents and memorabilia, very generously opened up his personal collection to me, offered cups of tea as I sifted through it, and made dozens of photocopies. Knud Kohr and Martin Krauß, who were in the midst of writing their own book on professional boxing in Germany at the time, kindly shared many of their findings with me. The film scholar Philipp Stiasny has kept me constantly updated on recent discoveries involving cinematic representations of sport during the Weimar era, particularly those involving women's boxing. Throughout all of my stays in Berlin, whether brief or extended, my friends Tine and Clemens Wischner have provided food, lodging, the latest news on that ever-changing city, and perfectly mixed Manhattans.

Because this book grows directly out of my PhD dissertation on the history of Weimar sports, I want to acknowledge a huge debt of gratitude to my advisor Rudy Koshar at the University of Wisconsin. He initially encouraged me to pursue this topic, offered steady support along the way, and gave me almost instantaneous feedback as I forged ahead in the writing process. I am proud to identify myself as one of his students. Jim Steakley, in Wisconsin's German Department, supported and guided me from my first days as a graduate student to the final submission of my dissertation. Moreover, he went through each chapter line by line, polishing the clunky translations and suggesting stylistic changes that made the end result much better. I have additionally benefited from the sage counsel and insightful comments of Laird Boswell, Suzanne Desan, and Myra Marx Ferree, all of whom carefully commented on the dissertation and advised me on how to go about transforming it into a book.

Since arriving at Miami University in 2004, I have had the great good fortune to be a member of the intellectually stimulating, professionally encouraging, and genuinely friendly history department here. I could not ask for better colleagues. In particular, Renée Baernstein has mentored me throughout the entire process of finding a publisher, polishing a manuscript, and securing a fighting chance at tenure. Along the way, Drew Cayton, Wietse de Boer, and Judith Zinsser have carefully critiqued multiple drafts, and Mary Kupiec Cayton has tactfully lit fires under me at critical points in the process of completing this manuscript. Almost the entire department read, commented on, and debated an early draft of my tennis chapter during an incredibly helpful departmental writing workshop. I thank all of them. Miami University itself has given me invaluable institutional support, too, from the always-friendly staff at the King Library and its Interlibrary Loan Department to the generous summer research funding that I received in 2005 to the Assigned Research leave in fall semester 2006, which afforded me the time off from teaching that I needed in order to return to Berlin for some necessary follow-up research.

At Oxford University Press, my editor Nancy Toff has been a terrific working partner in transforming the rough manuscript into this finished book, and Sonia Tycko has calmly and carefully answered all of my formatting questions and gently nudged me to meet critical deadlines. I am also grateful to the two anonymous readers for Oxford University Press, who read the entire manuscript with remarkable attention, care, and intelligence. The German Historical Institute in Washington, D.C., has also aided in the production of this book by subsidizing the procurement of publication rights to a number of the images that appear in these pages. I particularly wish to thank David Lazar for his help in this regard.

A number of friends actually agreed to slog through portions of this manuscript when it was in much worse shape than it is now, and they even seemed cheerful about doing so. Both Jonah Zelman and Ron Becker made it to the end of an earlier draft of the tennis chapter that was twice its current length, and they lived to tell about it. Ron gave me the idea of opening the chapter with a brief vignette of one male and one female player, and this suggestion helped me to rewrite all three chapters in a much more engaging style. Dave Becker wrote witty and astute marginalia on an earlier draft of the boxing chapter, and Mike Dahlie did the same for the track and field section. To the extent that this book appeals to a wider audience beyond historians, or even academics, I can thank them. I also thank Dave Ciarlo, my grad-school roommate and co-commiserator since the days of the preliminary examinations, for his friendship over the years. We paced each other as we wrote our dissertations and again as we finished our manuscripts, and we can at last see the light at the end of the tunnel.

Finally, and most importantly, I want to thank my mom and dad for their love. My dad always referred to the dissertation as my "paper," which somehow made it seem more manageable. And as I worked on turning it into a book, he never doubted that I would finish, even when I did. My mom always told me how proud she was of me, and I wish so much that she had lived to see the finished product. I dedicate it to her.

Contents

BODY BY WEIMAR

Nr. 34
28. Jahrgang

Berliner

Einzelpreis
des Heftes
25 Pfg.

Illuſtrirte Zeitung

Verlag Ullſtein & Co, Berlin SW 68

On the day of Friedrich Ebert's inauguration as president of the new German republic, the *Berliner Illustrirte Zeitung*'s cover photograph placed his physique, along with that of defense minister Gustav Noske, on full display for its readers to scrutinize. *Ullstein Bild/The Granger Collection, New York*

Introduction
Building a Better German

On August 21, 1919, Friedrich Ebert took the oath of office as president of the newly constituted Weimar Republic, Germany's first elected head of state and the leader of that country's postwar venture in democracy. To mark that auspicious day, the weekly *Berliner Illustrirte Zeitung* published a front-page photograph of Ebert and Defense Minister Gustav Noske in bathing trunks during a trip to the beach, their sagging bodies displayed matter-of-factly to a national audience. The photograph created a sensation. Harry Kessler reflected in his diary entry for that day that Ebert—pale, hairless, and insulated by a layer of fat—conjured a mental picture of the fictional, walruslike creature from Gerhart Hauptmann's 1896 play *The Sunken Bell*. That unfortunate cover image, Kessler added, had cast a pall over the day's inauguration ceremony.[1]

Few Germans had seen their leaders so physically exposed, and even fewer seemed to relish the sight. Within weeks, artists and political wags from across the spectrum began to repackage this image in satirical compositions, which they circulated as postcards, editorial cartoons, and photomontages.[2] The mere fact of physical exposure alone did not entirely account for the mixture of shock and derision. Instead, it was the condition of those exposed physiques. The magazine cover invited viewers to judge the bodies of Ebert and Noske, and those like Kessler did not particularly like what they saw. The droopy, frail appearance of these two men conjured visions of decline rather than prosperity. The *Berliner Illustrirte* thus confronted its readers with a vivid corporeal metaphor for the state of the postwar republic at its very inception. It was "soft," just like the men who governed it.

Across Germany, people of all political stripes, women as well as men, reacted to the nation's perceived softness by calling for a new physical body. Germany was by no means alone at this time in its concern for the fitness of its citizens. Dozens of countries across Europe, North America, and Asia focused attention on the physical body after 1918, seeking to rehabilitate war-weary populations and restore a measure of national health. Postwar Germans, however, demanded more of their somatic projects than mere rehabilitation. The nation's stunning military defeat prompted demands for a complete overhaul of society, culture, government, and even of the body itself. This drive for a new body inspired diverse and sweeping agendas in the postwar years, including the eugenics movement, state-sponsored welfare programs, nudism, vegetarian lifestyles, temperance campaigns, Bauhaus housing settlements, and every conceivable manner of sexual and familial reform.

One's physical self, according to the emerging ethos, had become a matter of concern to the nation as a whole, and that nation increasingly judged its citizens on the qualities and capacities of their bodies. No branch of postwar German body culture did more to heighten this level of self-scrutiny and to establish male and female ideals for the modern era than competitive sports. Already in April 1919, four months before the bare midriffs of Ebert and Noske graced newsstands across the country, the general-interest sports magazine *Illustrierter Sport* had proclaimed a dire need for the "healing of our national body," and it singled out competitive sportsmen and women as the figures who would lead the way.[3]

The emergence of competitive athletes as agents of a somatic revolution in the early 1920s would surely have surprised observers in Wilhelmine Germany. Sports like tennis, boxing, and track and field had only just arrived in the country during the closing decades of the nineteenth century, and most German elites had dismissed them as pointless, if not counterproductive. The kaiser himself clashed repeatedly with his son, the crown prince, over the latter's avid dedication to sports, which Wilhelm II saw as detrimental to his successor's physical and moral development.[4] Imperial Germany instead mandated rigid drills for its young men of military age, and it favored indigenous forms of communal, noncompetitive exercise, such as hiking or *Turnen*, for the rest of the male population. Women, thanks to the tight societal and sartorial constraints on their movement, had to make due with an even more limited palette of exercise options. As late as the First World War, most Germans openly scoffed at Anglo-American sporting sensibilities, and a German camp commandant once sentenced five British POWs to eight days of special detention for having initiated a spontaneous soccer game with a loaf of stale bread.[5]

By the 1920s, however, public attitudes toward competitive sports had begun to shift dramatically. Postwar Germans increasingly dismissed the Wilhelmine approach to physical exercise as having cultivated nothing but ponderously stocky men, artificially fragile women, and a terrible waste of human potential. If the bodies of Ebert and Noske did not inspire confidence, then neither did the stout frames of those prewar figures of national leadership, the kaiser and Field Marshal Hindenburg. The Weimar Republic needed an entirely new body, many Germans insisted, a modern body that would liberate the hitherto latent capacities in men and women alike.

Athletes provided the template for just such a body—sleek, stream-lined, and engineered for maximum performance. Not only did they project images of peak performance and efficiency, but they also exuded a distinctly modern spirit that captivated legions of postwar fans. Competitive athletes seemed unbound by the tethers of tradition and social convention. They concentrated single-mindedly on self-development, unleashed aggressive impulses, and took open pride in their own physical displays, all of which prewar Germany had discouraged, especially in women. To postwar Germans confronting an array of dizzying transformations, though, such characteristics now seemed both essential and liberating, and the media reinforced this sense by promoting sportsmen and women as models of modernity who would show an uncertain public how best to adapt to their changing world.

Athletes served this purpose so ably because they had star power in Weimar Germany, and, at least among their legions of fans, they had influence. Kurt Doerry, a former track and field athlete himself and editor of Germany's leading sports journal, *Sport im Bild*, referred to athletes in 1926 as the indisputable role models for the postwar generation.[6] "Sports are the thing now," he insisted, "and their victorious champions are the new heroes of our era, the heroes to which our youth look and whom they emulate with every fiber of their being." Athletes, for one thing, proved that the body still mattered. Even as mechanization steadily devalued muscle power in the economy, that same muscle power had greater value than ever down on the running track or tennis court. In addition, compet-itive sports contributed to an impression of the Weimar Republic as a postwar meritocracy, even when that promise remained unfulfilled in so many areas. Because sports competitions produced champions of both sexes and from all social backgrounds, though, it offered ostensible proof of the new republic's claims to emphasize talent and hard work over gender, ethnicity, and birthright.

Whether a scrappy boxer from working-class Berlin or a single young woman with a punishing serve and volley, those previously marginalized members of German society were now—thanks to competitive sports—landing on the front pages of daily newspapers, gaining entrée into the salons of high society, and translating athletic achievements into financial profit. Sports enabled young people to play a far greater role in the cultural life of the postwar years than they had prior to the war, and sports afforded the best among them an unprecedented degree of upward mobility. Through competitive sports, to borrow the famous phrase of the historian Peter Gay, outsiders might become insiders.[7]

In this and other ways, athletes exhibited a "self-made" quality akin to that which Henry Ford championed in his autobiography, whose German translation had become a runaway bestseller in the mid-1920s. As the cultural commentator Siegfried Kracauer remarked in 1927, "The faster a man runs, the more world-renowned his legs are. No limb is too insignifi-cant, even the fists or the tennis racket can make one's name."[8] Unlike the distant specter of an American industrial titan like Ford, an athlete's success felt attainable to young Germans, since most knew at least a local club champion, if not a regional or national one. The fact that athletes presented multiple ways in which to remake themselves, moreover—from muscular self-development to commercial self-marketing—made the quality of "self-madeness" seem within reach of a relatively broad public.

Health and fitness movements proliferated in Weimar Germany, and most of these promoted some idea of remaking one's body and oneself. Most of these movements, however, viewed the body primarily as a site of resistance to modernity or, at the very least, as a refuge from modern life's most harrying features.[9] Nudism, hiking, and gymnastics, to name just three strands of postwar physical culture, clearly positioned themselves as antidotes to the hectic, atomized, and high-pressured environment that so many cultural critics had come to associate with postwar society. These movements promised to liberate a "natural" body that the modern world had ostensibly placed under siege, and they certainly contributed to the discourse that surrounded health and the body in Weimar Germany.

They only tell half the story, though. Competitive sports presented a set of counter images and discourses on physical fitness and the body that, I argue, exerted an even more powerful influence on Weimar Germany. In stark contrast to the adherents of those other movements, male and female athletes eagerly embraced modernity in all of its rationalized, individualistic, commercial, competitive, time-oriented, and achievement-focused excess. Instead of fleeing "the tyranny of the clock," athletes pursued it. Sportswomen and men thrived in a world of measurement and record keeping, a world that continually pushed them to boost the output of their hearts, lungs, and quadriceps, just as it drove businesses to expand their production and employees to increase their productivity. Athletes, in other words, embodied precisely the elements of modern life that so many other branches of German physical culture rejected.

Athletes cultivated an explicitly "modern" body that featured a number of elements, foremost among them a lean, streamlined efficiency. Competitors in different disciplines modeled variations on this theme, of course, with a marathon runner developing a more aerodynamic profile than a heavyweight boxer, but the proscription against surplus flesh applied to all. Extra weight slowed the body down, and the modern body—like the society in which it operated—was all about speed. As the 1925 film *Tennis* breathlessly declared, "A fraction of a second that gets us to the ball more quickly often spells victory."[10] As a metaphor for what it took to get ahead in the Weimar Republic, that statement had meaning even for those women and men who may never have picked up a racket in their lives.

In order to attain that lean speed, the athlete subjected him- or herself to monitoring and outside direction, another component of the modern body. The boxer illustrated the heightened level of scrutiny better than any other athlete. His trainers regularly measured every contour of the fighter's body, from his neck down to his calves, all of which the press carefully reported. Laboring bodies throughout postwar German society came under scientific scrutiny, as physiologists and industrial engineers charted workers' heights, weights, and physical motions in an effort to boost performance.[11] In this, competitive sports led the way. The athlete increasingly authorized a cadre of experts, including coaches, managers, and physiologists, to determine diet, training program, and competition schedule. In much the same way that the rationalized assembly line shifted authority from the worker to the engineer, modern competitive sports subsumed more and more of an athlete's autonomy to scientific calculations and outside discipline.

This close monitoring of the athlete's body pointed to yet another component of the modern self: a competitive drive that manifested itself everywhere in postwar society from the playing field to the workplace to the bedroom. Hans Fallada's Weimar novel *Little Man, What Now?* illustrated this drive in the character of a men's clothing salesman, who, "sportsman that he is, is able to impart even to his present occupation a touch of real competition. Best record to date: one hundred and nine coats an hour, scrupulously brushed."[12] Such competitive spirit made the athlete a perpetual work in progress. Sportswomen and men restlessly experimented with new techniques, strategies, and regimens, all in the hope of cutting a fraction of a second from their previous times or driving a backhand return just out of the reach of their opponents. Such investments paid rich dividends, as Heinz Landmann forcefully argued in his 1928 essay "Hero Cult," in which the successful athlete basked in a public adoration "meant entirely for him, entirely for his character as it reveals itself in his peak performance, [and] above all in competition."[13]

As a corollary to this competitive mind-set, the modern athlete projected an individualism that stood in sharp counterpoint to the communal approach of other strands of German physical culture, like nudism and gymnastics. Competitive sports created hierarchies of ability and celebrated personal achievement. The tennis player, boxer, and javelin thrower pursued self-interest in the very act of vying for a championship title. Even in team sports, especially at the elite level, competitors sought to elevate their own profiles, since future opportunities depended on it. Like successful entrepreneurs and politicians, athletes were in the business of self-promotion, of beating the competition, of coming out ahead every time. Unlike most captains of industry and elected officials, though, athletes made this trait appear positively heroic.

Carla Verständig praised competitive sports in 1927 specifically because they instilled in women the element of assertive individualism.[14] Women had subsumed their own interests to those of others for far too long, she insisted, and noncompetitive practices like rhythmic gymnastics simply perpetuated this subservience by fostering "those characteristics that put up no resistance to the domination of the man." This explained why men kept pushing such exercise programs on women in the first place. Competitive sports, on the other hand, promoted everything that rhythmic gymnastics did not—strategic thinking, physical strength, aggressiveness, and personal ambition. Sports, Verständig concluded, emancipated. Walter Schönbrunn praised athletic self-interest on similar grounds in 1930, when he referred to athletes as the true "republican men."[15] Their individualism reflected the values of the new German democracy far better than the obedient conformity of communal gymnastics, which Schönbrunn dismissed as suited only to "the subjects of a monarchical government." Both Schönbrunn and Verständig agreed that athletes represented the modern ideal.

Not every German lived up to this ideal, of course. In fact, few did, and most probably did not even try. Although sports associations attracted growing memberships over the course of the Weimar Republic, their numbers always remained relatively modest as a percentage of the country's overall population.[16] Athletes nevertheless presented bodies and sensibilities that most Germans recognized as quintessentially modern and ideally suited to postwar society. The fact that so few Germans measured up to this ideal type might in itself point to another facet of Weimar modernity. Historian Reinhard Koselleck describes the ever-widening gap between the "space of experience" and the "horizon of expectation" as a hallmark of the modern age.[17] Athletes represented the sorts of individuals that many Germans wished to become and perhaps fantasized about one day becoming, even if those same Germans showed no signs of beginning that self-transformation. Moreover, athletes represented the types of citizens that many officials and commentators would have liked to see populate, and repopulate, the postwar nation. This discursive elevation of sportsmen and women to the status of national role models signaled a shift in social values and one that the athletes themselves had helped to initiate.

Historians of the Weimar Republic, unfortunately, have not demonstrated the same awareness of how significantly athletes shaped German society that commentators at the time did. Recent histories of Weimar Germany accord sports only a passing mention, if that, and studies of the New Woman have largely sidelined athletes from their analyses, even though a confident athleticism stood at the center of the New Woman's self-presentation. As the historian Michael Ott concluded in a 2002 review, the study of sports in Germany "has fallen between the cracks of the competing historiographical paradigms."[18] This is too bad, Michael Poliakoff has insisted, since the study of sports is "not a trivial pursuit...it tells a lot about the character, values, and priorities of a society."[19] Unfortunately, the scholarship on sports itself has also missed a number of opportunities to interweave athletic developments with broader historical transformations, and it often gives little sense of sports as an important agent of social and cultural change.[20] This field shows some promising signs of moving in a more integrative direction, but with a few notable exceptions, works that connect sports to society, and society to sports, remain a relatively rare breed.[21]

Studies of gender could benefit from a more holistic, integrative lens as well. Although the growing body of scholarship on men and masculinity in recent years has provided a welcome addition to our understanding of how societies construct gender, it has simply replicated the established practice of addressing men and women in isolation from one another. This practice runs even deeper in the field of sports history because nearly all of the athletic disciplines enforce a clear division between men's competitions and women's.[22] Societies, however, define men's and women's roles in a close and mutually constitutive relationship to one another, especially in the realm of sports. Rather than study male and female ideals in isolation from one another, therefore, scholars need to study them together, in order to get a sense of how gender operates in a society at any given time.

Male and female athletes shaped an explicitly modern sensibility in the postwar decades that extended far beyond the nation's playing fields and even its borders. Sports had become a cosmopolitan enterprise by the 1920s—nowhere more so than in places like Hamburg, Cologne, and Berlin—and this book illuminates both developments of specific significance to Germany and those that had a global resonance. Weimar Germany makes an ideal case study for the intersection of sports, gender, and "modernity" because its citizens, cultural commentators, and popular media devoted so much attention to each.

German fans idolized sports champions in the 1920s, lavishing almost as much attention on foreign athletes as they did on their homegrown stars. The Finnish runner Paavo Nurmi, the American boxer Jack Dempsey, and the French tennis sensation Suzanne Lenglen all enjoyed cult status in the Weimar Republic. They, too, provided templates for the modern man and woman, just as their German counterparts Otto Peltzer, Max Schmeling, and Cilly Aussem did. Because of that, all of these champions receive attention in this book. The existence of such transnational attachments on the part of everyday German fans also reminds us that cosmopolitan tastes and a fascination with the mildly exotic, a much-vaunted characteristic of Berlin's cultural avant-garde, extended to wider circles of postwar society.

Not only did much of the German public follow the comings and goings of sports stars in the 1920s, but the nation's media also devoted a tremendous amount of time to analyzing and debating the impact of these figures. Between 1920 and 1933, forty new general sports magazines appeared on newsstands across the country, along with eighty-one discipline-specific journals.[23] The general sports magazines, in particular, enjoyed wide popularity after 1918 by following a formula that blended straightforward reportage with society gossip, fashion, personality profiles, and plenty of photographs and illustrations. These magazines treated athletes as cultural figures and sports as a medium of popular expression. They, along with the daily sports pages, transformed athletes into household names, celebrities whose lifestyles outside the arena attracted as much attention as their accomplishments within it. Feature films, newsreels, pulp fiction, popular music, the visual arts, and a booming business in collectible trading cards further helped to make athletes some of the most recognizable people in postwar society.

German officials, commentators, and the media devoted at least as much attention to the ongoing transformations in postwar men's and women's roles, rights, and expectations. The war had killed approximately two million German men and left another four million with physical or psychological injuries that placed them under the temporary or long-term care of others, usually women.[24] In addition to the dependent positions of many individual men after 1918, the humiliating circumstances of the military defeat, as well as the subsequent economic crises and political instability, called into question male authority in general. Women, meanwhile, seemed only to have expanded upon the increasingly public and independent roles that they had played in German society during the war. In political terms, women gained the right to vote in 1919, and Article 109 of the Weimar Constitution specifically guaranteed them equal rights under the law. In economic terms, a small—but visible and growing—number of women began to establish themselves in the male-dominated, white-collar professions, as lawyers, physicians, journalists, and professors.

Partly because the lost war and the establishment of a new political system had so noticeably disrupted the gender order in postwar Germany, the Weimar media arguably concentrated greater attention on the issue of changing male and female roles than any other contemporary issue. They kept gender at the center of the nation's postwar conversation. In a 1929 essay that typified this sense of the earth shifting beneath one's feet, the novelist Robert Musil proclaimed that postwar Germany had given rise not just to a new woman, but also to "a new man, a new child, and a new society."[25] The natures of these new men and women occupied everyone from the mass-circulation *Uhu* to the lesbian journal *Garçonne*, the latter of which mused in 1931 on the distribution of various masculine and feminine traits, "we find all of these tendencies in both sexes."[26] This incomparably diverse and self-scrutinizing media landscape both reflected and fueled vigorous debates over how best to negotiate the changing expectations for men and women in a modern age.

This book concentrates on three sports in particular: tennis, boxing, and track and field. All three share the distinction of being individual, competitive sports that entered Germany in the last third of the nineteenth century. Each one, however, occupied a different class position, articulated a slightly different vision of modernity, and posed its own peculiar challenges to established gender roles. In chapter one, I examine the upper-class sport of tennis, which fully embraced women's participation during the 1920s and quickly established itself as the most visible female athletic pursuit of the time. Not only did tennis provide numerous examples of strong, talented women for the popular press, it presented images of sexually assertive and financially independent ones, too. If *Sex and the City* had taken place in

Weimar Germany, its producers might well have set it on a tennis court. Male players, meanwhile, cultivated a dandyish and openly sexual persona that ran entirely counter to the prewar Prussian emphasis on male stoicism and *Selbstbeherrschung* (self-control). In doing so, they posed a potentially alluring alternative to the physical and psychological toughness that anchored German masculinity and that so many of the era's businessmen, military veterans, and competitive athletes in other sports placed on robust display.

If tennis occupied an upper-class, female-oriented position in the constellation of interwar sports, then boxing had clearly seized the blue-collar, male-oriented one. Nevertheless, women engaged in various forms of boxing, too. Images of female boxers circulated widely in the 1920s, through advertising, films, songs, and popular literature, and these depictions presented a model of female strength and aggression. Even the bawdy, burlesque versions of female boxing that appeared on variety stages around the country carried a subversive message. By empowering women to behave "outrageously"—throwing punches, strutting around, demanding to be watched—these shows and their performers brazenly defied the standards of demure femininity. As female fighters were claiming active roles during the 1920s, male fighters were steadily, and consciously, assuming more passive ones. These men marketed their own impressive physiques to an adoring public for commercial gain, and they did so by employing strategies, and poses, that had characterized the peddling of erotic images of women for decades.

I turn my attention in chapter three to track and field, which represented a contentious middle ground in terms of class and gender. As male and female athletes adopted progressively more rationalized, all-consuming training regimes over the course of the 1920s, commentators and medical officials argued heatedly over the social and physical repercussions of the resulting bodies and personalities. Track and field advocates, meanwhile, sought to deflect these concerns by consciously positioning their sport as a foundational activity in the postwar project of national recreation. For male athletes, this meant presenting themselves as the embodiments of national strength, whose athletic training compensated for the military training that the Versailles Treaty so tightly restricted. Female athletes, meanwhile, played an entirely different role in the national project—as mothers of the future generation and, according to proponents of women's sports, as the standards of ideal motherhood itself. By the mid-1920s, track and field had sparked a firestorm over how sports, and greater female independence in general, would affect Germany's demographic future.

In researching this project, I have cast my net widely. I began by examining the journals of Germany's national associations of tennis, boxing, and track and field from 1919 to the early 1930s, since these publications often set the tone for the larger media coverage of competitive athletes. Federation journals were not mere public-relations mouthpieces for their respective sports; they frequently criticized their own champions, and their editorials reveal sharply contrasting visions of the future of the respective sports. I then looked at the general-interest sports magazines and at the sports pages of major daily newspapers that proliferated in the 1920s, particularly *Sport im Bild*, *Illustrierter Sport*, *Sport und Sonne*, and sports sections of the *Berliner Tageblatt* and *B.Z. am Mittag*, all of which mixed competition coverage with social analysis, cultural commentary, and celebrity profiles. These magazines and newspapers attracted a generally middle-class readership, but since sports fandom transcended every social divide in Germany, the magazines' readerships certainly did as well. The journal *Der Querschnitt*, although founded by an art dealer and clearly catering to the literary set, bore a certain affinity to those other sports magazines. It unabashedly celebrated boxing, as its subtitle "magazine for art, literature, and boxing" plainly showed; it published numerous photographs of leading athletes; and it even dedicated an entire issue to sports in 1932.

Finally, because sports influenced so many aspects of popular culture, I also delved into the general daily press; a number of popular, satirical, and sexual reform magazines; films; cabaret; the visual and plastic arts; advertising; music; and penny fiction. One source from this category, in particular, surfaces often in my narrative and deserves a brief introduction. The acerbic and reactionary writer Adolf Stein, who wrote under the pseudonym "Rumpelstilzchen," published weekly feuilletons in the newspaper *Tägliche Rundschau*, a part of Alfred Hugenberg's media empire and an important vehicle for Hugenberg's right-wing political agitation throughout the Weimar Republic. Rumpelstilzchen's feuilletons described the Berlin cultural and political scene with a decided focus on the offbeat characters and prominent personalities behind the news. As such, they provide valuable descriptions of many of the metropolis's happenings, such as the performances of female boxers and strongwomen, that otherwise escaped newspaper coverage. Rumpelstilzchen's writings also provide a valuable insight into an important current of hostility toward the broader social, cultural, and political transformations taking place in the Weimar Republic. That hostility, not surprisingly, targeted many of the changes that competitive athletes had helped to initiate, and Rumpelstilzchen's own analysis contributed to the debates surrounding postwar sportswomen and men.

This landscape of federation journals, sports weeklies, and the wider mass culture painted a picture of sports champions that sometimes stabilized, frequently challenged, and ultimately reshaped the notion of a modern woman and a modern man in Weimar Germany. The impressive physical feats of male and female athletes raised the level of expectations placed on the human body and opened up new routes to social and financial success. The steady improvement that an athlete showed in the size of his biceps or in the speed of her 100-meter dash, moreover, offered seemingly irrefutable proof that a rationalized training program and intense competition promoted progress. To the wider German public that followed this progress in the sports press while simultaneously grappling with competition and rationalization in their own lives, athletes offered lessons. By virtue of their own demonstrable success, athletes provided compelling models for negotiating the shifting sands of modern German society.

Many components of the modern self that competitive athletes ushered in over the course of the Weimar Republic outlived that system's demise. When the National Socialists came to power in 1933, they promoted women's sports with the same explicit goal of producing healthy mothers that officials and commentators had first articulated in the 1920s. The Nazi regime's celebration of the chiseled body—so infamously displayed in the monumental sculptures of Arno Breker and Josef Thorak and in the films of Leni Riefenstahl—advanced an ideal that already enjoyed widespread admiration in the Weimar Republic. When Germans again turned to sports as a form of national rehabilitation after the Second World War, East Germany, in particular, picked up on a number of impulses from the Weimar period. That regime's invincibility in so many women's events echoed the earlier triumphs of the Weimar Republic's female athletes in international competition. Part of East Germany's success unquestionably derived from performance-enhancing drugs, but it also stemmed from a dedication to training female athletes—one of the few countries to do so in the 1960s and 1970s. That too, was a legacy of the Weimar Republic.

Scholars have rightly celebrated the vibrant cinema, arts, and cabaret scene of Weimar Germany, but they have not paid enough attention to the fact that this period saw some of its most radical and lasting contributions in the arena of physical culture. As the French writer André Gide told his friend Harry Kessler in 1932, "Germany is thirty years ahead of France," an assertion that Gide based on Germany's innovativeness in four specific areas: "Architecture, public health, sports, and outlook [*Weltanschauung*]."[27] While architects created visions of the modern built environment, athletes energetically shaped a vision of the modern body, as sleek and efficient as any Bauhaus design and one that remains with us as an ideal to this day. The rapid pace of social and cultural change disoriented and overwhelmed many Germans after the First World War. Athletes—some of the most visibly successful adapters to this new environment—demonstrated to Germans how a new woman and a new man should function in the modern world.

Among those whom the media felt could most benefit from this demonstration were the government's own leaders—the very group whose sagging bodies had exposed the need for a new body back in 1919. The feuilletonist Joseph Roth argued in 1921, only half facetiously, that Germany's foreign minister needed athletic training more than he needed French. Because modern diplomacy required such incredible stamina, Roth wrote, the nation's top overseas representative "has to be steeled, as if for a boxing match."[28] Seven years later, Berlin's leading daily newspaper, *B.Z. am Mittag*, complained that Germany's eleven-man cabinet included only one genuine "sportsman," an embarrassingly poor ratio in comparison to that of Britain and America.[29] In 1932, after more than a dozen years in which German society and culture had celebrated sportsmen and women, the writer Sindbad took stock of the athlete's most exemplary traits. The athlete possessed not only a "sure sense of indomitable power," but also the ability to "brush aside in the simplest manner all complications that might interfere with his own personal happiness." After cataloging these laudatory traits, Sindbad asked simply, "Why are we still hesitating to have sportspeople govern us?"[30] The era of the athlete as societal standard had indeed arrived.

1

Disorder on the Court
Soft Men, Hard Women, and Steamy Tennis

When Hans Moldenhauer, the third-ranked men's player in Germany from 1925 to 1927, died tragically in an automobile accident on December 29, 1929, the nation's tennis establishment paid tribute to his famously artistic form. Walter Bing praised Moldenhauer's "inimitably graceful shots" in the pages of *Tennis und Golf*, the journal of Germany's tennis federation, and he lauded Moldenhauer's absolute refusal "in any situation, to violate...tennis elegance."[1] In fact, Bing presented him as a paragon of personal comportment, "the blonde player on whom one never noticed a hair out of place, or anything outwardly or inwardly unharmonious." Bing readily conceded Moldenhauer's lack of competitiveness, noting that he invariably opted for an aesthetic shot over a winning one and that he unhesitatingly sacrificed sure-fire victories in the interest of presenting "beautiful tennis." Again and again, Bing returned to Moldenhauer's stylish contributions to the game, saluting him as "a prototype of the elegant, nonchalant player" and "a gentleman in the best sense of the word." Moldenhauer was the embodiment of an appealingly debonair manhood, the quintessential gentleman of tennis.

Meanwhile, on the women's side, Cilly Aussem, a rising star in 1929 who would go on to reign as the German national champion at the end of the Weimar Republic, drew praise for an entirely different quality: her no-holds-barred determination to defeat her opponents. As early as 1927, the tennis analyst Bill Fuchs described Aussem in the *German Tennis Handbook* as one to watch because she played "the new, aggressive, net-attacking style of women's tennis" that was revolutionizing the entire sport.[2] He admired her competitive zeal and disciplined focus. At one point, Fuchs even suggested that Aussem soften her approach just a bit, if only to show female fans "how to embody competitive tennis charmingly" and how to play "manly, modern tennis attractively"—a "manly, modern tennis" that, ironically, he found distinctly lacking in the men's game itself.

Moldenhauer and Aussem reflected the divergent paths that men's and women's tennis had taken by the end of the Weimar Republic and that initiated changes in postwar German society as a whole. The commentator Paul Liebmann argued as early as 1926 that two types of tennis existed in Germany. He referred to the first type as "a purely social game" and "a pleasant amusement in the outdoors, an opportunity for flirting and catching some fresh air."[3] Liebmann reserved his highest regard for the second type, however, "the sport of tennis," which he described as "marked by goal-oriented practice and the holding of competitions, [and] which has shown a remarkable development in Germany." By the late 1920s, the spirit of "pleasant amusement" attached itself ever more exclusively to the men's game. The second type, meanwhile, the competition-driven "sport of tennis," seemed increasingly to animate the women's game, providing the era's most visible forum for women's newfound and formidable physical talents.

Precisely because of its status as one of the most socially acceptable female sports in the 1920s, tennis regularly attracted some of the best sportswomen that Germany produced. Physicians and educators had been promoting the sport for women since the late nineteenth century, largely because of the belief that tennis demanded little strenuous effort. That belief prompted the casual remark by the popular illustrated journal *Sport im Bild* in 1921 that anyone could play tennis, even "the weak sex."[4] While other sports in the 1920s conceived of themselves as male pursuits first and foremost, tennis rapidly established itself as a hallmark of the emerging "New Woman." Already by 1919, the sports magazine *Illustrierter Sport* made the claim that in no other branch of the sporting world "is the female sex so powerfully represented" as in tennis.[5]

Up through the early years of the Weimar Republic, tennis as a whole appeared as a "soft" game rather than a "hard" sport. As *Sport im Bild* had so dismissively pointed out, "anyone" could play it—provided, of course, that "anyone" had the financial means to join a club and buy the equipment. This posed a formidable barrier to entry, and tennis had a decidedly aristocratic reputation throughout the interwar period, which only further reinforced its soft image. Less a competitive physical contest, tennis seemed designed principally as a pretext for flirtation and afternoon socializing, a game that conjured visions of genteel luxury and fashionable posing. The Germans even coined the term *Kaffeetennis*, literally "coffee tennis," to designate a relaxing hour of courtside coffee and pastries that typically followed a quick set of tennis, or simply supplanted it altogether.

This genteel aura surrounded the men's game throughout the Weimar period. Female players, on the other hand, reinvented themselves as quintessentially modern athletes over the course of the 1920s, possessed of peak conditioning, sharp concentration, and competitive instincts. By the end of the decade, therefore, both male and female players appeared as gender renegades. The men offered German fans an updated version of the nineteenth-century dandy. The stylish, pleasure-seeking tennis player liberated himself from the imperatives that governed other Weimar-era sportsmen, whose discipline, rigor, and monastic avoidance of women formed the dominant image of the modern male athlete. Tennis players offered an alternative to that hegemonic masculine ideal.[6] According to the image that emerged in the sports press, the man of tennis trained lightly and, while on the court, demonstrated a far greater concern for artistic flair than strategic purpose. This dedication to aesthetics defied the increasingly businesslike and *sachlich* (coolly matter-of-fact) society that they saw around them. Furthermore, whereas boxers enshrined sexual abstinence at the center of their training ethos, tennis players considered partnerships with women—both athletic and otherwise—to be the very raison d'être of the game.

Female players, by contrast, increasingly projected images of strength, aggression, and self-sufficiency over the course of the 1920s. The media made these women's muscles into fetish objects, a task made easier by the much more revealing tennis outfits of the postwar period. Female tennis players had, in the span of the decade, remade their bodies from soft to hard, and when the German public sought a potent symbol of just how "new" the New Woman was, it looked no farther than the tennis court. The players, in turn, translated this iconic status into careers in business and sports journalism, providing examples of the "self-made woman" to a society that could scarcely conceive such a creature just a decade earlier.

By the early 1930s, the images that most Germans ascribed to tennis depended largely on the sex that played it. The male players insisted that men could lead stylish, indulgent, and even decadent lives, too. At the same time, female players boldly challenged the preexisting assumptions that had constrained women's horizons of possibility. While male players pursued pleasure, it was the female players who got down to business. These women presented athleticism, ambition, and a pursuit of the spotlight as acceptable options for postwar middle-class women, instead of lives confined to home and hearth.

Lascivious Leisure: Tennis as Lifestyle

Through the first decades of the twentieth century, German tennis remained the preserve of the elite, requiring natty attire, social connections, and a fat expense account. When British expatriates introduced Germans to tennis in the second half of the nineteenth century, the game drew its first adherents primarily in the wealthy, Anglophile trading ports of northern Germany and chic spa retreats like Wiesbaden, Baden-Baden, and Bad Homburg.[7] As a result, German tennis carried an exclusive, English-inflected cachet, and the German Tennis Association adopted the British model of propagating the game through elite clubs when it organized itself in 1902.[8]

The game's foreign provenance, along with its well-heeled tournament circuit around Europe, lent tennis a worldly, sophisticated air from the very start.[9] This distinguished tennis from the relative insularity, chauvinism, and cross-class appeal of Germany's homegrown physical culture. In particular, the *Turnen* (gymnastics) movement, which consisted largely of synchronized routines, had conceived of itself since the early nineteenth century as a unifying force for pan-German expression, more or less open to Germans of all backgrounds. Its gatherings invariably featured elaborate displays of patriotic pageantry and choreographed movements performed in unison. As its advocates constantly reminded the public in the 1920s, *Turnen* had sprouted from German soil. This made it, in their eyes, a more authentically Teutonic form of exercise than such competitive sports as tennis, which had originated abroad and had the further disadvantage of demanding a much greater investment.

The elite cosmopolitanism of tennis players awoke suspicion in these self-proclaimed patriots. German players competed abroad more often than at home, for instance, and they selected foreign doubles partners as a matter of course. Furthermore, they chose the south of France as their preferred destination for winter training, an especially galling affront to ardent German nationalists, who nursed strongly anti-Gallic animosities after the humiliations of the Versailles Treaty and the French occupation of the Rhineland. On top of all that, German tennis players displayed a flagrant tendency to speak English, an unpleasant reminder of that other wartime foe. Tennis officials themselves recognized this as a liability and tried to popularize German coinages as a means of tethering the game more firmly to a patriotic foundation, but neologisms like "*Schläger*," "*Spielfeld*," and "*Aufschlag*," never quite replaced "racket," "court," and "service" in the conversations of players and fans.[10] Such a self-consciously worldly outlook distanced tennis from other branches of German physical culture, and the Anglicized affectations further softened the male player's image in comparison to that of other sportsmen in the 1920s.

Added to this vaguely subversive openness, tennis players in Weimar Germany also exuded privilege, beginning with the noble surnames that guaranteed them admission to clubs in the first place.[11] The association of tennis with nobility seemed most jarringly pronounced during the economic turmoil of 1918–24, when few but the bluest bloods had the money and leisure to take up the game. One 1919 article in *Illustrierter Sport*, in attempting to make the case that tennis players, too, had suffered during the war, instead underscored their clear class advantages. In it, the author bemoaned the "increasingly severe shortage of household and kitchen help" that had prevented many avid players from spending time on the courts, apparently because these men now had to draw their own bathwater. Immediately after decrying the lack of servants that had purportedly so burdened these players, however, the author then protested, without irony, against "the mistaken inclination of the broad masses...to view tennis exclusively as a luxury sport."[12] A commentator in *Sport im Bild* made a similarly tone-deaf appeal for sympathy by complaining that the economic crisis had made it exceedingly difficult for many players to conduct their customary winter training on the Mediterranean.[13]

Early coverage of tennis tournaments after the war consistently generated the impression of players as blithely oblivious to the economic realities that affected the rest of German society. F. W. Esser, for instance, prefaced his report on a 1920 tournament by meticulously setting the luxurious scene: "I am sitting at tea in a wicker chair in front of the charming Swinemünde Tennis Clubhouse on the shady garden terrace; in the corners, geranium petals in bloom allow their red light to play off the decorative shrubbery that has been trimmed in the shape of a pyramid."[14] At a time when skyrocketing inflation forced city dwellers to scavenge for food, and many had long since resorted to a barter economy, reports like this presented an incendiary contrast: a life composed entirely of topiary and ease. One December 1926 cover of a sports weekly illustrated a similarly ingrained elitism. It featured a drawing of Germany's top male athletes in various sports, each holding his Christmas wish list. The purse-lipped caricature of Dr. Heinz Landmann, the 1924 German men's tennis champion, had scribbled just one thing on his: "Protect tennis from the plebs!!"[15] While female players began to shed their veneer of exclusivity by the mid-1920s, as the Weimar Republic in general became more socially fluid, male players never quite did. In fact, as the magazine cover suggests, some even dedicated themselves to preventing just such a possibility.

The patina of gentility situated men's tennis within a matrix of class and gender, since gentility conveyed not only wealth and good breeding, but also a certain delicacy. The perceived idleness of male players reinforced a centuries-old sense of the nobility as "unproductive labor."[16] Because this noble idleness had historically suggested both a reluctance to do hard work and an incapacity for it, it struck many as not only economically useless but as slightly feminine, to boot. George Mosse has argued that the German bourgeoisie redefined masculine ideals in the nineteenth and early twentieth centuries in explicit opposition to the perceived softness of the nobility, a perception that historian Marcus Funck, in turn, has connected to the Eulenburg scandal of 1907, in which several aristocratic officers in the kaiser's inner circle stood accused of engaging in homosexual activity.[17] In the wake of this scandal, German men further distanced themselves from aristocratic-officer sensibilities, which had oriented around the refinements of court society, and they instead sought a "hardened masculinity." The image of male tennis players as pampered nobility, therefore, whose entire milieu triggered associations with the courtier society that the Eulenburg scandal had discredited, contributed to the coding of men's tennis as a "game" for dandies rather than a "sport" for athletes and, therefore, not a means of forging the hard man.

DER WUNSCHZETTEL UNSERER AKTIVEN

Hamburg, 24. Dezember 1926   3. Jahrgang Nr. 13   20 Pfg.

A purse-lipped Dr. Heinz Landmann, standing closest to the Christmas tree, holds his personal holiday wish list, on which he has written simply, "Protect tennis from the plebs!!" *Deutsche Nationalbibliothek Leipzig*

At the same time, though, the media appealingly linked tennis with the good life. It presented tennis as a lifestyle untouched by financial worries or the Pietist dictates of hard work and self-control. The daily newspaper *B.Z. am Mittag* presented an idyllic fantasy for its readers by describing a "typical" tennis vacation in 1928: "You don't run and sweat yourself to death. Instead, you laze about, relax, bask in the sun, listen to jazz, play a little bit of tennis, and spend the rest of the day playing bridge."[18] The term *Kaffeetennis* captured precisely this ideal, with the emphasis decidedly on the *après*-match refreshments and conviviality. Richard Goerring, writing in a 1928 issue of *Tennis und Golf*, worried that film representations of tennis had reinforced this reputation.[19] How, he wondered, should the average cinemagoer know "that drinking coffee under a veranda decorated with flowers [and wearing] white pants...are not the only pleasurable things about tennis," given that most depictions of tennis in the movies consisted almost entirely of those images alone.

Goerring proposed a public-relations campaign modeled on those of the soccer and boxing establishments, both of which sought middle-class respectability after the war. Whereas soccer and boxing wanted to soften their images, though, Goerring wanted to harden that of tennis, to make people see its merit "as a competitive sport." Goerring overlooked the possibility in his editorial, however, that tennis might very well have benefited from precisely that soft image. The notion of leisure masquerading as physical activity would have appealed to a certain number of men, who worked hard enough in the rest of their lives and nourished dreams of idle afternoons. The notion of sipping coffee under a flower-bedecked trellis might not have seemed half bad, especially if one could do so under the socially acceptable cover of engaging in a sport. The game's worldly sensibility simply heightened the fantasy. When the journalist Sebastian Haffner fondly recalled the tennis club of his youth in the 1920s as "a piece of the globe in the middle of Berlin," he spoke for those German men who appreciated the game's sophistication and whiff of worldliness.[20]

Marcus Funck, in tracing the bourgeoisie's rejection of aristocratic masculinity in the early twentieth century, argues that Germans increasingly associated the nobility with sexual decadence as well as effeteness, yet another quality that set it apart from the virtuous bourgeoisie.[21] Tennis's own noble pedigree, therefore, reinforced its equally pervasive reputation for licentiousness in the Weimar period, which drew heavily on precisely the stereotype of the aristocratic rake.[22] Unlike other physical activities, tennis placed a premium on debonair self-presentation, and it afforded seemingly endless opportunities for flirtation, since men and women regularly played against one another in official matches of mixed doubles and informal games of singles. In the German popular imagination, tennis served just as much as a catalyst for romance as it did as a form of physical exercise. The co-founder of the German Lawn Tennis Federation, Robert Hessen, himself openly adopted this view, and players before the war jokingly referred to tennis clubs as "engagement kennels."[23]

By the 1920s, though, the tennis court resembled a singles bar more than a marriage market, given that players had seemingly abandoned the goal of forming long-term, monogamous relationships. German society had grown more permissive during the Weimar Republic, and male and female players alike expressed a degree of sexual frankness unheard of before the war. Hans Egon Holthusen referred to the prevailing sensibility in Weimar Germany as one of "aesthetic-erotic revolt," and tennis players were right there at the barricades.[24] The Weimar-era neologism "Tennisflirt" described the coy glances and double-entendres that volleyed back and forth across the net with greater intensity than the ball itself.

Burghard von Reznicek prefaced a 1932 book on tennis with the question, "Isn't [the tale of] a tennis flirtation on the aquamarine shore of Lake Geneva...oftentimes worth listening to just as much as an academic rehashing of a heated battle on a clay court?"[25] In a book that purported to focus on tennis as a serious sport, Reznicek instead framed it from the outset as a collection of indiscretions about the rich and amorous. When Paula von Reznicek—a tennis player herself as well as a society fixture and Burghard's ex-wife—asked rhetorically of her female readers in 1928, "Haven't you sometimes felt the sweet excitements of tender eroticism during or after athletic exertion?" she presented tennis as a form of foreplay.[26] She again made her case for the inherently sexual nature of the game in another 1928 piece, when she wrote that French champion René Lacoste "eroticizes the balls and us like no other," which might also have explained the growing legions of women in the stands at tennis tournaments.[27]

Germans associated male athleticism with a strict self-denial—of food, alcohol, sex, and pleasure—that physically and psychologically hardened the sportsman for competition. The manner in which tennis openly celebrated male sexuality clearly distinguished its adherents from those in other sports. It also marked a deviation from the larger masculine ideal of *Selbstbeherrschung* (self-control) that had formed the bedrock of male behavior throughout the nineteenth century.[28] The historian Petr Roubal argues, with respect to *Turnen*, that "chastity was considered a major virtue to be expected of a young gymnast" and that "sexual intercourse with women [was] regarded as a moral weakness and a danger to the gymnast's body."[29] Men's sports in the nineteenth and twentieth centuries commonly saw their mission as one of redirecting men's passions away from sex. Soccer took off in Victorian Britain, for instance, in part because pedagogues like Edward Thring promoted its beneficial release of pent-up energy that would have otherwise found an outlet in masturbation.[30]

Tennis, on the other hand, gave every appearance of stoking libidinal impulses rather than rechanneling them. Otto Froitzheim, Germany's top tennis player throughout the 1910s and early 1920s, contributed to this impression with his legendary dalliances, including with the film star Pola Negri. Leni Riefenstahl wrote of Froitzheim that "he was much gossiped about, not only because of his prowess at tennis, but also because of his innumerable love affairs," and she admitted to having lost her virginity to Froitzheim in his Berlin apartment.[31] An early 1933 cartoon in *Tennis und Golf* drew on precisely this image of the lascivious male player that Froitzheim had helped to create. Under the heading, "The illustrated tennis report," the cartoon depicted an older man flirting openly with a younger woman sitting at a courtside table. The caption's tennis-related double-entendre—"He scrapped the singles in order to concentrate himself better on the mixed doubles"—once again suggested that, when it came to the men's game, competition took a back seat to amorous pursuit.[32] Not by accident did Vicki Baum choose to make Pix, the dapper casanova in her 1930 stage comedy *Pariser Platz 13*, both a clothing model and a tennis player.[33]

Tennis's somewhat louche reputation extended to same-sex relationships as well. In a 1920 issue of the gay magazine *Die Freundschaft*, for example, one man's personals ad for a tennis partner hinted at the expectation of something more: "Tennis partner...sought by 18-year-old beginner (1m, 62cm tall). Prefer a man up to 30 years old, masculine character, idealist, preferably English-speaking, foreigner O.K., possible study of the language together."[34] In the 1928 tennis novel *Das weiße Spiel* (The White Game), several players argued heatedly over which classical god best represented the game of tennis: upon Günther's suggestion that

Der illustrierte Tennisbericht:

„. . . . Er strich das Einzel, um sich besser auf das Mixed
konzentrieren zu können."

The male player as a flirt: This "illustrated tennis report" playfully explains that the man has "scrapped the singles in order to concentrate himself better on the mixed doubles." *Universitätsbibliothek der Humboldt-Universität zu Berlin*

"the god of tennis is Eros," the debate ended in unanimous agreement, and conversation promptly switched to the latest gossip.[35]

The sexualized image of the male tennis player placed him in the position of the pursued as well as in that of the pursuer, and this combination of active and passive roles further fashioned his articulation of a softened masculinity. In the 1930 short story "The Partner," Bert becomes the object of his female tennis partner's seductive designs.[36] Not only does she literally call the shots on the tennis court—deciding when her partner has hit a ball deep—but she also directs their impending liaison in an internal monologue that forms the narration of the story. Bert, she decides, would "have to be trained" as her lover and coaxed along under her world-wise tutelage. Given Bert's apparent willingness to let her make the first move, the woman confidently resolves to "take the offensive" and expose the "amusing impracticality [that] lurks behind my practical tennis partner."

A June 1926 article, dispensing advice at the onset of the summer vacation season, saw male players as especially vulnerable to the assertive advances of women and cautioned them, "If a lady comes on to you, that is no reason to become intimate with her on the tennis court."[37] Indeed, once the tennis ace Johanne has set her sights on Günther in *Das weiße Spiel*, she makes all the moves. Johanne picks him up on their first date, drives him to her favorite restaurant, and even orders his entrée.[38] A 1929 cartoon poked fun at this image of male passivity when it showed a man serving a tennis ball, under which the caption stated, "The entire world marvels at Meier's bomb-like serve in tennis." "Only his wife knows...," the caption continued, "...where he got it from," and the second panel revealed that Meier had built up his serving strength by beating dust out of the household rugs at his wife's behest—the male player as hen-pecked husband.[39] The 1925 short story "Mixed Doubles," meanwhile, featured a husband looking helplessly on as his wife flirted openly with her partner on the other side of the net.[40] In countless stories like these, the tennis court redrew the rules by which men and women interacted. The strength of this reputation motivated a number of men to insist that their fiancées quit their tennis clubs within a few days of consenting to marriage. "Whoever became engaged and still wanted to play the 'flirt's game,'" notes historian Christiane Eisenberg, "would have demonstrated a questionable commitment to marital fidelity."[41]

The overt passions on display in the world of tennis marked a fascinating exception to the sociologist Norbert Elias's argument that the rapid expansion of male and female sports after the First World War was predicated upon the imposition of tight self-control over one's basic drives.[42] Tennis not only imposed no such restrictions on personal conduct, it seemed to encourage just the opposite. The game appeared singularly ill suited, therefore, to fostering the "companionate marriages" that many Weimar commentators in the last half of the 1920s advocated as the foundation of healthy, stable families. This marital model, based on a 1927 book by Americans Ben Lindsey and Wainwright Evans, emphasized the importance of mutual respect and compatibility between husbands and wives, and it counseled newlyweds to postpone childbirth for several years until their marital partnership had revealed itself as stable and had established a healthy degree of mutual trust and understanding.[43]

This notion of marital teamwork evoked clear parallels to the camaraderie of the playing field, and a number of observers saw sports as the perfect way to create the sense of shared purpose in men and women that laid the foundations of a companionate marriage. Erik Schwabach's 1928 book, *The Revolutionizing of the Woman*, for instance, advocated co-ed sports as a way to teach women "that there can be a community with men that lies clearly beyond a lustful sexuality."[44] Despite tennis's incomparable ability to bring the two sexes together in a common athletic pursuit, though, tennis nurtured exactly that atmosphere of "lustful sexuality" that the advocates of companionate marriage warned so strongly against. Instead of promoting friendship and cooperation, a role that many marriage reformers had clearly envisioned for sports, tennis seemed only to encourage infidelity and jealousy.

Whereas conservative critics denounced tennis for putatively undermining monogamy, however, many men and women were undoubtedly drawn to the game in part by that very promise. Tennis beckoned those who sought an attractive and liberating alternative to home life and a thrilling release from moral restraint. Even in the relatively emancipated atmosphere of Weimar Germany, the expectations of forming a family still circumscribed many middle-class men's and women's lives. Tennis held the allure of a lifestyle as much as a sport, and that lifestyle bespoke style, ease, and wild oats.

Men at Play: The "Soft" Masculinity of German Tennis

Weimar Germany's media tended to portray the men's game as an overly refined and aesthetic product of the leisured nobility rather than of the dynamic, new professional classes, as more "soft" than "hard." Tennis had established itself as the vanguard of female physical culture because, unlike other sports, it welcomed women and naturally attracted the most athletically ambitious among them. Men's tennis, on the other hand, faced competition from a whole array of athletic pursuits that promised far greater athletic status, like boxing, soccer, hockey, cycling, and track and field. As a result, the most driven and trailblazing men of athletic talent, who might otherwise have reinvented and modernized the game, typically gravitated to other sports instead.

If boxers and sprinters possessed more instantly recognizable masculine cachet in the 1920s, however, the tennis player shaped an alternative masculinity that melded certain aspects of postwar society, such as overt sexuality, with some of the sensibilities of the nineteenth-century upper class. The player's elegance and worldly charm, for instance, revived some of the values of Wilhelmine Germany's male nobility, minus that class's military tradition of discipline and reflexive national service.

The careful way in which players carried and presented their bodies—their bearing, movement, and posture—contributed to their postwar aura of elegance. The historian Heikki Lempa has traced a "sensitive" masculinity that emerged in nineteenth-century Germany in opposition to the hegemonic militarized, *Turnen*-influenced variant.[45] This sensitive masculinity expressed itself, among other ways, through one's carriage while ballroom dancing, promenading along boulevards, and participating in other forms of genteel leisure. The male tennis player of the 1920s clearly incorporated elements of this earlier sensitive masculinity into his own self-presentation, particularly the emphasis on the aesthetics of movement.

Germany's male players also had a marked air of the *Lebenskünstler*, roughly "an artist of living well," about them, a bon vivant who understood his principal vocation as the pursuit of the good life. These men never took the game too seriously and certainly did not dedicate themselves to it in the way that other athletes did to their sports. As a character in *Das weiße Spiel* put it, her club's best player was a man "devoted to luxury and everything easy in life."[46] A sprinter looked red-faced and sweaty after a race, and a boxer's postfight visage often resembled raw meat. The male tennis player, on the other hand—whether competing in a championship match or strolling on the veranda—took pride in appearing dapper, polished, and unhurried in all circumstances. *Sport im Bild*'s breezy preview of men's tennis fashions in 1926, for example, declared, "The gentlemen want to make life effortless for themselves during tennis," a goal apparently best achieved "in white linen knickerbockers with white wool socks and shoes."[47] Articles like this one overturned the dominant image of a highly focused, achievement-oriented sportsman and offered, instead, a softer ideal for those postwar men who wanted nothing more than to "make life effortless for themselves."

The tennis player's entire sun-tanned, relaxed body advertised the fact of his living well. As the historian Bernd Wedemeyer-Kolwe has argued, Germans in the Weimar Republic looked for physical markers of leisure, especially a tan, which symbolized "spare time, freedom, liberal attitudes, and health, as well as a modern lifestyle."[48] It also indicated a willingness and ability to spend money on oneself, as commentators regularly observed. One 1926 article, ostensibly about the recent results of a men's tennis tournament, took time to comment admiringly on the dashing way that top-ranked Heinrich Kleinschroth "wore his camels' hair coat."[49] Such depictions of the nattily attired male player acknowledged that men, too, now took part in a world of consumption that had, since the nineteenth century, oriented itself primarily toward women.[50]

Tennis also enshrined "fair play" and scrupulous politeness in its competitive ethos more overtly than some other sports, which further shaped the player's alternative masculinity. So new was the concept of "fair play" in German physical culture, in fact, that the language itself lacked a suitable equivalent for the term when tennis began gaining popularity. The Germans borrowed the English word itself, therefore, as well as the ethos. Even then, as George Mosse has argued, fair play "was not an important ingredient in the makeup of the usual German hero."[51] The central value of fair play, a value that itself points to the tendency in men's tennis to eschew aggressive competitiveness, marked yet another distinguishing feature of the male player's athletic persona.

Tennis und Golf frequently complimented the German men's team on its sportsmanlike conduct in international competition, even going so far as to rhetorically transform athletic defeats into moral victories. In one such case in 1928, that magazine took direct issue with a Berlin newspaper that had described the German loss to Britain as a "tragedy." A "game between good comrades" can never be a tragedy, *Tennis und Golf* corrected. "Sports is only a tragedy when someone wins or loses in an unsporting manner. Our players have won well and, what is more difficult, lost well."[52] The following year, the journal put forward Hans Moldenhauer as a "role model for Germany's tennis youth," not because of his winning performances on the court, but because of "his fairness toward his opponent and the umpire."[53] *Sport und Sonne*, not surprisingly, chose two male tennis players to illustrate the value of fair play to its readers in 1928. The caption beneath a full-page photograph of two boys shaking hands at the net instructed readers, in a clearly pedagogical tone, that "the defeated player congratulates the winner."[54]

Some commentators, however, did not share this view that male players offered worthy role models, good sportsmanship notwithstanding. A 1927 article in the yearbook of the German Tennis Association typified the ambivalence of even some of the sport's own officials. In it, Bill Fuchs evaluated Germany's highest-ranked men, including Philipp Buß, whom he described as "overly thin" and "not a powerful, vigorous player." After underscoring Buß's unimposing physical presence and lack of force, Fuchs did pay compliment to his finesse, noting that "he possesses, along with Froitzheim and H. Kleinschroth, the finest hand among all the German players."[55] Fuchs counterposed this passage on Buß with an admiring, almost fawning description of another male player, Walther Dessart, about whom he wrote:

> Equipped with a truly athletic body, opposed to all manner of cheap showmanship and posing, Walther Dessart is the downright paragon of a competitive athlete of the first order. It seems an accident to us that Dessart achieved the status of . . . tennis champion. If he had gone in for rugby or crew, he would have made no less of a name for himself.[56]

By opposing Dessart's "truly athletic body" to Buß's "overly thin" one, Fuchs dismissed exactly the type of build most common among tennis players and revealed his concern over the apparent absence of "truly athletic" players among the men. Fuchs seemed genuinely astonished that Dessart had even chosen tennis in the first place, given that his skills and build would have found a better athletic outlet in a sport like rugby or rowing. The entire tone of the passage held men's tennis in lower regard than other sports and suggested that it did not deserve a sportsman of Dessart's caliber. And that passage sprang from the pen of one of the game's ostensible advocates.

Finally, Fuchs's attention to the "fine hand" of Buß underscored the sense that male players favored elegance over power as the principal goal of the game. By praising Dessart's lack of "posing" as an exception in men's tennis, Fuchs took a swipe at the perceived tendency of male players to favor style over substance. A 1928 article, lyrically titled "On the Beauty and Rhythm of Tennis Strokes," encouraged precisely such a stylish approach when it declared that the aesthetics of play count more than winning points: "It may be that the beautiful player is not always the best player, but it should remain a goal just the same to carry out the task as perfectly as possible."[57] This admonition to inject some artistry into every point echoed that of the tennis coach in Kasimir Edschmid's *Sport um Gagaly*, who advised his young charge to hit the ball "much more melodiously, but just as hard," and who appreciated another player for hitting with the precision of a man and the gracefulness of a woman.[58] Similarly, in *Das weiße Spiel*, a male character gladly sacrificed two games in the second set of a tournament match "solely in order to make a few very artistic shots."[59]

Some fans, at least, appreciated such gestures. The tennis player William Schomburgh argued in 1928 that those who watched matches did so "in order to watch the sport that they love in its perfection," which they did not define as synonymous with "winning."[60] For these aficionados, the performance counted far more than the outcome. A 1929 article in *Sport im Bild* rhapsodized, "Even the hardest stroke of the master has a certain lightness and yielding elasticity; the fastest volleys still trace the most wonderful curves."[61] The reporter tempered each description of strength in this passage with a countervailing one that stressed the shot's beauty. In this, he simply followed the pattern of the German sports press as a whole, which generally saw tennis as "more than most of the other games, an aesthetic-rhythmic sport," to use the words of another article that appeared the following year.[62]

This attention to the choreography of a match and its attendant invitation to subjective appreciation situated tennis alongside dancing or figure skating, rather than with a combative sport like boxing or an intensely competitive one like track and field, in which only the objective assessment of the clock or the measuring tape mattered. That same 1929 *Sport im Bild* article consistently reminded its readers to concentrate on the artistry more than the outcome: "the lesser hero [is] not always the one who loses. To return the cunningly thought-out and most maliciously placed balls of your partner with a spirited, elegant stroke—that is what true sport is all about." Those players who insisted on winning points with their "maliciously" tactical shots, the author implied with a sneer, coarsened the game and should not provoke a response in kind.

Hans Moldenhauer exemplified the propensity of Germany's male players, even the top-ranked elite, to invert the Bauhaus mantra by putting form ahead of function. The daily *Berliner Tageblatt*, reporting on a German tournament against a visiting Australian team, noted with a sigh that Moldenhauer "unfortunately usually places more value on cutting a good figure than on ambitious competition."[63] Conrad Weiss, too, offered a mildly critical assessment of Moldenhauer's tennis when he eulogized the player in a 1930 issue of *Tennis und Golf*. Weiss called attention to Moldenhauer's passivity—"He gladly allowed himself to be led"—and pointed out that teammates instinctively protected him, "instead of forcing him to become self-sufficient, hard, and a fighter."[64] Here, Weiss seemed to implicate the very culture of German men's tennis in shaping Moldenhauer's noticeably soft approach to the game. Weiss also reinforced the pampered aura of the men's game by noting that Moldenhauer's father, a wealthy manufacturer, had indulged the player as a teenager and even procured some scarce tennis balls via neutral Sweden for the young Moldenhauer during World War I, a period of extreme rubber scarcity.

Two weeks after Weiss published his obituary of the deceased Moldenhauer, Hermann Rau volunteered his opinion of the player's legacy. Rau, too, commented on "a certain delicacy, a certain loveable weakness" that had radiated from the dapper Moldenhauer, who "was, by nature, no fighting machine [and] also no tactician." Still, Rau viewed Moldenhauer as a positive representative of German tennis and suggested that his many fans saw him as a standard of good form: "His groomed appearance, his elegant, athletic figure, his fabulously fluid, harmonious bodily movement, and his shots of unmatched stylistic beauty were enough to make him a darling of the public."[65] Rau understood all too well that Moldenhauer's athletic ethos deviated from that of other sportsmen, but he nevertheless held up Moldenhauer as an ideal in his own right—debonair and sensitive, an attractive alternative to an aggressive masculinity. In fact, one police lieutenant used tennis to instill just such a refined sensibility in his men, including gentleness and proper manners. After explaining that the sports of track and field and boxing helped his men to develop speed, agility, and sharp reflexes, the lieutenant then justified his decision to introduce tennis on the grounds that "no other active game [is] so suitable for teaching the participants social grace and good form."[66]

Many commentators genuinely appreciated the unique qualities that tennis brought to the world of men's sports, even if they expressed it in a very backhanded way. The sports editor and former track star Kurt Doerry saw the game's principal value in its accessibility to men of all ages. Doerry wrote in 1929 that older men "can only, in rare cases, go in for competitive sports that demand the exertion of the body's entire strength," but, he added cheerily, "the man over forty can still take part in tennis and golf tournaments."[67] Tennis, according to Doerry's taxonomy, counted as a leisure activity rather than a sport, but also one that placed fewer strains on the body and promised many more years of enjoyment than did the more intense forms of activity.

A satirical piece in *Der Querschnitt* similarly downplayed the game's athleticism when its author wrote that she would rather date a tennis player than an actual athlete. She described her ideal as "mid-sized men who don't engage in anything more vigorous than bridge and weekend tennis, [and who can accompany us] to performances [and] amuse us, while the heroes are sent to bed by their trainers."[68] Even though this author considered the tennis player to be the antithesis of a strapping sportsman, she still wanted to date him. Only the player, after all, could devote himself to women and life's other pleasures. Osbert Sitwell offered an even franker assessment of tennis when he dismissed it as "a harmless, dumb, quite pleasant game."[69] He did, however, appreciate its players' good looks, writing that "competitive athletes look remarkably ugly, except, perhaps, those in lawn tennis." Unlike the *Querschnitt* piece, Sitwell's article did, at least, implicitly include male players in the category "competitive athletes."

According to the physiologist Fritz Giese, tennis appealed especially to men of refined, artistic tastes. "The Beau-Brummel-type, the dandy, the model of an Oscar-Wilde-esque orgy of colors...will seek an aesthetic sport that agrees with his milieu," he observed, including "the horse, the stylish car, and international golf or tennis."[70] Giese reinforced the player's fashion-plate status by tracing his lineage back to nineteenth-century Ur-dandy Beau Brummel. His invocation of both Oscar Wilde and an "orgy of colors," moreover, suggested decadent self-indulgence and a sensibility that bordered on the flamboyant. Giese intended this as a swipe at tennis, but, like so many representations of the game in the Weimar period, the passage offered an alternative reading to its audience as well. The lifestyle that Giese presented of snappy clothes, international travel, "stylish cars," and equestrianism could well have appealed to a generation of men shaped by the memory of wartime and inflationary deprivations.

In Volkmar Iro's 1926 depiction, the tennis player does not have a care in the world. He "comes to tennis at mid-morning somewhat blasé and absent-minded," Iro wrote. Not only that, he's a little bit of beefcake, too: "a slender, smooth-shaven, cute young man...looking like an Apollo statue and as tan as a Malay."[71] The male player, as rendered by Iro, may not have exuded strength and virility, but he looked good, slept late, and had plenty of luck with women. Because of this reputation for relaxed good looks, the image of the male player became a staple of advertisements. Elida skin lotion praised the "wonderful tan of his skin" and pledged that "everyone could look like him," if they used that product.[72] Odol mouthwash insisted that its oral rinse contributed every bit as much to a man's outward appeal as his carefully chosen tennis outfit.[73] Ads like these targeted a consumer-oriented male demographic in postwar Germany that admired the player's lifestyle and wished to emulate it.

If much of the wider Weimar media depicted tennis players as enviable, refined and attractive, sports reporters often presented them as stubbornly outdated. In sports reportage, male players came across as quaint vestiges of an earlier era, a far cry from the rationalized training and aggressive tactics of other countries' players—and of the German women. *Sport im Bild* published an interview in 1928 with an Australian player who described Otto Froitzheim as a graduate of the "old, solid school" of tennis, not the modern methods of the French, American, and Australian players.[74] The captain did compliment Froitzheim's mastery of the fundamentals, but he essentially dismissed Germany's best male player as fusty and behind the times.

In men's tennis, as in so many areas of business, culture, and social organization, America represented the future. The *Berliner Tageblatt* prefaced its 1931 assessment of the state of the German men's game by first contrasting it with more rigorous sports. "Track and field athletes compete [and] boxers fight," but one "plays" tennis, the article gently needled.[75] The Americans were changing all of that, however: "When America's Davis Cup team trains, they play tennis only on the side. They sprint, they box, they swim, because modern tennis demands conditioning." Like the earlier 1927 yearbook entry by Bill Fuchs, this article saw far greater value in other sports. In fact, it reserved the greatest respect for those tennis players who played the least amount of tennis and instead spent their time on more rigorous activities. The Americans' cross training worked wonders, the article concluded. "The broad-shouldered boys from over there" had remade tennis "from a game into a competitive sport." They changed it from soft to hard. Hans Kreitner exclaimed that "the American is the manliest tennis player in the world," a quality that he attributed to the American players' willingness to appropriate combative sports, like boxing.[76] The Americans, Kreitner observed, "want to decimate at any cost. Their will focuses on the 'knockout.'"

Gottfried von Cramm, ranked Germany's second-best player in 1932, embodied German tennis's genteel, cosmopolitan ideal at the end of the Weimar Republic, complete with an aristocratic background and famously Anglophile tastes. Cramm began his tennis ascent in 1928, when he joined the Berlin club Rot-Weiß and achieved his breakthrough in the Davis Cup competition of 1932. Cramm's entire public image centered around his manners, lineage, and appearance. If the nickname "Big Bill Tilden" conjured the American player's towering athletic frame and forceful strokes, Cramm's nicknames—"The Tennis Baron" and "The Gentleman from Wimbledon"—highlighted his well-bred sophistication. His immaculately groomed good looks generated attention, too, and female members of Rot-Weiß reportedly whispered that "even if he only plays half as good as he looks, he'll soon be world champion."[77] Cramm's careful attention to appearance never flagged, either. The newspaper editor George Salmony recalled that Cramm "never took advantage of the permissible freedom of movement afforded by more comfortable shorts, and, from Melbourne to Helsinki, remained instead true to his blossomy white, perfectly tailored long pants."[78] Like so many of his compatriots, Cramm gladly sacrificed freedom of movement to the interests of propriety and good taste.

Cramm, not surprisingly, played a conservative style of tennis, too. In a preview of a 1931 tournament against a visiting South African team, the *Berliner Tageblatt* wrote: "Against the modern technique of [his South African opponent]...von Cramm will have a tough go of it."[79] As it turns out, Cramm did win on the following day, but his reputation as an old-fashioned player had clearly influenced the prognosis. A photograph that accompanied a report of his victory nicely portrayed the comfortable world of German men's tennis that Cramm exemplified. In it, he and his opponent, each smartly dressed in their club jackets, relaxed at a well-appointed table. The caption said simply, "After a long, hard match, peace-fully [enjoying] coffee and cake...on the terrace of Rot-Weiß."[80] *Kaffeetennis* was indeed alive and well at the courtsides of Germany's men's matches, in persnickety defiance of the modernizing trends in the rest of the tennis world, and the rest of German society, too.

If Cramm represented the stubborn center of men's tennis at the end of the Weimar Republic, then Daniel Prenn, Germany's top-ranked player in 1932, represented its up-and-coming fringe. His success suggested that modern methods were beginning to make inroads into this staid subcul-ture, before the National Socialists cut his career short in 1933. Whereas Cramm sported a noble surname and the proper pedigree, Prenn came from a middle-class family, and his Jewish parents had only just immi-grated to Berlin from St. Petersburg after the October Revolution in 1917.[81] Prenn pursued a career as a civil engineer alongside the one in tennis, and his own rise from an immigrant Jewish background to the #1 ranking offered a perfect example of the upward mobility that sports had begun to foster. In this, he mirrored a larger trend in Weimar Germany of prewar outsiders, such as Jews, becoming postwar insiders in business, politics, and culture.[82] Prenn had climbed as high as the #6 ranking in the world by 1932, the first time that a German man had cracked the tennis top ten since before the war.

Despite his success, however, Prenn continued to be seen, and to see himself, as something of an outsider in German tennis. For one thing, he possessed precisely the fast-paced, hard-hitting, and aggressive style that officials found so lacking in his countrymen. Prenn attributed this approach to his own outsider status as a Jew living in Germany. In a 1929 interview with a German-Jewish newspaper, Prenn directly ascribed his aggressive style to his personal background, saying that a thousand years of oppression had made Jews particularly combative.[83] Prenn's acceptance within the tradition-bound world of men's tennis remained always tenta-tive, and he confronted anti-Semitism throughout his career. After a 1929

Davis Cup match victory in Berlin, Count von der Schulenberg, a member of the national tennis association, derisively remarked, "the Jew would win, of course."[84] The fact that a German-Jewish newspaper carefully described how Prenn had gradually warmed even "radical right-wing spectators" to his side during a 1932 match indicated the level of visceral hostility that he sometimes had to overcome, even as the country's best player.[85]

In 1932, *Tennis und Golf* explicitly contrasted the styles of Prenn and Cramm. Prenn, it wrote, "is the fighter even in training, the brains, the man who will achieve success by force of his will." The article continued, "It's quite different with von Cramm...during training before a big match, he tries more to establish his 'touch,' his feel for the ball. Here, too, he is the 'spit and image' of Moldenhauer."[86] Like Hans Moldenhauer, Gottfried von Cramm embodied the artistry and light-hearted ease that formed such central components of the male player's public persona. Even in the mid-1930s, at the peak of his career, Cramm's biographer describes one of his most breathtakingly close matches as an "elegant...duel inside the white lines, not the epitome of a competitive game determined by power and strength."[87] Cramm nevertheless enjoyed very high regard among German fans, and his articulation of a genteel masculinity appealed to a segment of the male public that perhaps felt otherwise alienated from the overly aggressive culture of men's sports.[88]

Thoroughly Modern Cilly: The Hard-Hitting Players of Women's Tennis

In the earliest years of the Weimar Republic, the media accorded female players even less respect as athletes than they did the male players. German sports fans just after the war generally regarded women's tennis, if at all, as simply a less taxing version of the men's game. F. W. Esser's press dispatch from the 1920 tennis tournament at Swinemünde expressed a typical disregard for women's matches. Only at the conclusion did he acknowledge that women had competed at all, and then only to dismiss this oversight as inconsequential: "Pardon me, my dear lady! But my skill at observation is not soft or kind enough to...properly and charmingly capture the tennis game of the graceful women."[89] Esser had relegated the women's matches to a dainty sideshow, and his protestation that he lacked the requisite "soft" observational skills implied that the very act of reporting on these competitions would have impugned his credibility as a sports journalist and, apparently, his self-respect as a man.

Apparently unbeknownst to Esser, however, a dramatic transformation in women's tennis had already begun, as Suzanne Lenglen, the legendary French champion who attracted a devoted German following, launched a revolution in the game. At a time when observers routinely commented on the easy-going approach of male players, they were already marveling at Lenglen's dynamism. George Salmony recalled Lenglen's ability "to catch the most impossible ball and to catapult it back with the force of a middle-gauge howitzer."[90] If the male player evoked a dandy, his female counterpart had metamorphosed into a piece of military hardware. Lenglen provided the public with a symbol of women's growing public prominence by achieving a level of athletic success unmatched by anyone else in tennis, of either sex. Hermann Rau asserted in 1929, "the most outstanding tennis figure of all time is a woman, Suzanne Lenglen."[91]

The women's sports magazine *Damen-Sport und Damen-Turnen* had already cast Lenglen as a symbol of gender equality—perhaps even superiority—in 1919, when it touted the fact that she had defeated male opponents as a fifteen-year-old and "proved that women had and could have the same thrilling style in lawn tennis as the men."[92] Heinrich Mann echoed this sentiment seven years later, when he wrote that Lenglen "can do what men do, too, only better."[93] Her unassailable dominance in the first decade after the war pushed other women in the sport to adopt the same aggressive athleticism, and she inspired a generation of future champions, including Helen Wills and Cilly Aussem.

Lenglen's status as a trailblazer extended to her 1926 decision to turn professional, which overturned both social norms and tennis traditions. Georg Lehmann framed her decision as a praiseworthy example of upward mobility, which, in contrast to one popular narrative of female advancement in Weimar Germany, Lenglen had achieved without a strategic marriage.[94] Her life story, which mirrored Weimar morality tales of men reinventing themselves through the new opportunities of the postwar era, demonstrated that a woman with initiative could make it big, too. Lenglen herself presented the switch to professional tennis as an act of self-emancipation in a 1928 interview with *Sport und Sonne*: "Why shouldn't I think about my future now that everyone for whom I've played has made their fortune? Will the people who have become rich through me one day take up my [cause] when I need them?"[95] Women would have easily identified with Lenglen's frustration over her dependence on men and her vulnerability to abandonment, and many of them no doubt sympathized with her interpretation of this personal decision as a blow for equality.

The press celebrated Lenglen as a one-woman industry. According to *Die Leibesübungen*'s 1927 article "What professional athletes can earn," Lenglen had taken in almost a million dollars during just one four-month tour that year. The article then admiringly listed her other business enterprises and projects, including public appearance fees, film roles, and royalties for articles that she published in newspapers and fashion magazines.[96] The sports commentator Willy Meisl compared Lenglen's matches to professional fights, the epitome of a hype-driven moneymaking sports event.[97] Emil Lenk, meanwhile, commented tartly on Lenglen's media omnipresence: "There is no newspaper [or] magazine from which Suzanne's picture does not leap out at us."[98] Here, Lenglen implicitly offended against the female domestic ideal. She not only did things that no woman had previously done, but she did so in an unrelentingly public manner.

Thanks to Lenglen, female tennis champions enjoyed the inside track to tastemaker status, capable of influencing fashion and behavior in realms far beyond the tennis court. Lenglen's ubiquitous headband, for instance, launched a fashion craze in Germany. Because competitive tennis demanded unhindered physical movement, female players wore revealing outfits that pushed women's fashions in general toward shorter hemlines and greater functionality. Players appropriated from the men, too, by donning ties, knickers, and visors, and, in so doing, they both propagated and legitimized the gender-bending styles that had emerged in the subcultures of the German metropolis, where tuxedos and monocles served as unofficial uniforms in lesbian nightclubs.[99]

The highly visible, popular, and attractive female players of the postwar period drew thousands of new female adherents to the sport as well, especially after Germany stabilized its currency in November 1923 and the economy began to improve.[100] The five "golden years" of relative prosperity in the Weimar Republic enabled tennis to make inroads with new social classes, since the cost of equipment and club memberships now fell within the budgets of more and more white-collar workers.[101] The women's game, in particular, appeared to welcome the middle classes and reward their talents. Women's tennis in Germany began to diverge from men's. While the latter continued to spit-shine its debonair image, female players energetically modernized their sport by incorporating rigorous training, encouraging tactical innovation, and pursuing commercial opportunities.

F. W. Esser may have blithely ignored women's tennis in his 1920 dispatch from Swinemünde, but journalists by the end of the decade paid more attention to the female players than they did to the males. "When a female sports champion shows up on the street, she is surrounded and followed as if leading a parade," Emil Lenk wrote in 1928. "She braves a crossfire of cameras, appears on posters, in all the movie theaters and display windows, and in journals and magazines."[102] Burghard von Reznicek noticed the transformation of the "modern female tennis player into a completely different figure than her predecessors." She was a star, with all of its benefits and payoffs: "If Wills, the world champion, wants to go into film, or if she, a well-known illustrator, arranges an exhibition of her sketches, the type-setting machines of the world press will bow down [before her] with greedy joy."[103] Increasingly aware of their formidable market appeal, female champions translated tennis success into both cultural influence and financial gain.

The media attention itself opened up a number of professional opportunities for players, who regularly contributed commentaries to magazines and pioneered sports reportage as a profession for women in the Weimar Republic. The articles and books by champions like Ilse Friedleben, Nelly Neppach, and Paula von Reznicek, in turn, shaped the bold public face of women's tennis in the 1920s. Women also governed their own clubs, which provided a sanctuary from the constricting social roles that still prevailed in many German homes. These clubs provided members with valuable leadership experience and the opportunity to form independent social networks. As Paula von Reznicek declared, "We make the rules, can do and have done what we want, can come and go without having to ask.... We preside over the situation that we have created!"[104] Men had used similar clubs and associations for centuries as a refuge from domestic life, and now women claimed the same prerogative for themselves. These were institutions, as Reznicek proudly reminded her readers "that we have created."

Tennis proved such an effective vehicle for the articulation of new women's roles in part because it packaged remarkably subversive elements within the nonthreatening veneer of a sport that had long identified itself as suitable for women and had seamlessly incorporated many elements of traditional femininity. Every self-respecting "modern" woman in the Weimar period had to pursue a sport, and tennis seemed both far sexier and far less "masculinizing" than a pursuit like track and field. When Elsa Hermann described the ideal postwar woman in her 1929 book *This Is the New Woman* as someone who "refuses to be regarded as a physically weak being in need of assistance" and yet remains "appealing in her appearance," she may well have had the female player in mind.[105] Two years earlier, *Sport und Sonne* had crowned tennis "the most beloved women's sport" specifically because it allowed "feminine grace to blossom" and because the resulting "tennis contours gratify the beholder."[106]

The "gratifying contours" of the Weimar player, though, differed noticeably from those of her prewar forebears. Tennis had given "feminine grace" an entirely new meaning. While they may have avoided the purportedly masculine qualities of sprinters and shot putters, female players nevertheless crafted a new vision of femininity that featured competitiveness, independence, and a hard, muscular physicality. They athleticized beauty standards in the 1920s and contributed to what historian Ken Montague has called the "internalization of the corset," in which exercise replaced an elastic garment as the mechanism for streamlining the body.[107] Johanne, the protagonist of Scheff's *Das weiße Spiel*, embodied this new ideal. She not only played unbeatable tennis, but she had perfectly toned legs—"vivacious limbs, like a thoroughbred"—that stoked men's fantasies.[108]

Men found German tennis champion Cilly Aussem's athleticism so attractive that a 1932 article joked about her receiving "Thirty marriage proposals on every game day, which increases by 220 percent on the South American tour."[109] Aussem and her fellow players owed their physical condition to the introduction of carefully calibrated training techniques in women's tennis. Initially inspired by the principles of the American industrial engineer F. W. Taylor, such rationalization had made its influence widely felt in Weimar Germany. From business organization to kitchen layout, the doctrine had inspired both religious devotion and visceral hostility, and it transformed women's tennis, along with the bodies of its top players.[110]

Lill, the heroine of another pulp tennis novel, had clearly absorbed the dogma of Taylorized training. Early in the novel, she barks exercise commands at her fellow tennis player Bine like a drill sergeant: "Straighten the knees!…more vigorous back work, down to your tailbone! Better balance between your muscles and your shoulder blades!"[111] Lill subsumed every aspect of her personal life under the greater goal of winning tournaments, from training to diet to relationships. She approached tennis matches against male opponents with such a cool-eyed focus on winning that her parents lose hope of her ever dating one of those men.[112]

Before the war, women's tennis languished in a dull consistency, complained a women's magazine in 1930: "ball back and ball forth, the female rivals stood anchored to the baseline, apparently determined to wait for Judgment Day." All of this changed in the 1920s, though, the article continued, as women "gained competitiveness and energy, in addition to pacing and spirit, [and] have become genuine sport-ladies, who know how to fight doggedly and to the last ball."[113] If the men's game at this time still seemed to expect little more of its players than linen pants and a family title, the women's game now demanded training and a thirst to win. As Annemarie Kopp argued in her 1927 article "Competition and Femininity," sportswomen put the lie to the simplistic equations of "feminine and weak, masculine and strong."[114]

A pair of 1928 cartoons in *Sport und Sonne* illustrated the results of this revolution in women's tennis. The top drawing presented a women's Wimbledon match in 1907 as a docile game akin to backyard badminton. Cumbersome outfits encased each player's body, and when one of them inadvertently allowed a glimpse of her calf from underneath the ankle-length skirt, the exaggerated shock of the onlookers expressed the overall prudishness of *fin-de-siècle* sensibilities. The fact that only a handful of onlookers even bothered to attend the match further underscored the women's relatively marginal status in the sport. The bottom illustration, on the other hand, showed a women's match in 1927, its lightning speed indicated by a flurry of dotted lines that charted the path of the ball. Players leapt and volleyed, returning nearly impossible shots. Their skills riveted the capacity crowd, which seemed not the least bit distracted by the sight of completely exposed arms and thighs. The caption marveled, "How the times have changed."[115]

Cilly Aussem, the German women's champion at the end of the Weimar Republic, illustrated the ambitious athleticism of the new breed of female players. Ilse Friedleben described her as a carefully trained, thoroughly rationalized tactician:

Miss Aussem has achieved an astounding, machine-like accuracy in her shots and wonderful footwork through systematic, excellent

Frauentennis in Wimbledon 1907 und 1927

(Sporting & Dramatic News)

WIE HABEN DIE ZEITEN SICH VERÄNDERT!

This 1928 cartoon highlighted the dramatic transformation in women's tennis by juxtaposing a Wimbledon women's match in 1907 with one in 1927. The caption exclaims, "How the times have changed!" *Author's collection*

training. She is capable of outstanding performance through her physical fitness, the rare equilibrium of her nerves in combination with a very goal-oriented will and undaunted competitiveness, [and] a lucid judgment, which conducts things soberly and cold-bloodedly to her own advantage.[116]

This description could scarcely have differed more from typical depictions of Germany's best male players at the time. The entire tenor of the passage bespoke the engineered power and efficiency of modern industry, whose business titans, like Aussem herself, exhibited a "goal-oriented will and undaunted competitiveness."

Aussem honed her aggressive technique in 1930 with the help of Bill Tilden and reaped her biggest dividends in 1931, when she captured the French and Wimbledon championships. She signaled to the public that the same modern approach that had already transformed tennis in other countries had finally arrived in Germany, via the women. In 1932, Rafael Schermann even analyzed Cilly Aussem's handwriting, claiming to have discerned in it her fundamental drive to dominate on the court: "Her strong will gives her psyche an element of the masculine. As a fighter who wants to wrest a victory under any circumstances, she is a formidable figure."[117]

The press praised this transformation. Already by 1924, one essay referred to women's tennis as "one of the most demanding sports" and applauded "the physical strength, stamina, and, above all, energy" of the player Ilse Friedleben.[118] Burghard von Reznicek echoed this praise of Friedleben in 1932, when he extolled her "incomprehensible energy and toughness, beyond which smoldered a desire to win."[119] Richard Goerring, meanwhile, gushed in 1928 over another female player's "serve of manly force."[120] Goerring, though, quickly reassured readers that this player "hits like a man and yet still remains a feminine Eve" and so tried to contain her hard-hitting athleticism within a reassuring limit, albeit one that he never clearly defines.

Alfred Kremer pushed those limits farther in a 1928 commentary, in which he argued that women possessed an innate "ambition and dedication that almost surpass a man's."[121] Horst Wagner agreed. "The woman is very often completely consumed by a matter that only concerns the man superficially," he declared in a 1931 article on tennis that contrasted the male player's frivolity with the female's resolute focus.[122] A cut-throat attitude toward winning—apparently so absent in the men's game—had come to define the women's game, a reflection, according to many observers, of the long-underestimated nature of women in general.

The press took this point even further when it suggested that a martial mentality had emerged in the new generation of female players, akin to that of the mythological Amazons.[123] When Paul Weeks referred to female players in 1930 as a "legion of Amazons," he implicitly broached the possibility that they would someday displace men in competitive tennis, just as the female warriors of lore had supplanted men in warfare:

In no branch of physical culture have the influences of women's emancipation...become more visible than in tennis. Today, we see...our tennis courts populated by a legion of Amazons, steeled through sports. The woman increasingly stands out in tennis. She has already surpassed the man in numbers and is on the way to coming as close as possible to matching him athletically. The accomplished player's technique scarcely lags behind that of the man.[124]

Tennis provided a stage on which women could establish their equality, in Weeks's estimation, and perhaps even their superiority.

Rix Grusemann, another tennis-playing character in *Lill*, wore her Amazonian qualities like a suit of armor. The author described her as looking like a "young man in a woman's skirt," an impression that her bearing and gait only further reinforced.[125] Rix freely appropriated men's clothes and a masculine persona, an unorthodox self-presentation that had clearly prepared her, or perhaps forced her, to take care of herself. "I've adopted just enough from the men...that I'm man enough to defend myself against them," she declared at one point.[126] For women like Rix, who had chosen an independent life and never intended to find a husband, tennis cultivated a valuable measure of resolve and self-reliance, and it provided a space in which those qualities received acceptance and encouragement. Tennis promised not only a physical transformation, in other words, but a psychological one as well.

An early match in *Lill* illustrated the raw aggressiveness of the new female players, as the heroine "murders the ball" with her punishing forehands and "dances bloodthirstily along the net."[127] A 1932 cartoon, appearing in the last year of the Weimar Republic, underscored the reputation for intensive competitiveness that female players had earned over the course of the preceding decade. In it, a female player chews out her hapless male partner in mixed doubles. "Screw up!" she shouts at him, while pointing sternly at the ball that he has just hit into the net, as if reprimanding a disobedient child.[128] The beauty and hygiene industry, recognizing this growing competitiveness in women's tennis, increasingly positioned its products as contributing to winning matches, since simply looking pretty on the court no longer sufficed. A 1927 ad for "4711" cologne featured a young woman hitting a backhand, under which the text asserted, "The female champion needs two things: unremitting training and—'4711'!"[129] Rather than suggesting that women "make life easy for themselves," to quote the 1926 article on men's tennis fashions, this product promised to "ward off exhaustion" that comes from a strenuous sport, in order that women could push themselves even harder.

As female players reinvented their game and themselves in the 1920s, observers speculated as to how the top-ranked women would match up against their male counterparts. Men and women had played against one another, formally and casually, since the sport began, and not just in mixed doubles. As early as 1907, a Hamburg tennis club sponsored a tournament in which male and female players officially vied against one another in singles competition.[130] What had appeared as a novelty event before the war became commonplace after it. Some of these mixed-sex matches foreshadowed the famous "Battle of the Sexes" between Bobby Riggs and Billie Jean King in 1973 by casting them as part of a larger struggle for

Gewitterbildung

This 1932 cartoon captures the gender stereotypes in tennis, as the competitive female player calls her submissive male partner a "Screw up!" after he has flubbed a shot. The subtitle reads, ominously, "Gathering storm." *Universitätsbibliothek der Humboldt-Universität zu Berlin*

gender equality. *Damen-Sport und Damen-Turnen* argued in 1918 that male players could find in female opponents "evenly matched, if not actually superior opponents."[131] The article imputed broader social consequences to these on-court competitions, and it concluded that tennis "enables ladies to prove their skill as equal to that of men," a statement that applied to all of society.

Ten years later, Horst Wagner argued that women's "basic ground strokes are almost of the same power" as men's, suggesting that male players could not necessarily count on having an advantage even in physical strength.[132] *Tennis und Golf*, also in 1928, expressed the belief that "women's competitive tennis is at the level of the men's game, technically and tactically."[133] It added that women played an even more spectacular and crowd-pleasing game than the men. Heinrich Mann had already conceded in 1926 that women could beat men in tennis, and he added, "tennis is only an analogy—they can win in business and everywhere."[134] Mann ascribed a vanguard role to tennis in paving the way for other social advances, a sport that served as an inspiration as well as an analogy. Dr. Friedrich Messerli concurred in 1928 that "in athletic relationships, the woman can be, without question, as good as the man."[135] In tennis, women seemed on the verge of confirming this thesis. In the same year as Messerli's provocative assertion, Helen Wills defeated Fritz Mercur, and did so shortly after Mercur himself had taken down the great Bill Tilden. To contemporary commentators familiar with the transitive property in mathematics, this chain of events raised the unsettling possibility that Wills played better than Tilden. Some, like Hermann Rau, frantically downplayed the significance of the Wills-Mercur match, but the top-ranked Australian player John Hawkes showed a great deal more humility. He confessed to a German magazine "that he would have to play in absolutely top form to be able to beat Wills."[136] Hawkes then suggested that his teammates, even in their best form, still might not stand a chance against her.

Germany's advertising industry began to play up such battle-of-the-sexes scenarios with increasing frequency after the onset of economic stability in the mid-1920s. A 1927 advertisement for eyeglasses showed a woman taking on two men at the same time, suggesting that it took both guys to match the skills of this one woman and make for an interesting match.[137] Two years later, a coffee advertisement presented a similar two-on-one match-up, which the woman decisively won. As one member of the vanquished male partnership exclaimed, "Aren't you just a fine little chap, Kitty! You beat us in tennis."[138] The text predictably credited its brand of decaffeinated coffee for Kitty's victory, at least in part. Even after the two men vowed to undergo their own six-week program of decaffeination and then take on Kitty in a rematch, though, she accepted the challenge with such confidence that a repeat victory seemed assured. Even without their coffee jitters, this advertisement implied, Kitty could beat these guys. In novels of the period, too, female players often beat their male opponents, and handily. The character Cissy in Arthur Schnitzler's 1924 novel *Fräulein Else*, for instance, steamrollered her cousin Paul in three straight sets, and Gagaly Madosdy, the heroine in Edschmid's *Sport um Gagaly*, crushed all male comers in match after match.[139]

In addition to superiority in certain head-to-head competitions, women contributed far more than men to Germany's international tennis standing. The nation boasted a formidable cadre of up-and-coming female players by the end of the 1920s, including Cilly Aussem, Ellen Hoffmann, and Hilde Krahwinkel, which contrasted with the far shallower bench on the men's side. *Sport und Sonne* focused almost entirely on the women in its 1927 assessment of the country's tennis prospects, relegating the men to the penultimate paragraph and then dismissing them with the comment that "unfortunately, no one here can be compared to a Cilly Aussem."[140] In January 1930, *Tennis und Golf* wrote that "the male players must content themselves with playing second fiddle," and in August of that same year, it declared: "Once again, we must—as so often in recent times—count on our ladies, when it comes to the wresting of national honor."[141] At the end of 1930, Aussem ranked second in the world and Krahwinkel ranked as the world's tenth-best player, the first time that two Germans had occupied positions in the top ten since 1914, when two men had claimed those spots. As Hermann Rau conceded in 1931 with a heavy sigh, "German women's tennis is at the moment much, much stronger than men's tennis."[142]

Walter Bing, on the other hand, did not begrudge women their vanguard position one bit. He praised "the string of [tennis] victories by our German women" in 1928 as an example of how far the nation had rehabilitated itself since the military defeat ten years earlier, and he crowed that his country's female players had "long since surpassed [those of] France."[143] Moreover, Bing insisted that Cilly Aussem's victories throughout that year represented the very best of German tennis, male or female. When Aussem captured the 1931 Wimbledon singles championship, Rumpelstilzchen saw it as proof to the world that "our will to live has not been extinguished." He gleefully continued, "The Englishmen's eyes nearly popped out of their heads" when they realized that Germans occupied both spots in the women's finals.[144] Aussem's victory coincided with the German boxer Max Schmeling's heavyweight title, but Rumpelstilzchen only mentioned Schmeling's success after first trumpeting that of the German women.[145] Here, sportswomen embodied the German "will to live" at least as much as, if not more than, the men. From scarcely receiving a footnote in the sports reportage of the early 1920s, Germany's female players now enjoyed top billing just one decade later.

The emancipatory spirit of women's tennis composed only one aspect of its modern image, and many women who fancied themselves in step with the times adopted the look of a tennis player, even if they had never served a ball in their lives. "In order to be modern, you take part in 'sport,' or you at least wear sports clothes. It's enough in most situations simply to be thought of as athletic," observed the commentator Carla Verständig in 1930.[146] As early as 1918, the magazine *Damen-Sport und Damen-Turnen* had criticized such *poseurs*, who "only dedicate themselves to tennis in order to parade around with the racket."[147] Herr von Dorsday, a character in the novel *Fräulein Else*, understood the appeal of such posing, given his belief that the tennis look enhanced the attractiveness of any woman. "When someone looks that good with a racket," he tells Else, "she's allowed to carry it as ornamentation."[148] Tennis conferred fashionability and social cachet in the 1920s, providing a model that many men favored and that many women followed.

The media commonly attributed Germany's newfound appreciation of athletic femininity after the war to the pervasive influence of the United States, with female tennis players among its principal agents. While men's tennis held onto its air of fusty Englishness, the women seemed to channel the dynamism of the American spirit. In 1927, the newspaper *8-Uhr Abendblatt* divided postwar German women into three categories—the "Gretchen," the "Girl," and the "Garçonne."[149] Whereas the Gretchen conformed to traditional ideals, the other two types projected something very new: a physical and sexual independence. Both the Girl and the Garçonne played sports, and both displayed traits closely associated with the tennis player and with American culture, which exerted a powerful pull on the Weimar Republic. The Girl, for instance, flirted energetically with her male partners, just as so many of the female players in the pulp fiction of the interwar period did. The Garçonne, meanwhile, displayed a coolness and ambition that marked her as a formidable representative of her own interests and a disarmingly assertive woman.

Paula von Reznicek commented on the transformation of the German women's game by creating a fictitious dialog between a "normal" player, who treated tennis as a hobby, and an "abnormal" one, who drove herself relentlessly.[150] "Normal" pleaded in vain to her companion that "three hours of training [per day] is reasonable, but five to seven—insanity!" This passage gives an indication of the extent to which female players had rejected earlier limits on female physical activity. Even three hours per week might have struck prewar society as excessive, but "Normal" viewed three hours per day as more or less par for the course by the 1920s. "Normal" continued to catalog the training excesses of "Abnormal," including the latter's decision to turn down a plum film role that had been offered to her. "Abnormal" explained that the filming would have cut into her workouts at precisely the moment when her coach was vowing "to make me 'Suzanne-like' [Lenglen] within three weeks."

"Normal" finally screamed in exasperation, "you're crazy! You consider yourself desirable, masculine, and passionate, and [yet] all because of the stupid sport of tennis, you forget everything erotic!" This outburst not only presented "desirable" and "masculine" as mutually reinforcing qualities in a woman, rather than mutually exclusive ones, but it also indicated the centrality of athleticism to the new standards of female attractiveness. The entire passage, however, also expressed Reznicek's own concern that, in the competition between the two souls of German women's tennis, the "Girl" was losing out to the "Garçonne." Whereas "Normal" viewed flirtation—"everything erotic"—as central to the game, "Abnormal" focused only on winning. Reznicek's sympathies clearly lied with the former. Even that character, however, trained with a dedication that would have shocked her prewar forebears, even if she stopped short of her friend's level of intensity.

Both the Garçonne and the Girl, moreover, exhibited an uninhibited sexuality. The Garçonne, however, had decisively shed any trace of the flirtatious coquette. She did not lure the man; she pursued him, and this display of aggressive sexuality both inflamed fears of a declining public morality and dovetailed with a number of stereotypes that had attached themselves to the female player. As the writer Stefan Zweig observed in

1929, women in the 1920s had moved from sexual object to sexual subject—"from waiting to be chosen to free choice"—when it came to liaisons of all types.[151] This extended to the possibility that women might pay for those liaisons, too, as the film director Billy Wilder recalled in a brief story about his earlier stint as a taxi dancer for the wealthy female guests of a Berlin hotel.[152] Historian Atina Grossmann writes that even sex reformers themselves expressed a certain shock during the Weimar Republic at the "the sexual shamelessness of the young single women who came to them demanding birth control."[153]

Popular culture in the Weimar Republic increasingly equated tennis with nonmonogamous, nontraditional, and, above all, nonreproductive sex. Women might flirt with their female teammates, for instance, as they did in a 1927 short story that appeared in the lesbian magazine *Die Freundin*. In it, Ruth tries to win the affections of Lia, her opponent on the tennis court. After the match, Ruth dreams about the object of her unrequited love and wonders if Lia noticed that Ruth had purposely let her win. It turns out that Lia had noticed and even found it exciting. As she later teases her increasingly jealous boyfriend, "it is so terribly amusing to have a woman do the courting for a change!"[154] Married women orchestrated liaisons on the court, too, taking to heart the signature song of Fritzi Massary, who asked nonchalantly in a 1932 operetta, "Why shouldn't a married woman have an affair?"[155] Johanne, the heroine of *Das weiße Spiel*, presented herself as "ultimately too modern a girl to believe in marriage for love's sake," a philosophy that freed her to pursue her fiancé's tournament opponent, Günther. When Günther proposed marriage to Johanne at the end of the novel, the sheepishness of her own assent reflected the liberated sexual fashion of the time: "I'm almost embarrassed...to love and marry him. How un-modern!"[156] When that other tennis-novel heroine, Lill, declared, "We want to be free...and not merely sheep on the marriage market," she spoke for a generation of women coming of age in the Weimar Republic.[157]

Paula von Reznicek would certainly have echoed Lill's remarks here. Again, though, she did not wish to see the defiant self-sufficiency of the Garçonne so thoroughly dominate women's tennis that no vestige of the Girl remained. In her 1928 handbook for the "modern lady," Reznicek asked somewhat wistfully, "Where is the tennis flirt? Today it's [only] fierce, hard-fought competition," an observation that she could well have extended to German society as a whole.[158] A fellow tennis player, Beverley Nichols, went even further in her criticism when she ridiculed the typical women's match in the pages of *Querschnitt* as "a genderless orgy."[159] The archconservative Rumpelstilzchen had weighed in on this trend as early as 1924. Intense training was making female tennis players "too manly," he decided, "...and gradually takes away the girlish softness for which our sex so gladly plays the knight in shining armor."[160] Lacking softness, these women threatened to make tough men irrelevant. Coming just six years after a war in which many women had proven their ability to get along without men reasonably well, and at a time when women were taking on increasingly prominent economic, political, and cultural roles, Rumpelstilzchen's comments revealed his own deep anxiety, undoubtedly shared by many men, about patriarchal decline.

Women, on the other hand, felt a greater need for self-sufficiency than ever before, and tennis presented an ideal training ground for this quality. It encouraged women to compete directly against men, after all, just as they would need to do in so many other areas of society. F. P. Weidemann drew a clear connection between female athleticism and societal transformation in a 1928 book on German sports: "The woman has become more independent, [and] to a greater degree she is man's competitor in the struggle for one's daily bread."[161] As the principal expression of female athleticism, tennis served as both a metaphor and a catalyst for far greater changes in the Weimar Republic. If marriage seemed like a distant or even an altogether undesirable goal for many German women after the war, tennis offered an alternative lifestyle.

If the image of the female player in the Weimar media did not look much like a marrying type, she looked even less like a maternal one. *Sport im Bild* lamented in 1924 over how few of Germany's best female players had raised families, even after getting married, and it urged women, in a tone that suggested a lost cause, to choose children over a glamorous tennis career.[162] An article two years later presented the modern woman as torn between motherhood, on the one hand, and "the winning of so many more tournament victories in tennis," on the other.[163] Competitive tennis led to spinsterhood, it insisted, and it mocked the "muscular" player "who will spring around [on the court] until her old age, at which time…she will suitably decorate her childless home with silver trophies."[164] The female player, with her slim hips, small breasts, and firm body, looked like the very antithesis of a stereotypically maternal form. She did look modern, though. As the cultural historian Sander Gilman argues, women generally did not wish to appear "reproductive" during the 1920s, and the popularity of breast reduction surgery increased markedly during this period.[165]

When the journal *Die Literarische Welt* referred to the woman who "would now and again unleash a child from her splendidly trained flanks as if driving a Slazenger tennis ball with her racket," it managed the tricky feat of reconciling tennis with motherhood while nevertheless employing one of the least maternal metaphors imaginable.[166] *Sport im Bild*, meanwhile, continued its own urgent campaign to raise the birthrate in women's tennis by publishing the sweetly pro-family piece "Our Tennis Children" in 1926, authored—ironically—by the happily childless tennis star Paula von Reznicek.[167] The article claimed to refute "those philistines" who insisted that "a tennis-playing mother [is] not suitable to raise children," but the perceived need for its publication in the first place lent it an air of mild methinkst-thou-dost-protest-too-much.

Reznicek herself clearly desired a public life without domestic responsibilities, and, in this regard, she typified the assured independence of so many female players in Weimar Germany. Her 1928 handbook for the new woman, *Resurrection of the Lady*, glorified a lifestyle free of children. She also represented a model of the self-made woman, having begun her career as a secretary. She honed her skills on the court, however, to win national and international tournaments and, in February 1930, became the very first German—man or woman—to win a tournament in Paris since the war.[168] She played an aggressive style of tennis as well. In games of mixed doubles, she often took charge, as when she partnered with Hans Moldenhauer, whom she "guided by her shrewd head," according to one third-party observer.[169] By successfully pursuing a career as an author and commentator, even as she maintained her success on the tennis circuit, Reznicek popularized an athletic ideal for women and significantly shaped the public image of the female player.

Reznicek seemed to place little value on marital monogamy, either, since she talked regularly and enthusiastically about the opportunities for women to strike up courtside affairs.[170] After marrying into her noble surname, she divorced fellow tennis writer Burghard von Reznicek and later married the auto-racing champion Hans Stuck. Throughout the period, she cultivated a very visible, and fabulous, lifestyle. On the evening of her historic 1930 tennis victory in Paris, *Tennis und Golf* reported that "the happy champion gave a cocktail party in her hotel," attended by diplomats, socialites, and literati.[171] *Der Querschnitt* crowned Reznicek "Germany's first and foremost female sports journalist" in 1932 and, in a nod to her social-insider status, praised her skills as a "talented teller of anecdotes and indiscretions."[172]

New Women, New Men

Players like Reznicek, Cilly Aussem, Suzanne Lenglen, and so many others did not single-handedly overturn centuries-old assumptions about and expectations of women, of course. Tennis did, however, create an important vehicle for women's postwar self-transformation. Precisely because women's participation in tennis did not appear as overtly threatening as their involvement in most other public activities, such as politics, science, or the law, tennis offered women a widely sanctioned venue for showcasing their skills and themselves. Players enjoyed status, visibility, and an unrivaled opportunity to launch trends and set standards. The imperatives of an increasingly competitive sport pushed these women to build strength, increase speed, and tone bodies. Its increasing commercial appeal enabled some to earn their own money, whether through the sport directly or in its burgeoning tertiary sectors, such as club organization, instruction, sports reportage, commentary, and fashion.

Above all, tennis encouraged women to pursue personal goals and pleasures unapologetically. Through tennis, women exhibited an ambition and competitiveness that had previously found few outlets and that resonated with the American-influenced business climate of the 1920s. The aggressive pursuit of victory or sexual satisfaction for one's own sake stood in opposition to the long-standing expectation in German society that women sacrifice their own satisfaction to the demands of husbands, sons, and family life. Female tennis players represented an outright rejection of the maternal expectations imposed on women by a German state that had elevated motherhood to a national duty.

If the female player openly defied many of Germany's most cherished societal norms, the male did as well. Just as tennis enabled women to articulate a harder image that encompassed muscles and ambition, it also opened up to men an alternative to the discipline and aggression that still formed the bedrock of German manhood. It provided a stage, in other words, for the presentation of a softer masculinity. Within this alternative, men could enjoy a refined lifestyle that included genteel manners, stylish clothes, lax discipline, and an appreciation of aesthetics. In addition, they could embrace open expressions of sexuality, in stark contrast to the ascetic rigor and intense self-sacrifice of most other competitive sports of the period, particularly boxing. Men's tennis, in fact, appeared downright hedonistic. The fantasy lifestyle that it projected would have appealed to some who had come of age in an era of wartime scarcity and skyrocketing postwar inflation. After generations of men stoically fulfilling their social duties, an opportunity to concentrate instead on personal pleasure could taste like liberation. This invitation to self-indulgence, moreover, came in the guise of a sport, a socially acceptable pastime for men that made it all the easier for some to embrace if they could afford to do so.

Such a man of tennis presented an ideal counterpart, perhaps even a necessary analog, to the female player. Both of these figures shaped and reflected larger changes in Weimar society, in which men, too, found themselves in new roles. Millions of wounded veterans depended on women for their support and care after 1918, suddenly placing legions of men in an unaccustomedly passive role. In the era of department stores, popular cinema, and mass advertising, men saw themselves as consumers as well as producers. New standards of physical appearance gradually imposed themselves on men, too, driven in part by the visibility of sports celebrities and matinee idols.

The legendary permissiveness of Weimar society, furthermore, allowed for the more open expression of male sexuality as well as female. In this regard, particularly, the man of tennis provided an apt model for his age. Whether as the roving lothario or the available object, male tennis players gave in to their desires, rather than suppressing them. This image of the sexual man juxtaposed two contradictory stereotypes. On the one hand, his lack of self-control marked the male player as sensuous, undisciplined, and—therefore—unmanly. On the other hand, it contributed to his reputation as the most overtly heterosexual athlete of his day. The National Socialists, significantly, seized on precisely this hedonistic reputation in their effort to cast tennis as a Jewish game and propagate the anti-Semitic trope of the lascivious Jew.[173] In an era that not only challenged the norms of gender and sexuality, but also restlessly experimented with new lifestyles and modes of social organization, tennis acted as one of the most prominent catalysts for change, the effects of which far outlasted the Weimar Republic.

2

Belle of the Brawl
The Boxer between Sensationalism and Sport

In 1926 Bertolt Brecht began outlining the story of a man who rein-vented himself through boxing and amassed a tidy fortune in the pro-cess. A longtime fan of the fights, Brecht nevertheless did not wish to write about the action inside the ring. Instead, as his notes for this never-completed novel indicate, Brecht wanted "to see how a man earns fame and fortune through boxing and how he begins to translate that fame into even more money—in short, how a man 'makes himself.'"[1] Under the working title *The Renown*, Brecht's completed fragments explore the life of a prizefighter who went by the nickname "Gorgeous George," a good-looking man who modeled part time for a hat company and so enflamed female passions that women pursued him "like a pack of blood-thirsty hounds."[2]

Brecht sought to explain how and why the male boxer had become an iconic figure in the Weimar Republic and the standard of postwar mascu-linity.[3] In the aftermath of what many Germans saw as an emasculating military defeat and in the midst of economic and social transformations that seemed to render men increasingly redundant, the pugilist repre-sented something essentially male: the genuine "hard guy." He could dish out a bruising, and he could take one, too. His sinewy body, stripped of fat through disciplined training, functioned like an anatomical suit of armor. The boxer established an ideal for the Weimar man who had grown soft, and even decadent, in the modern metropolis.

At the same time, the prizefighter flourished in precisely that deca-dent metropolis. He marketed his carefully crafted persona and body without inhibition, and he thrived on the patronage of the leading commercial and cultural elites of Weimar society. Brecht understood the boxer's ambiguous relationship to modernity, as both antidote and exem-plar, from close-hand observation. He claimed to have modeled his pro-tagonist on his friend, the German prizefighter Paul Samson-Körner, but he certainly had the French light heavyweight Georges Carpentier in mind as well. Carpentier shared not only a first name with Brecht's protagonist, but also his heartthrob status. The Weimar press positively swooned over Carpentier's handsome features in the early 1920s, and one sports weekly eagerly anticipated a feature film that gave the fighter "the opportunity to display his athletic physique."[4] Carpentier's acting talent was beside the point, the article gushed, since he was "so strong, so noble, and *soooo* good-looking!"

Male fighters may have dominated the world of German boxing in the 1920s, but they did not monopolize it. In 1921, the same year as that anxiously anticipated Carpentier film, Weimar fight fans could also witness the spectacle of women boxing in the ring. Walter Rothenburg, Germany's foremost fight promoter, published an article on one such series of female bouts that took place in Hamburg, which he began with an eye-popping statement: "No man, even if he had earlier been the biggest Don Juan, still risks it in this day and age to approach a lady on the street. The reason: the woman is beginning to box!"[5] German men faced a revolution in gender relations, Rothenburg implied, with the female pugilist leading the charge. After all, he continued, such a woman had more than just self-defense in mind: "She wants to exact revenge—sweet revenge! She wants to smash the man's ribs in, the ribs from which she was born." This report, which appeared in *Boxsport*, the official journal of Germany's boxing establishment, indulged in somewhat mocking hyperbole, but Rothenburg did see women's boxing as an indication, even if an extreme and rare one, of a newfound aggression and physicality on the part of postwar women. The female fighter augured—or perhaps spearheaded—greater changes to come.

Like her male counterpart, the female boxer, too, shaped a new postwar standard, and she reflected similar ambiguities—part self-empowerment, part self-exploitation. On the one hand, the Hamburg event had an undeniably burlesque feel to it that tapped into a long tradition of lowbrow flesh peddling that came in the form of variously contrived and orchestrated "catfights." On the other hand, Rothenburg discerned something new and potentially transformative here: a desire for "sweet revenge" that assumed a male opponent, not a male patron.[6] Moreover, the burlesque elements on display in Hamburg had clear analogs in the world of men's boxing. Rothenburg's winking comment that "the 'legwork' of the ladies seemed to interest [the spectators] the most" found its equally voyeuristic corollary in the women who went after Gorgeous George "like a pack of bloodthirsty hounds."

The figure of the boxer in the Weimar Republic subverted longstanding male and female roles, and it helped to shape new ones. The manner in which a boxer expressed raw, sustained, and public violence, for instance, had few antecedents for men in prewar German culture, let alone for women. In this, the fighter seemed to channel the brutality of an entire era that witnessed battlefield slaughter, street fighting, and political assassinations. In the case of the male fighter, the media often attributed this violence to the fighter's lower-class origins, whether real or imagined. In doing so, the media and prizefighters themselves helped to popularize a working-class chic among many middle- and upper-class men, particularly those in cultural circles who increasingly sought to cultivate a tough, purportedly blue-collar masculinity that would stiffen their soft edges. The female fighter's expression of violent aggression proved even more transgressive, since she was thereby claiming one of the most stereotypically masculine behaviors for herself. In the increasingly precarious postwar environment, in which women competed for jobs, political influence, and even husbands, such a trait appeared well worth cultivating.

The boxer also held out the tantalizing prospect of self-reinvention, presenting to his or her audience the possibility of "making" oneself anew. Hopeful tales of working-class prizefighters who had risen to fame and fortune abounded in the Weimar Republic, and each example of a successful prizefighter offered ostensible proof that such hopes lay within every aspiring boxer's reach. Women rarely dreamed of growing rich from boxing, but pugilism nevertheless provided them, too, with a vehicle for crafting entirely new personas. The boxing ring afforded women a rare space in which to create the types of unrestrained, larger-than-life personalities that society otherwise denied them. Many more women adopted the sport's training practices, such as workouts on the punching ball or sandsack, and some even sparred in the ring. These boxing drills instilled strength, coordination, and physical self-awareness, skills that the writer Vicki Baum, for one, credited with boosting her overall confidence and determination in professional interactions and contract negotiations.[7]

The pugilist's fame and fortune derived from the marketing of their bodies as well as their fighting skills, and it tapped into a public voyeurism that directed itself every bit as much toward the male form as toward the female one. Part of the financial success of the male prizefighter stemmed directly from his self-presentation as a heartthrob in films, photographs, and the ring itself. He, placed himself in the hitherto unaccustomed role of male object. In so doing, the prizefighter focused an aesthetic attention on the male physique that supplemented the Weimar period's otherwise more pragmatic corporeal concerns of health and performance. Women, of course, had long submitted themselves to such aesthetic attention, and the titillating spectacle of woman-on-woman fighting that had emerged in the grittier entertainment venues of the nineteenth century had only fueled appetites for this daring fare. Female boxers subtly redefined the nature of this sexual appeal after the war, however. They incrementally shifted their sport out of the tawdry realm of burlesque, where it had taken off in the early 1920s, and into the positively fashionable boxing-inspired fitness programs by the middle years of the decade. The image of a woman in boxing gloves, fresh from a workout on the punching ball, graced the covers of national magazines and promoted a stylish new ideal of modern womanhood.

Pugilistic Performances: Playing the Part of the Boxer

To sports purists in the 1920s, boxing matches remained indelibly tainted by the crass, sideshow novelty acts that comprised the entirety of most Germans' exposure to pugilism in the Wilhelmine period. When the famed Wintergarten Theater introduced curious Berliners to the technology of cinema in 1896, for instance, its debut film featured the now hackneyed stunt of pitting a man against a kangaroo in the boxing ring.[8] Unlike Britain and the United States, which had cultivated strong boxing traditions since at least the middle of the nineteenth century, boxing had existed only on the shadowy margins of German society prior to the First World War. A number of local laws and police prohibitions banned or sharply curtailed the sport throughout most of Imperial Germany, and authorities in the larger cities repeatedly cracked down on public fights and raided the clandestine ones that did take place.[9] This precarious legal status before 1918 helps to explain pugilism's shallow roots in the prewar German populace. A national boxing federation first formed in 1912, much later than in the rest of western Europe and North America, and only a few boxing clubs managed to establish a low-profile presence before the war, primarily in British-influenced port cities like Bremen, Hamburg, and Stettin.

The German public in the late nineteenth century could, nevertheless, watch fistfights in certain popular entertainment venues, such as circuses, yearly markets, and burlesque theaters, a few of which featured women. A native of Vienna by the name of Caterine Baumann, for example, claimed unofficial titles for herself in boxing, wrestling, and weight lifting on the sideshow circuit, which she then used to promote a tour of the United States in 1913.[10] Male boxers relied heavily on these same popular venues, since they comprised most of the available arenas in which to perform, compete, and earn money prior to 1918. The future German and world heavyweight champion Max Schmeling recalled disliking boxing as a kid in the 1910s precisely because of its association with lowbrow entertainment, commenting, "I never saw great fighters, but instead only 'show boxers' at fairgrounds."[11]

With the collapse of the German monarchy and the declaration of a republic in November 1918, progressive politicians, not to mention legions of budding entrepreneurs, called for a legal tabula rasa with respect to many areas of government regulation. As a consequence, the new German government either lifted or ignored prohibitions that regulated public conduct and "decency" in many areas, including boxing. Almost overnight, the public and well-publicized "big fights" established themselves as fixtures in the postwar popular culture. Throngs of German spectators, many of them completely unfamiliar with the sport, crammed into sports arenas across the country to watch the "manly art of self-defense."

German boxing gained its initial injection of talent in these early years from a cohort of young fighters who had learned their craft in British prisoner-of-war camps during the war, including such early champions as Hans Breitensträter, Kurt Prenzel, and Adolf Wiegert. Fight fans commonly referred to this entire first generation as "Knockaloe Boxers," in reference to the internment camp on the Isle of Man where many of these men had been held after their capture. The postwar presence of British soldiers in the Rhineland gave another boost to organized boxing in the Weimar Republic and contributed to Cologne's emergence as one of the sport's hotbeds in the 1920s. Because Great Britain had long adopted an evangelizing attitude with regard to spreading competitive sports, British camp guards and occupation troops viewed the instruction of Germans in boxing as part of England's larger civilizing mission. Many of those guards and occupying soldiers considered the Germans to have conducted the war in an unsportsmanlike manner, including the use of poison gas, zeppelin raids, and unlimited submarine warfare, a perception that made the project of instilling a sporting spirit in that people seem all the more urgent. As a German commentator in 1922 noted of the circumstances under which his fellow countrymen had acquired the skills of boxing: "Strange that it first took a war to bring us this method of increasing our strength—[and] from the land of the enemy."[12]

Despite a cadre of trained fighters and solid institutional support for boxing after 1918, though, the same crass sensationalism that had adhered to pugilism in Wilhelmine Germany remained the driving force behind popular fights throughout the Weimar Republic. The historian Modris Eksteins has called modernism "above all, a culture of the sensational event," and boxing matches fit into that culture seamlessly.[13] A carnivalesque atmosphere animated many fights, in which the boxers performed in the roles of their self-cultivated personas, while staging a series of signature gimmicks in the manner of circus entertainers.

A black boxer who claimed to have held a prewar welterweight title and who fought under the name of "Dixie Kid," for instance, staged exhibition matches in Berlin in the 1920s in which he fought the entire bout with one foot rooted to the spot on the canvas where he had dropped a handkerchief.[14] Meanwhile, another young boxer launched his career as "Sabri Mahir, the Terrible Turk," building an impressive record by fighting only pre-selected opponents and later achieving even greater fame as a boxing trainer to Berlin's cultural luminaries.[15] Bertolt Brecht's 1926 story "The Left Hook" even blended a boxing match with a drag show when he described his protagonist entering the ring for one bout wearing a "perfect pair of lady's shorts, lavender. It was the most coquettish thing that you could possibly imagine."[16] Brecht continued by describing how this fighter "went around as if in the theater," an apt description of the attitude adopted by so many prizefighters at the time.

Spectators loved the outrageous performances. At men's bouts, they readily suspended their disbelief, even as commentators openly groaned at the obviously scripted and rehearsed nature of some of these fights. Christopher Isherwood recounted one such performance in 1932 at Berlin's Lunapark amusement park:

> One of the boxers is a Negro. He invariably wins. The boxers hit each other with the open glove, making a tremendous amount of noise. The other boxer, a tall, well-built young man, about twenty years younger and obviously much stronger than the Negro, is 'knocked out' with absurd ease. He writhes in great agony on the floor, nearly manages to struggle to his feet at the count of ten, then collapses again, groaning. After the fight, the referee...calls for a challenger from the audience. Before any bona fide challenger can apply, another young man...jumps hastily into the ring and strips off his clothes, revealing himself already dressed in shorts and boxer's boots. The referee announces a purse of five marks; and, this time, the Negro is 'knocked out.'
>
> The audience took the fights dead seriously, shouting encouragement to the fighters, and even quarrelling and betting amongst themselves on the results....The political moral is certainly depressing: these people could be made to believe in anybody or anything.[17]

Isherwood interpreted the response of these spectators as gullibility, but they may just as likely have been thoroughly accustomed to treating boxing matches exactly as they would any other dramatic fiction that they watched on a popular stage, by willfully overlooking inconsistencies and giving in to the pleasure of a riveting and action-packed story.

Boxers themselves adroitly blended physical prowess, sexual exhibition, and astute showmanship. Kurt Kaufmann, whom the *Berliner Tageblatt* proclaimed "the strongest man in Berlin" in 1931, displayed the genius for self-promotion that marked any successful prizefighter. He once received 50 marks for pummeling an amusement-park strongman in a boxing contest, before going on later that day to have himself crowned Berlin's "most beautiful man."[18] Both of Max Schmeling's cinematic starring roles involved playing characters who started out in varieté theaters, the setting for so many pugilistic spectacles. Boxing even took on the role of dinner theater in a scene from Fritz Lang's 1928 film *Spies*, in which table after table of elegantly dressed couples watch a men's fight in the intimate and sophisticated setting of a nightclub.[19] Once the match has ended, liveried waiters whisked away the makeshift boxing ring in order to make space for an orchestra and dancing.

A more explicitly sports-related setting did not necessarily alter the audience's expectations, either. Even at the officially sanctioned bouts that took place in big-city sports arenas, crowds clamored for drama, sensation, and blood, not the athletic prowess that the self-styled boxing aficionados appreciated. Frustrated officials even strived to groom a "proper" appreciation of the fights over the course of the 1920s, with limited results.[20] As late as 1928, the commentator Curt Gutmann bemoaned spectators' complete failure to appreciate the sport of boxing: "They want to see pounding [and] grabbing, until one or the other boxer or, better yet, both collapse; the ultimate denouement would be a 'double K.O.'"[21] The German public, in Gutmann's exasperated opinion, viewed boxing as less a noble contest than a fairground cockfight.

To the actor Fritz Kortner, though, therein lay the value of boxing. It communicated a truth about postwar society better than any drama or visual artform ever could: "As mercilessly, as furiously as the boxers go at one another, so bitterly do we all fight for our existence."[22] Even as the fights reflected the political violence and street fighting that rocked the first several years of the Weimar Republic, they may have provided a small measure of reassurance to the watching throngs as well. "Violence, yes, but divided into tolerable doses," writes the historian Birk Meinhardt with regard to Weimar Germany's boxing fever. "And the most important thing: you weren't drawn into it, you remained a spectator."[23] Many stages served such a pressure-valve funtion in the early 1920s. Berlin's "Cabaret of the Nameless," for example, encouraged audiences to vent their hostility by hurling taunts at the performers onstage, a practice that prompted the author and critic Erich Kästner to dub it "a padded cell for the metropolis."[24]

Critics duly noted, and lambasted, the sensationalistic nature of boxing in Germany. Ernst Haberlandt derided the prizefights as lowbrow spectacles that had "just as little to do with sport as skat tournaments, hunger artists, premieres of the fattest man, the thinnest woman, and so forth."[25] Volkmar Iro dismissed the boxing champion in 1926 as a commercial sell-out, and Bernd Ruland described the boxing ring in Weimar Berlin as a space where "the contours between sport and carneval, competition and public amusement blended together."[26] After nearly a decade of trying to raise public appreciation of the skills required in pugilism, *Boxsport* sighed with resignation in 1927 that people continued to "see boxing as a type of variety-show number."[27] Bertolt Brecht, on the other hand, applauded the boisterous spectating habits of Germans and even encouraged playgoers to watch theater as if they were at a boxing match.[28] Much to the chagrin of discerning German fans, though, most spectators inverted Brecht's mantra by watching the fights as if they were theater—lowbrow, fairground theater.

Given the German public's tendency to view all boxing as an outrageous and extreme type of theatrical performance, the distance separating the women's boxing that appeared on varieté stages from the men's boxing that often appeared on those very same stages would not necessarily have appeared all that great to the ordinary spectator. Female boxers, in fact, joined a crowded field of tough, physical women during the Weimar Republic who elicited both fear and fascination from the crowds of onlookers who witnessed their feats. The "iron queen," Martha Farra, for instance, built a career in the early 1920s on her ability to bend horseshoes, bite through chains, and pound nails with her bare hands.[29] A contemporary of hers, Käte Sandwina, claimed the title "strongest woman in the world" for her capacity to break chains and withstand the impact of automobiles being driven over her. After hearing that Sandwina planned to open a school in Berlin for the purpose of instructing other women in these skills, the feuilletonist Rumpelstilzchen exclaimed, "Egad—the entire Kurfürstendamm will be overrun with Brunhildes. At that point, the men will surely mince about in high-heeled shoes and brassieres."[30] Despite Rumpelstilzchen's mocking tone of dismissal, this passage also conveyed the clear discomfort that this physically imposing woman had elicited.

A cover illustration by Walter Trier for the humor magazine *Frechheit* tapped into this same idea by depicting a muscle woman hoisting a sofa over her head, on which several bookish men delicately perched.[31] Audiences undoubtedly viewed female pugilists and strongwomen in multiple, overlapping ways—by turns ridiculous, provocative, enticing, funny, titillating, inspirational, astonishing, and just plain frightening. Bernd Wedemeyer argues that such performances invariably contained "a dangerous, irresistible erotic thrill," something on which Fritz Giese commented, after witnessing a 1925 match-up in Berlin between "fighting broads." "The male spectator is entranced by these 'ladies,' who provide him the elevated pleasure of switched roles," Giese insisted, at a time when "switched roles" formed a staple of popular entertainment throughout Germany.[32]

Ernst Hanfstaengl recalled accompanying Adolf Hitler to watch women's boxing at Lunapark during one of Hitler's early political visits to the capital city. The bouts at this venue definitely veered in the direction of burlesque, with "the women in abbreviated trunks and shirts, mincing around and landing an occasional tap." Hanfstaengl did add that "Hitler was riveted" by what he saw.[33] Rumpelstilzchen proved equally engrossed by an evening of women's boxing at the Metropol Theater in 1921, an aggressive free-for-all that included "impulsive pummeling" from the evening's chief draw, Ilona Kowacs.[34] At one point, Rumpelstilzchen noted, the referee banished Kowacs to her corner "because of her unfair fighting methods (she kicked her opponent in the shins)," in response to which she then "goes up to the manager and hurls a tin pail at his head." In creating and performing such an over-the-top persona, Kowacs publicly acted out in a manner that, to say the least, radically rejected the prewar imperative of female docility. Act or not, the boxing ring afforded Kowacs with the liberating opportunity to unleash some raucous aggression.

In a review of another women's boxing event, this one in 1922, Rumpelstilzchen interlaced ridicule with a surprising concession that some women had the potential to fight skillfully. "The manly broad...could certainly train herself in boxing," he allowed.[35] As for the evening that he had just witnessed, however, Rumpelstilzchen concluded that "these little ladies...have no idea what athletic toughness is." The boxers, though, had already shown a certain amount of "toughness" by stepping out on stage in the first place and engaging in behavior that so thoroughly pushed the boundaries of female respectability. To the women in the audience, meanwhile, these fights may have provided the vicarious thrill of watching someone else do exactly what they had always wanted to do themselves and may even have encouraged a very few to overcome their last remaining reservations.

Female performers, meanwhile, incorporated the movements and affectations of boxing into their own artistic productions. Kickline troops expertly replicated the gestures of the prizefighters, partly in parody and partly in homage. The Max Schmeling film *Knockout* opened with precisely such a scene of chorus girls in boxing outfits replicating a stylized bout. The dancing team of Trudi and Hedi Schoop took this several steps further by pantomiming every aspect of a championship match, from muscle cramps to victory ceremony.[36] The expressionist performer Valeska Gert, meanwhile, developed a dance titled "Boxing Match," in which she re-created the sparring of the professionals so expertly that her audiences would cheer her on as if they were watching an actual fight.[37] Such reenactments of boxing by women challenged the categorization of pugilism as fundamentally male. These performances also presented boxing itself as a piece of choreography, an aspect that many spectators had already learned to appreciate. The sports sociologist Jennifer Hargreaves argues that fans have always understood boxing "to be like ballet," an understanding that the collage artist Hannah Höch conveyed in her description of two boxers during a 1924 fight that she witnessed as "very fine dancers."[38]

Female boxers undeniably foregrounded the theatrics of pugilism, but no more so than the males did, as Christopher Isherwood's description of the fight at Lunapark so aptly illustrated. The worlds of entertainment and boxing overlapped in the Weimar Republic, and audiences derived a similar voyeuristic pleasure from the sport, regardless of the sex of the fighters in the ring. "Masquerades...were a feature of cultural life" in Weimar Germany, writes Ian Buruma, and few people in that era could masquerade with the skill and gusto of the boxer.[39] By appropriating and then exaggerating the aggressive behavior of some men, female fighters like Ilona Kowacs engaged in a type of drag that exposed the performative nature of masculinity, even as they claimed many of those masculine qualities for women, too.

If the pleasure of drag performance derives from "the recognition of a radical contingency in the relation between sex and gender," as Judith Butler argues, then these boxing performances by women suggested that male prizefighters performed in drag as well, from the the exaggerated pre-fight rhetoric to the puffed-up, arm-pumping victory celebrations.[40] The idealized figure of the male boxer in Weimar Germany represented, in almost every way, what Butler calls a "hyperbolic version of 'man,'" and, as such, an "inapproximable ideal" for the boxer who found himself compelled to take on that role.[41] The highly performative and imitative nature of these female boxing performances on popular stages across Germany did not fundamentally differ from the bouts contested by men on those very same stages. German audiences assumed a degree of artifice in the boxing performances of men and women alike in the 1920s, but those performances offered liberating messages nonetheless.

Raising Pain: Violence, Stoicism, and Taking it Like a Man

In 1929, the conservative sports journal *Sport und Gesundheit* published the poem "The Champion Boxer," which lionized the fighter's "atavistic feelings," his capacity to inflict punishment on an opponent and to absorb it himself.[42] "Blood flows in streams," the poet rhapsodized, and "the nose swells." Boxing did not just inure the fighter himself to such violence, either; it ostensibly inoculated the spectators against an aversion to brutality as well. This, according to the poet, made boxing critical to postwar society: "Humanity was becoming so terribly pacifistic. You are the hero who quenches the ancient thirst for blood." In other words, the pugilist would vanquish the encroaching peacenik sentiments that threatened to erode the nation's mettle.

Some in Germany nurtured a belief that the nation had lost the war because it simply could not withstand the suffering, sacrifices, and violence that attended modern armed conflict. To their thinking, Germans, especially those on the home front, had lost their nerve—too coddled by the comforts of the *belle époque* to stomach a brutal struggle when their leaders called upon them to do so. Writings like "The Champion Boxer" presented pugilism as a necessary and timely corrective. If modern society had softened Germans, then pugilism would reinstill the toleration of violence, even an appreciation of it, and thereby banish whatever pacifist impulses had crept into German society. Boxing, more than any other sport in the Weimar Republic, cultivated a specifically violent masculinity, which the sport's enthusiasts cast as a national necessity.

As a consequence, the male boxer emerged as a postwar hero of almost unparalleled status. A poll taken in 1930 showed that heavyweight champion Max Schmeling enjoyed a higher name recognition among Germany's fourteen-year-olds than any other major figure in the interwar period, higher even than the novelist Karl May, whose wildly popular adventure books had nearly the same status among young people then that the Harry Potter series does today.[43] This lionization of the prizefighter revealed Germany's changing conception of ideal manhood since the Wilhelmine era. Because of boxing's close association with working-class ruffians and carnival hawkers, almost no one prior to the war would have singled out the sport as exemplary of manly attributes. Drill sergeants and strict schoolmasters—not the shady purveyors of back-alley brawling—forged the ideal man in the kaiser's Germany.

The 1919 Versailles Treaty drastically reduced the German military's size and composition, however, and therefore army training could no longer fulfill its role as the country's school for manhood. Sports, including boxing, stepped into this vacuum by virtue of their claim to impart physical fitness, discipline, and skills that might prove useful in hand-to-hand fighting. One of Schmeling's nicknames, the "Black Uhlan," explicitly linked the boxer to warriors of yore by simultaneously evoking Schmeling's jet-black hair and the fearsome Uhlan, a nineteenth-century Prussian cavalry lancer. The image of the lone, heroic fighter, who relied on nothing but strength and instincts, moreover, offered an inspiring and nostalgic counterpoint to the anonymity of modern, mechanized warfare.

The rise of the boxer also coincided with a dramatic decline in the social value accorded to *Bildung*, the liberal emphasis on science, the arts, and moral self-development that had formed the cornerstone of middle-class values and aspirations in nineteenth-century Germany. By the 1920s, business achievement and material success had eclipsed *Bildung* in the popular imagination, a process to which the prizefighter himself had contributed in significant ways. The legendary sums that he received for his fights, for example, appeared to show that upward mobility no longer depended on an esoteric appreciation of Schiller, Brahms, and the Greek tragedies, but instead on talent, aggression, and a well-toned body.

The satirical magazine *Simplicissimus* visually represented the new social order on one 1930 cover by depicting the heavyweight champion Max Schmeling towering over the two principal symbols of German greatness in an earlier time, Goethe and Bismarck.[44] The ironic subtitle, "What progress—from Goethe via Bismarck up to Schmeling!" lampooned a society in which a boxer commanded more respect than a world-class poet and a legendary statesman. Gustav Stresemann, the Weimar Republic's Nobel Prize–winning foreign minister, had observed the declining status of *Bildung* and corresponding rise of the boxer with similar chagrin. In a 1927 speech, he expressed his "strongest aversion" for the way in which "individual professional boxers…are being more or less branded as national heroes."[45]

To many Germans, though, the prizefighter embodied resurgent manhood. When *Boxsport* complained in 1925 about how "many denaturalized men and women are running around now," it specifically blamed

society's "systematic battle against natural fighting instincts... and the 'elevation' of defenselessness and pacifism to an ideal—even an athletic ideal!!!"[46] Despite the rampant paramilitarism that characterized the entire Weimar period, *Boxsport* nevertheless perceived a postwar society firmly in the hands of effete malingerers. Like the poet above, it claimed that boxing would shake Germany out of its pacificist torpor by nurturing those "natural fighting instincts" that postwar society had suppressed in men. Back-to-nature youth movements, which surged in popularity after the war, had only produced "effeminate creatures," the journal lamented, who "go out to the woods or meadow Sunday after Sunday with guitars and girls to dance in circles and tell fairy tales." Quoting the boxing champion Ludwig Haymann, it concluded, "It is not poets, thinkers, and dreamers who will bring Germany back to its place in the sun, but, rather, hard—iron hard—constitutions."[47] Only a solid training in pugilism would prepare German boys for the fights to come.

Der Querschnitt, one of Germay's leading cultural journals, praised boxing as a "pure men's sport" and maligned those who would dare to criticize it as "men with women's sensibilities."[48] Alfred Flechtheim, the journal's founder and a prominent art dealer in Berlin, avidly pursued boxing, as did the playwright Bertolt Brecht, the theater director Erwin Piscator, the author Vladimir Nabokov, the artist George Grosz, the sculptor Rudolf Belling, and the conductor Leopold Stokowski, to name just a few of the cultural figures who took up pugilism in the 1920s.[49] Boxing undoubtedly appealed to these men for a number of reasons, including the inherent drama of man-to-man combat.

At the same time, these artists and intellectuals revealed a particular attraction to the sport that stemmed from a self-conscious attitude toward their own perceived effeteness, a self-consciousness that further underscored the declining masculine status of *Bildung*. By publicly associating themselves with a sport that articulated a tough, working-class masculinity, these men sought to bring their own images into closer alignment with the qualities that Weimar society increasingly valued.[50] Flechtheim revealed as much when he declared, with an almost audibly puffed-out chest, "Through boxing a man is made hard and powerful... a real guy."[51] The writer and critic Kurt Tucholsky, however, found this tendency ridiculous, and he chided his fellow literati in 1929, "Fight! But don't shout that you're a fighter. One grows hoarse from listening to this. And has to laugh over the strongman pose."[52]

Intellectuals, however, understandably felt as though society continually questioned their masculinity. The media, after all, regularly mocked the nation's once-celebrated cultural ideal of *Dichter und Denker* (poets and thinkers) for the alleged uselessness of their lofty pursuits and, even worse, the effeminacy of their sensibilities. Fritz Löbl felt that Germany had placed far too much emphasis on *Bildung* in the past, at the expense of manhood-building physical skills. "German writers, if you do not want our young boys to become sissies instead of men, then take your foreign colleagues as an example and come out strongly in favor of boxing," he implored in the monthly *Sport und Sonne* in 1929.[53] Löbl emphasized boxing's raw aggression as just what future generations needed in order to stiffen their spines.

A 1923 poem, meanwhile, succinctly captured the prevailing attitude of the post-*Bildung* era: "You can't defend yourself with thoughts, you have to grab the boxing glove."[54] The poet Karl Kaiser, another product of German *Bildung* who subsequently tried to shed that identity, echoed this sentiment. In his 1931 poem "Boy, become a man!," Kaiser wrote that "life means combat" and advised his young readers to seize it "with your fists."[55] The poem presented boxing as a rite of passage and as essential preparation for survival in the new social order. Given a postwar culture that increasingly valorized the athlete and ridiculed the intellectual, it was little wonder that so many of Weimar Germany's cultural elite chose to publicly perform their own masculinity—and refute the intellectual's reputed softness—by turning to boxing, the most aggressively violent sport of them all.

German culture's increasing celebration of aggressive force, itself a product, in part, of the popularity of boxing, began to reshape the sport by the middle part of the decade. In particular, fans of boxing began to deride the British style, in which judges awarded points to fighters based on how skillfully they had performed in the ring, similar to a fencing match. Instead, Germans more and more favored the American style of boxing, which emphasized the knockout blow. The commentator Ludwig Will glorified offensive fighters who went for the knockout, as the title of his 1926 *Boxsport* essay, "The Will to Destroy," plainly indicated.[56] Defensive fighters lacked "the two greatest masculine characteristics," which Will listed as "battling with a do-or-die attitude and courageous determination." Men needed ruthlessness, not style, Will declared, because "fighting means the destruction of the opponent, and his destruction means victory. That's true in all combat sports and also the central point in war." Will explicitly linked the winning-by-points strategy to England, referring to both the strategy and the country as "overly cultivated and, in principal, outdated." Rudolf Hartung insisted that the point system suppressed a man's natural destructive urges. The boy who acts out violently, Hartung argued in 1927, "possesses more genuinely manly characteristics than some 'men,'" and he argued that German society should actively encourage the youthful *"furor teutonicus*...whose goal and reward lies not in 'point' values...but rather in fervent strength itself and in the instinct for blood."[57]

Bertolt Brecht belittled the point system as fundamentally emasculating, too. "The principal mortal enemies of natural, unaffected, and plebeian boxing are those scholars who sit ringside and tally points in their head," he sneered.[58] Brecht's celebration of boxing as "unaffected and plebeian" explained part of the sport's cachet among so many intellectuals: it represented precisely the blue-collar toughness that they felt personally lacking. Working-class masculinity had begun to challenge the hegemony of the middle-class variant in the 1920s, and German boxers led the charge.[59] A "slumming" chic circulated in cosmopolitan circles, as some Germans affected an attitude of coarseness, rather than refinement. Brecht's loathing of the ringside "scholars," a category to which he arguably belonged, highlighted his own embrace of the new-style masculinity and discomfort with his image as an intellectual.

Because prizefighting demanded that its heroes withstand punishment as well as dish it out, the boxer in Weimar Germany represented, in the words of Tony Jefferson, "the supreme emblem of the hard man."[60] Fans venerated these athletes for their seemingly limitless capacity to absorb punches and continue to fight, for proving that they were, as enthusiasts at the time put it, *"hart im Nehmen"* ("able to take it"). A 1922 report noted that police officers had incorporated boxing into their own training because, even if a belligerent did manage to land a punch, "the hardened man isn't bothered by it."[61] A 1925 book on boxing drove home the point that a stoic ability to "take" a blow reflected manly toughness every bit as much as the capacity to land one.[62] The 1927 serialized novella *The German Tornado* went so far as to claim that a boxer "could not possibly know excessive sensitivity, since…he is used to tolerating blows and punches, regardless of the intensity," suggesting once again that the sport served as a useful inoculation against any weak-kneed tendencies to give up a fight.[63]

The premium placed on a man's ability to take it assumed heightened importance after 1918 because of the perceived causes of Germany's defeat. The kaiser had declared at the onset of hostilities in 1914 that the country with the strongest nerves would win the war, a statement that haunted Germany four years later when it loomed as an indictment of their psychological mettle. Not only had the country's civilians purportedly shown themselves incapable of "taking" the wartime sacrifices, but the phenomenon of shell shock, male hysteria, and the naval mutinies of October 1918 had—according to some observers—revealed that same incapacity in even the soldiers and sailors. No less a figure than General Erich Ludendorff was said by many to have lost his nerves. As historian Paul Lerner writes, "The male hysteric…haunted the German imagination" in the Weimar Republic, since he indicated a man "who shrank from life's difficulties" and ran from a fight.[64] By contrast, the boxer symbolized the anti-hysteric, the man who attacked life's challenges head on. Adolf Hitler, not surprisingly, praised this quality in the boxer. "Above all, the young, healthy body must learn to suffer blows," he wrote in *Mein Kampf* and drew an analogy between the individual capacity to endure suffering in the pursuit of victory and the national one.[65]

Boxers took noticeable pride in the bruises that they had received in their fights, visible proof of their capacity to take it. These wounds testified to the bearer's manly honor, much as the dueling scar had done for the aristocracy and the striving middle classes during the Wilhelmine period. The fact that wounded veterans were desperately trying to conceal their own injuries through the use of facial prostheses at the same as boxers were proudly displaying theirs showed how the physical markers of a fight had taken on radically divergent meanings in the Weimar Republic, depending on the context. A veteran's injuries only underscored his impotence in the face of mechanized combat and reminded his countrymen of a humiliating defeat. A prizefighter's bruises, on the other hand, symbolized a dogged resilience in hand-to-hand engagement. They also communicated the implicit boast, "you should see the other guy," a boast unavailable to those who had served in the vanquished German military. The correspondent Hans Natonek felt that boxing had a lesson to teach society precisely in the way that it honored the bruised and the beaten. "The teary eyes of beautiful women turn toward the defeated in the ring, who receives his well-earned laurels just as the victor does," Natonek wrote. He added, in an implicit and poignant contrast between the respect that injured boxers received and the relative neglect with which society had handled its returning war veterans, "Nothing of the sort happens in real life. The beaten is left, unnoticed, to his own future."[66]

The sports columnist Kurt Doerry described the genuinely fight-hardened pugilist in 1922 as sporting a "punched-in nose" and "mostly deformed ears."[67] Rumpelstilzchen certainly had this image in mind when he lowered his own estimation of the boxer Franz Diener solely because Diener "still did not have much of a bashed-in saddle-nose."[68] Max Schmeling recalled feeling mortified by his own smooth and bruise-free face as a young man in the early 1920s. Upon returning from the gym, Schmeling's pals would taunt him with the question, "Whom are you really fighting, your grandmother?"[69] Desperate to give himself the visage of a bona-fide fighter, Schmeling confessed, "I punched myself...until my nose turned blue." This fetishization of the broken nose showed how an appearance of having "taken it" contributed centrally to so many men's identities as boxers. Schmeling's self-inflicted bruise, meanwhile, also recalled the surgically constructed dueling scars to which some nineteenth-century men turned when they longed for the social cachet that the scar provided, but had no intention of engaging in actual swordplay.[70]

The violent masculinity of pugilism appealed to women in the Weimar Republic as well, both those who watched the fights and those who took part in them. By celebrating or engaging in violence themselves, these female boxing enthusiasts staked a claim to masculine behavior for women, too.[71] Germany's press, in fact, engaged in a heated debate over the "masculinization of the woman" in the 1920s. Some of this discourse reflected shrill hyperbole, but it also focused attention on the very real dynamic of women adopting masculine traits, behaviors, and prerogatives for themselves. Many women in Weimar Germany may well have shared the sentiments of Jenni Olson, a boxer in the early 1990s, who felt that the sport brought out "a male-ness" in her.[72]

Observers in the 1920s clearly perceived masculine qualities in Germany's sportswomen, as we have already seen from characterizations of female tennis players (see chap. 1). One lovestruck male character in the novel *Sport um Gagaly* swooned over its heroine, a crack tennis player, specifically because she had "the assets of a man expressed in a woman."[73] At a 1925 conference, Dr. Margarete Streicher spoke of a "certain masculine influence" that she had observed in all areas of female physical culture since 1918.[74] Rumpelstilzchen's above-mentioned reference to "the manly broad" who "could certainly train herself in boxing" also acknowledged the presence of masculine female athletes. Female spectators, too, commonly exhibited violent impulses, especially when they entered the boxing arena to watch the big prizefights. Paula von Reznicek, in her 1928 handbook on living the life of a "modern" lady, enjoined women to attend the fights as an assertion of their independence. "We are not stereotypes anymore," she insisted as she urged others to join her in embracing the violent spectacle of boxing.[75]

Some men welcomed this female patronage of the sport with open arms. Erwin Petzall, for example, dusted off the well-worn theory of the woman's civilizing influence in order to support his own argument that female attendance would curtail the notoriously crude behavior of male spectators.[76] As Petzall plainly stated, the woman's "presence will contribute greatly to the disciplining of the male public."[77] One male fan alluded to exactly this type of dampening effect when he complained to *Boxsport* in 1925 that women should not attend the fights. Men want to "yell to our heart's content at boxing matches," he explained, "and not be restrained out of respect for the weaker sex."[78]

According to most observers, however, this fan need not have given the slightest thought to offending "the weaker sex." Instead, female spectators seemed even more excited by the violence than male ones. Rumpelstilzchen attributed this to nature. By way of proof, he pointed to the "cruel feline instinct" of two women whom he had recently observed at a 1924 bout, who "lick their lips in deep satisfaction after watching the left eyebrow of one boxer ripped open."[79] A 1928 article in *Sport und Sonne* ventured a similarly biological explanation for women's appreciation of violent spectacle when it described boxing matches as environments in which "[female] nature reveals itself as cruel, cold and lascivious."[80] After witnessing the lusty reaction of one female fan, in particular, the correspondent decided that "this woman has only one regret: that we don't have bullfights here yet."

In the story "Inge and the Boxing Match," Inge's escort called the female fans "wildcats, who are intoxicated by the sport."[81] Inge, attending a bout for the very first time, arrived at the same horrified conclusion when she noticed that several nearby women had "an expression that she had only seen flare up in Madrid at the bullfights." Where commentators like Petzall expected women to provide examples of civilized conduct, others pointed in the opposite direction, describing female fans as the most unrestrained and violence-loving in the house. The psychoanalyst Horst-Eberhard Richter recalled his own mother as the one who pushed him into boxing as a child in the early 1930s. After telling her that his schoolmates were taunting him, his mother simply replied, "hit back!"[82] The prizefights of the Weimar period seemed to place exactly this female encouragement of violence on full, public, and—to many German observers—disturbing display.

The fact that so many women appeared able and eager to watch violent brawls fed a sense of alarm at the apparent coarsening of German society as a whole, suggesting that years of warfare, political street-fighting, and assassinations had dulled moral sensitivities and inured the population to suffering. Officials supported such a development up to a point, since tougher citizens would endure the hardships that their forebears between 1914 and 1918 ostensibly could not. When women shifted from stoically tolerating suffering to openly encouraging it, however, their behavior veered into the threateningly masculine and outright brutal. If *Boxsport* attributed the postwar "denaturalization" of men to their repression of the fighting instinct, then the "denaturalization" of women stemmed from their unleashing of it.[83]

This specter of unleashed female violence and the denaturalized woman caused Germany's press to talk about, fret over, and argue against women's competitive boxing out of all proportion to its actual practice. The female boxer symbolized the masculine woman, and the exercise advocate Martha Werth declared as early as 1921 that boxing was inherently unwomanly.[84] Erwin Petzall, who had argued so strongly in favor of women attending the fights as spectators, nevertheless decreed in that same 1925 article that "the practice of fist fighting by women is obviously something unnatural."[85] A physician attending the 1925 Berlin conference on women's sports likewise insisted that "we [women] don't want to knock our opponent to the ground in a competition. That's not at all our psychic makeup, and therefore we don't box."[86] Dr. Elsa Matz, attending a 1929 conference on women's sports, explicitly warned that those who engaged in intrinsically male activities like boxing "would become masculinized and coarsened" themselves.[87] Even the lesbian magazine *Garçonne*, in a 1931 article, regretted the fact that some doctors had recognized boxing as a women's sport, since its practice so plainly jeopardized one's womanhood.[88]

These admonitions against female boxing and its putatively masculinizing influence in the 1920s did not deter some women from stepping into the ring and displaying precisely the masculine attributes of aggression, toughness, and violence that worried medical officials. The period of hyperinflation that stretched from 1918 to 1924 marked the heyday of women's bouts, in part because of an anything-goes atmosphere during these years that encouraged iconoclasm and the most daring forms of cultural expression. To some extent then, women's boxing appealed for no other reason than its sheer radicality. Looking back upon the early Weimar Republic from the vantage point of 1931, Hans Ostwald presented the inflation years as a topsy-turvy time in which "many things that otherwise took place in secret appeared openly in the bright light of the public stage."

In this environment, Ostwald continued, "it was the women who…completely transformed themselves."[89]

The shock value of women's boxing, in fact, just as likely attracted women to the practice as deterred them from it. The female boxers' transgression into a male sphere represented emancipation and a fulfillment of the new republic's promise that men and women would enjoy equal rights and equal opportunities in all areas of society. In this light, women's boxing seemed positively liberating to many women, just as the appropriation of other male prerogatives in the 1920s did, from monocles and neckties to autoracing and solo flying—the manlier, the better. In addition, female boxing tapped into a general sense after the war that individuals needed to fend for themselves, a sense felt perhaps most acutely by the growing ranks of unmarried women. Finally, and quite apart from any practical or political consideration, some women simply liked to do it, and boxing's booming popularity in Weimar Germany naturally attracted dedicated female adherents as well as male ones. These women, in turn, benefited from the high consumer demand for fistfighting spectacles on those relatively rare occasions when they did stage public women's bouts.

Press accounts do record the existence of organized contests between female fighters in the early 1920s, although it remains unclear who sanctioned these matches or how seriously the competitors and spectators took them. The bouts did seem to draw sizable crowds, though, even during a time when soaring inflation could quickly put the pinch on wages and savings. A brief 1921 notice in the journal *Boxsport* mentioned a program of "Five ladies' boxing matches and two matches between blacks and whites" that took place in Koblenz.[90] The event presented itself as a novelty, but the placement of men's bouts on the same evening's billing as women's fights not only blurred the boundary separating the two but also cast the women's bouts in a more competitive light. Furthermore, as the reporter noted, these fights took place in a sports arena, and not on a varieté stage, which established the expectation of a bit more fist fighting and a bit less showmanship. A very brief follow-up report two weeks later noted only that, despite a postponement and very expensive tickets, the event had sold out.[91]

Erwin Petzall made a fleeting reference in 1925 to "a few practical experiences with actual women's boxing," which he made a point of distinguishing from the "ladies' fights" that featured on burlesque stages. Petzall never elaborated on the nature of these bouts, however.[92] Other references to women's boxing events in the first half of the 1920s also distinguished them from the bawdy productions that crowded the popular stages. A 1922 article on a match in Frankfurt, for instance, noted that the audience could have gone to any number of nearby clubs to see women in skimpy boxing costumes. Instead, it had shelled out dear money to watch women step into the ring and punch one another.[93] The American heavyweight champion Jack Dempsey witnessed a women's boxing match during his Berlin tour that same year, and it apparently made a big impression on him, since he reportedly talked about nothing else for the entire evening.[94]

The paucity of newspaper coverage regarding women's boxing almost certainly speaks to the relative rarity of these events, but it may also reflect the fact that such bouts straddled the gray zone between sports and entertainment, with the result that editors either did not know how to cover these events or simply did not care to do so. The women's boxing matches that did take place in the Weimar Republic's early years showcased female aggression and violence to a degree unprecedented anywhere else in German culture, with the possible exception of a largely underground S/M scene in the country's largest metropolises.[95] Like that subculture, women's boxing attracted male spectators with the illicit promise of violence by and/or to women. Jennifer Hargreaves argues that men's desire to watch women's boxing has, throughout the twentieth century, derived in part from the sport's "potential as a surrogate for male brutality against the 'weaker' sex."[96] A similar desire, though, seemed to animate the crowds at men's fights as well.

Despite the rarity of competitive women's matches in the postwar years, they had created enough of a concern by 1921 that the German Association of Amateur Boxing called for their explicit prohibition.[97] The association cited a number of reasons for this move, including a fear that the presence of women's boxing would impede the efforts of men's boxing to emerge from the shadow of its own show-business reputation and to establish itself as a respected sport. Four years later, the Federation of German Fist Fighters issued a prohibition against women fighting men, in light of the perceived threat of another Weimar-era spectacle, albeit an equally rare one.[98] These bans, however, may have done more to open up the possibility of women's boxing than to shut it down. The act of prohibiting something itself can provide, in Judith Butler's words, "*the discursive occasion* for a resistance," and the bans themselves may only have served to advertize the fact of women's boxing in the first place.[99]

A 1928 article in the *Berliner Tageblatt* seemed to confirm many men's worst fears of the threat posed by aggressive women with trained fists.[100] It reported the criminal proceedings against Anita Wiznowski, "a big, rough woman, a positively colossal broad," who stood accused of aggravated robbery. She had beaten up a cattle trader and taken all of his money, a story made all the more harrowing by virtue of her earlier career as a prizefighter in traveling sideshows. The victim, according to testimony, "received from her a terrible hook to the chin, which sent him down for the count." Wiznowski apparently ran a regular criminal operation, assigning to her two male underlings the task of emptying the unconscious man's pockets, for which she gave them a 1 percent cut of the resulting loot. Wiznowski later stole another man's wallet, too. When asked by the judge why he had let her steal his wallet, this second victim replied sheepishly: "I already knew Anita's hard punches. And I thought: It's better to just leave it to the criminal police to take care of the matter." Wiznowski received twenty-one months in prison, but her initial criminal success demonstrated the harrowing fact that a particularly formidable female boxer could easily overpower, or simply intimidate, most men.

The specter of the violent woman surfaced with remarkable frequency in the popular culture of the Weimar Republic, with one of the earliest depictions taking the form of a female boxer in Ernst Lubitsch's 1919 film comedy *The Oyster Princess*.[101] It starred the famously tomboyish actress Ossi Oswalda, who played a business magnate's volatile and violent daughter, also named Ossi. In a pivotal early scene, she attends a morning meeting of the ladies' temperance society, at which each member chooses from among the previous night's haul of drunkards the one whom she wishes to "reform." When the particularly handsome and inebriated Prince Nucki staggers into the room, all of the women instantly vie for the right to treat him. Ossi organizes a solution to this impasse: "We'll deal with the dispute through a boxing match." The women change into their fight clothes, line up in two rows, and begin to spar. Gradually, women limp out of the room, rubbing sore legs and backs, and, after a few minutes, only Ossi and one other remain. Ossi chases the woman briefly, before knocking her to the floor for a ten-count.

Scraps of clothing litter the room as Ossi turns to Nucki and ominously warns, "Now it's your turn." Visibly cringing, Nucki braces himself for one of her flattening blows. Instead, Ossi seductively removes her boxing gloves and kisses him sweetly. The playfully naughty conclusion, in which her removal of the gloves mimicked a striptease, suggested a scene straight from the burlesque stage. The contest itself, however, presented the aggressively confident and violent side of women's boxing that emerged as an equally prominent image in Weimar Germany. And Ossi's suggestion to box in the first place slyly appropriated the age-old tradition of rival male suitors dueling for the hand of a woman. This time, however, women fought over the man. The boxing match asserted a woman's right to claim something by physical force, since Ossi did not rely on emotion or logic to make her case for treating Nucki, but on her fists alone. Furthermore, even as Ossi coquettishly sheds her gloves, she remains decisively in charge—the seducer and not the seduced. She calls for the carriage to take them back to her place, and she declares her determination to take responsibility for Nucki's "private treatment."

The sight in 1919 of so many women competing on screen over one man paralleled the situation in which many women of marrying age found themselves at the time, given that they far outnumbered marriageable men after the war. The media made this a topic of heightened concern throughout the Weimar era, as indicated by a 1921 article that urged women to dress more fashionably, lest they suffer the "fate that is caused by the decrease in men who are interested and able to marry."[102] Female audiences, therefore, could easily have read the message of *The Oyster Princess* as: "Learn to box, because you're going to have to fight for a man."

In an environment of "surplus women," boxing appeared as both an apt metaphor and a useful skill. The scene in which Ossi and her friends rehabilitated helpless drunkards also resonated with the millions of scenes that played out on a daily basis across the nation, in which able-bodied women cared for male veterans disabled by the war.

The 1923 Austrian film *East and West* presented an even bolder depiction of the violent female boxer. The Yiddish star Molly Picon played a rebellious young woman who appears in the opening scene wearing boxing gloves.[103] Picon's character has even packed her punching ball for a trip to Galicia to attend a cousin's wedding. Just after her arrival, Picon blithely devours the entire meal that had been prepared for the breaking of the Yom Kippur fast, in reaction to which the family matriarch sends her to her room. Picon works herself into a violent rage on the punching ball before storming back into the kitchen and knocking the woman out cold. Like Oswalda, Picon, too, appropriated a number of masculine traits in addition to boxing, including repeatedly defying the Orthodox community's careful segregation of the sexes by disguising herself as a man. Picon's gender-bending appealed strongly to the men, just as Oswalda's had, and Picon, too, remained firmly in charge of events throughout the entire film. By the conclusion, she had remade her male love interest to fit her own designs, inspiring him to modernize his appearance and forego Talmudic studies in favor of a business career.

Alongside these cinematic depictions, the specter of the aggressive and surprisingly powerful female pugilist surfaced in jokes, songs, and cartoons of the period, particularly in situations where she knocked out her husband or fiancé. The popular Berlin cabaret singer Claire Waldoff belted out a song about her fictional neighbor, Frau Meyer, who boxed so well that she regularly flattened Herr Meyer.[104] Her fists instilled such fear in him, the lyrics continued, that he avoided her as much as possible. *Boxsport* published a humorous piece in 1925, meanwhile, in which a man solicited the help of his wife in teaching their children to box. As the lesson begins, he asks his wife to throw a demonstration punch at him, which he anticipates easily parrying. Instead, his wife lands the left hook with such power and precision that the man drops to the floor, blood pouring from his nose.[105] Although played for comedic effect, these jokes drew on perceptions of the violent woman and her capacity for a well-landed punch. To some observers, female boxers not only heralded the emancipation of women, but also threatened the subjugation of men.

Made from Scratch: Selling the Self-Made Slugger

Boxing could seem liberating for men and women alike in the Weimar Rebublic. This stemmed in part from the fact that the lifting of all legal sanctions against the sport had coincided with the end of the monarchy and the expansion of the franchise in 1918. Like the greatly expanded democratic politics, boxing afforded new opportunities. As one female pugilist insisted after an evening of women's bouts in 1922, "if other women can have themselves elected to parliament, why shouldn't we be allowed to box?"[106] This woman seemed to see political rights as paving the way for athletic ones, but the influence cut both ways. Boxing promised its practitioners a destiny shaped by their skills and hard work alone, and that mentality had implications in Weimar Germany that stretched beyond the world of sports. Max Schmeling subscribed to that outlook and helped to propagate it among his fans. In his first memoir, published in 1930, Schmeling wrote that through boxing, "you can be whatever you want to be."[107] Indeed, boxers provided some of the most prominent examples of being whatever one wanted to be that the Weimar Republic had to offer.

For Hein Müller, who reigned as Germany's light heavyweight champion in the late 1920s, a youthful foray into the sport of boxing led to a complete metamorphosis. A 1929 profile of Müller described him before he entered the sport as "a tiny, pale boy of ninety pounds, so tiny, so pale, and so light." Several years of dedicated training in pugilism, however, had transformed him into a powerful, imposing figure, and the profile concluded that "Müller provides the living example of what courage, tenacity and hard work can achieve."[108] This same desire to remake one's body motivated Weimar intellectuals to engage in boxing drills themselves and to work out in the same gyms that the top-ranked pugilists did. The theater director Erwin Piscator erected a punching ball and other exercise equipment in his bedroom, while Carl Zuckmayer, Egon Erwin Kisch, Curt Bois, and others chose to train at Sabri Mahir's gym and "boxing salon," which attracted almost as many cultural luminaries in the 1920s as did the legendary Romanisches Café.

Gay men recognized the transforming power of boxing, too. For one thing, it built the sort of taut physique and macho image that would overturn stereotypes and attract other guys like a magnet. In 1920, the gay magazine *Freundschaft* appealed to both of these advantages when it declared, manifesto-style, "Do away with the powder, make-up, and perfume, which are only good for the ballroom! Through training, physical exercise, and sports...genuine friendships will flourish. The super virile men among us will embrace this suggestion without hesitation."[109] In addition, boxing promised to develop in its practitioners an ability to defend themselves with their fists, a huge asset to any gay man who wished to live openly in Weimar German society, its legendarily permissive atmosphere notwithstanding. In a 1920 letter to *Freundschaft*, one reader recommended the critical necessity of sports like "wrestling, boxing, [and] weight-lifting," in light of social hostility toward Berlin's increasingly visible homosexual subculture.[110] Those who did not take up the sport themselves often cultivated a patron relationship with those who had. As the sexologist Magnus Hirschfeld had observed in 1904, wealthy gay men had a history of supporting struggling fighters in exchange for the latter's services as bodyguards and, implicitly, companions to their benefactors.[111]

Prizefighters took pride in the results of their physical training, just as their fans took pleasure in it. Boxing reportage lavished attention on every square inch of the fighter's body, painstakingly recording its measurements as if diagramming a high-performance engine, and references to the athlete as a "fighting machine" rapidly became a cliché of boxing journalism.[112] When the literary magazine *Die Weltbühne* referred to Breitensträter as a "mechanized wonder" who was "put together in an admirably functional manner," they could as easily have been quoting from the latest car advertisement or Walter Gropius's Bauhaus manifesto.[113] Hermann von Wedderkop, who replaced Flechtheim as publisher of the literary journal *Querschnitt* after its first year, described Breitensträter's body as an engineering marvel, "built entirely according to machine-like guidelines."[114] Through photographs, statistics, and rhapsodic descriptions like this one, the press focused readers' attention on the boxer's impressively self-made body, which it established as a postwar standard of physical perfection.

In a 1925 book on boxing, Gustav Schäfer could scarcely contain his swoon as he lovingly detailed the manner in which a well-trained fighter's "hips become lithe and relaxed....The stomach loses its fat and instead gains muscle....The shoulders become broad and muscular from the workouts on the punching bag."[115] By proclaiming the sport's power to craft broad shoulders and washboard abs, this passage acknowledged that postwar men viewed their bodies as just as central to a successful self-presentation as women did. In the words of the sociologist R. W. Connell, the boxer's narcissistic attention to his own body stood in opposition to "the dominant construction of masculinity as outward turned."[116] His unassailable status as an icon of manliness, however, paved the way for other men in Weimar Germany to express a similar narcissism of their own.

Pugilists remade their spirits as well as their flesh. The boxer subjected himself to an austere lifestyle that denied the pleasures of eating, drinking, smoking, and sex. In 1922, *Boxsport* praised the monastic air of the "true champion" and his "renunciation of the cruder sensual amusements of an overly refined cosmopolitan culture."[117] In so doing, the boxer reasserted the importance of *Selbstbeherrschung* (self-control) to manly comportment, in stark contrast to the male tennis player who indulged his every impulse. Boxers typically cloistered themselves in rural camps for weeks prior to a fight, where they remade their bodies through rigorous training and their psyches through rigorous abstaining. The 1927 story "The German Tornado" reminded readers that a genuine fighter "has to submit not only to a strict physical diet but also to an exceptionally painstaking spiritual one."[118] *Boxsport* concluded in 1922, with echoes of a puritan sermon, that the "immoral person" would invariably succumb to the superior "spiritual fist" of the self-controlled fighter.[119]

Weimar Germany's champion boxers pursued social and cultural transformation, too. The sociologist Loïc Wacquant refers to the ring as the fighter's "stage," on which he could "construct a heroic, transcendent self" that overcame his proletarian background.[120] Because so many champions of the 1920s had risen out of a working-class milieu, their personal biographies suggested that lack of family privilege no longer presented an insurmountable obstacle to wealth and status in the new Germany. Boxers exemplified the process whereby "outsiders" of the prewar period—in this case working-class sluggers—became "insiders" in the postwar one.[121] Prizefighters enjoyed ex officio insiderhood in the 1920s, such that Max Schmeling served as a judge for the very first Miss Germany pageant in 1927, even though he had only just begun his boxing career and had yet to win a major title.[122]

To working-class youth, the boxer's life story presented a tantalizing route to fame, fortune, and social status. Even if exceedingly few men actually "made it"—Christiane Eisenberg estimates that only a fraction of the five hundred to seven hundred professional boxers in the entire Weimar period earned a decent living at it—the German media nevertheless established the prizefighter as a financial success story.[123] "Everyone who is a good boxer moves into the professional class," observed the daily *Frankfurter Zeitung* in 1928, "in the hopes of earning the famous mountain of gold that one reads so much about in the newspaper."[124] A would-be manager promised a young blue-collar boxer just such a mountain of gold in the 1925 story *The German Devil*, "Man, if I looked and punched like you, I'd be a famous and rich man in a couple of weeks!"[125] The boxer, not surprisingly, quickly fulfills this prophecy. And he found a real-life counterpart in Hein Müller, who, as a 1929 magazine profile reminded its readers, illustrated a prizefighter's dramatic ascent "from common origins."[126] Boxing's rags-to-riches reputation even lured successful athletes away from other sports, including the German shot-put champion Ludwig Haymann, who sacrificed his eligibility for the 1928 Olympics— and a likely gold medal—for a shot at the big purse.[127]

The media reinforced this reputation by frequently expressing far greater interest in the boxer's earnings outside the ring than in his achievements inside it. When Schmeling returned from his 1929 U.S. tour, one report cut straight to the bottom line: "Not only did he earn a great deal there in his fight against Paolino [Uzcudun], with a $72,000 take, but he also did a good business with the exhibition fights at twenty-six locations."[128] That same year, the boxing journal *Boxwoche* ran a cover illustration of Schmeling, smartly attired in a business suit and merrily rolling along atop a silver dollar.[129]

The promise of exactly this kind of a fortune had propelled Schmeling into boxing in the first place. "When I heard what [Dempsey] earned," Schmeling recalled in 1929, "my courage, my drive, and my determination only grew." He immediately added that the European championship bout, "which I won in two-and-a-half minutes," had netted him a cool 25,000

A 1929 cover of the boxing journal *Boxwoche* presents Max Schmeling merrily rolling atop a silver dollar coin after his remarkably lucrative tour of the United States. *Courtesy of Volker Kluge, reproduced in 100 Jahre Max Schmeling—ein Brandenburger (Förderverein Kurort Bad Saarow, e.V.)*

marks.[130] That same sum would not even have raised an eyebrow two years later, as commentators came to associate increasingly lavish incomes with the Schmeling name. When he pocketed $130,000 for winning the world heavyweight championship in 1931, for example, *B.Z. am Mittag* yawned, "It does not involve so terribly much money this time."[131] Delivered at the height of Germany's economic depression, this remarkably jaded comment demonstrated just how inflated the financial expectations for successful prizefighters had become.

The fact that Schmeling's income in 1929 already far surpassed that of the Nobel Prize–winning author Thomas Mann highlighted once again how radically postwar society had reevaluated the relative worths of the mind and the body, at least when it came to sports. Under the headline "Two Powerhouses," the satirical magazine *Ulk* featured a caricature of Schmeling towering over Mann, even though the latter stood atop a stack of six of his famously thick novels. The caption juxtaposed two quotations from news organizations, the first announcing that Mann had received 200,000 marks for his Nobel Prize in literature and the second reporting that Schmeling's next fight had already guaranteed him $250,000, the equivalent of 1,050,000 marks.[132] In case anyone in Weimar Germany wished to place a monetary value on *Bildung*'s relative decline vis-à-vis "biceps culture," this cartoon provided it. At the same time, it portrayed Schmeling as a boxer who had indisputably "made" himself, with a vengeance.

The ability to exploit one's fame beyond the world of boxing became another established part of the prizefighter's idealized narrative of self-madeness. Active and retired boxers negotiated advertising contracts, hawked photographs of themselves, and even opened nightclubs, as the ex-fighter Franz Diener had done in Berlin in the mid-1920s. Even more importantly, prizefighters quickly discovered that they could parlay their name recognition into careers on the silver screen, just as Hans Breitensträter had done in 1921, at the very beginning of his boxing career. At first Breitensträter just performed stunts, but he got the lead in *The Master of Death* later that year, a film that naturally featured him in a fistfight.[133] Even minor German fighters could often land a part or two, as Carl Peterssen did when Alfred Hitchcock cast him in a 1928 English boxing film, one of that director's very first features.[134] Never one to pass up a money-making opportunity, Max Schmeling epitomized the prizefighter-cum-matinee-idol, too, and he starred in the two most prominent German boxing films of the era, *Love in the Ring* (1930) and *Knockout* (1934).

The boxer Kurt Prenzel also made a well-publicized transition to the silver screen, but because he managed this almost entirely thanks to the patronage of his wife, the successful film actress Fern Andra, Prenzel did not wholly qualify as a self-made man, at least according to the exacting standards of the German media.[135] Instead, commentators highlighted his dependency on Andra, who owned a production company and enjoyed much broader name recognition. *Rumpelstilzchen* even suggested that Andra had smothered Prenzel in her oversized shadow. Andra's habit of bestowing such expensive gifts on her husband as a new car, the feuilletonist insinuated, had turned Prenzel into a kept man. Rather than Prenzel having remade himself, *Rumpelstilzchen* believed that Andra had done the remaking. "Under her influence, under her aesthetic effect," he wrote, "the champion boxer Kurt Prenzel...is among the most elegant men in Berlin today."[136] This was not meant as a compliment.

In contrast to men's tennis, in which calling a player "elegant" represented the highest praise, the term had a pejorative ring in boxing. After reporting in 1924 that Prenzel planned to play the role of a dandy in a forthcoming revue sketch, a reporter for *Boxsport* expressed concern. "If they [boxers] look like an 'Elegant', that does nobody any harm," he assured readers, but "to be an 'Elegant' only, that's something that they should never be." Prenzel had not yet reduced himself to the level of an "Elegant only," the reporter insisted, but "he does seem on the road to becoming one."[137] Prenzel had clearly "made it," and he had done so in part through his boxing, which had no doubt attracted Fern Andra to him in the first place. His further development beyond that point, however, and especially his later status as a film actor and dapper man about town, derived more from the efforts of his wife than himself. Moreover, as both Rumpelstilzchen and *Boxsport* readily pointed out, the direction of this remaking had deviated in important ways from the standards set by the sport.

Boxing afforded women an opportunity to remake themselves, too, even though female boxers never even came close to making the sort of money that the sport dangled before its male prizefighters. Some women who boxed in semi-competitive or burlesque venues after the war did manage to earn a modest income doing so, but the real nature of the female boxer's self-making was much more physical and psychological than financial. Through training on the punching ball and sandsack, workouts in the boxing gym, and sparring with male or female partners and coaches, women refashioned their bodies and spirits in ways similar to that of the male fighter. These women developed a leaner and stronger body, a greater sense that they could defend themselves, and an aggressively self-confident new image.

A few women were already engaging privately in various forms of pugilistic training before the First World War. A 1909 photograph for the Ullstein publishing house, for instance, shows two well-dressed women in boxing gloves sparring with one another in what the caption described as a boxing school for women.[138] After the war, the practice became much more public. In the 1920 film *Steuermann Holk*, a character played by the cinema idol Asta Nielsen, famous for her gender-bending roles, takes boxing lessons from a black champion.[139] Whereas publicly staged bouts between women had enjoyed their brief florescence during the inflationary period that ended in 1924, boxing exercises for women grew steadily throughout the 1920s and enjoyed their greatest media visibility during the last years of the decade. By the end of the Weimar Republic, workouts on the punching ball or sandsack had become instantly recognized markers of modern womanhood. Boxing drills never attracted the devoted female following that tennis did, but its outré status did draw a number of self-consciously modern women, including some of Weimar Germany's most prominent celebrities.

Two women take boxing lessons in 1909. *Ullstein Bild/The Granger Collection, New York*

German sports journals regularly showed these women engaged in the very same drills and exercises that the male prizefighters performed, suggesting that the gap separating men's physical abilities from women's was not all that great to begin with and was in the process of narrowing. By engaging in boxing drills, women also claimed strength and aggression as qualities that they, too, needed to cultivate. When the newspaper *Hannoversche Allgemeine* proclaimed in the early 1920s that "the woman has awoken from the passivity of the last century to active life," nothing illustrated this awakening more forcefully than female boxing.[140] Carla Verständig declared in 1927 that society had falsely constructed a notion of female passivity. On the contrary, she wrote, women demonstrated through their involvement in sports the very same steely will that their male counterparts did.[141] The postwar era required female self-sufficiency, after all, in which women fended for themselves.

When *Sport im Bild* published a photograph in 1922 of two young women in athletic attire boxing one another while a third one coached them from the side, it pointed toward a new era in women's combat sports. Whereas earlier female boxers—what few there had been—had trained under the tutelage of men, this photograph showed a woman taking on the coaching responsibilities, too.[142] The sport itself, like its adherents, was becoming more self-sufficient. By the end of the decade, female boxers appeared on the covers of sports magazines with surprising frequency.

A 1930 issue of *Sport und Gesundheit*, for instance, featured a photograph on its cover of a young woman in boxing gloves helping her opponent back to her feet.[143] The caption described their sparring as "fun-loving," but the well-outfitted gymnasium in which these women boxed suggested that they approached the workout with a certain amount of seriousness. Moreover, the caption's identification of the women as "two film beauties" framed their boxing workout as a contributor to their toned figures and an important element in their self-presentation.

By the middle of the 1920s, it was no longer unheard of to see women training in the most famous gyms, sports schools, and boxing studios in Germany, where they received expert coaching and rigorous instruction in the fundamentals of pugilism. The College of Physical Education in Berlin began to instruct its female students in boxing in 1923, including not only the techniques and skills necessary for workouts on the sand sack but also lessons in fistfighting.[144] In an apparent effort to preempt the potential concerns of cultural conservatives, one article emphasized that the program segregated men and women during boxing instruction, rather than teaching them in coed classes. The 1925 course catalog for Berlin's Sportpalast included individual instruction for women on punching technique and footwork.[145] Athletes in other women's sports, moreover, incorporated boxing drills into their own training programs throughout the 1920s as a means of improving strength, agility, and mental performance.[146]

In 1926, a full-page photograph of a woman intently working out on the punching ball appeared in the sports magazine *Arena*. Its caption declared, "Today, the woman boxes," a statement that functioned both as a description and an imperative.[147] Paula von Reznicek, in her 1928 handbook for the modern lady, recommended to all of her readers that they incorporate a similar workout on the punching ball into their morning *toilette*. The accompanying illustration, in which a woman dressed only in shorts and boxing gloves concentrated on her boxing drills, linked modernity, athleticism, and a toned beauty within the figure of the female pugilist.[148] The poem "Her Cares," from the same year, made an identical linkage between pugilism and modern womanhood. "You are responsible for your figure," it lectured its readers, as a preface to its prescription of daily boxing drills to help them to meet that responsibility.[149]

In a two-page spread in 1928, *Sport und Sonne* stressed the tremendous health benefits that boxing provided to everyone, "including the ladies."[150] The author of this article, Max Leusch, nevertheless discouraged women from engaging in actual bouts and instead assured his female readers, "It's sufficient if you pursue boxing as exercise and gymnastics and not as a competitive sport." Leusch labeled this type of pugilism "Gentleman's boxing," which already implied that women would be participating in the very same regimen that had drawn so many white-collar males to the sport during the Weimar Republic. In this, Leusch echoed the boxing coach Gustav Schäfer, who had advocated boxing drills for women in his 1925 book and similarly insisted that both practices offered

Morgenarbeit

Heute boxt die Frau

The sports magazine *Die Arena* decares that "today, the woman boxes" and features an attractive woman working out on a punching ball. *Zentralbibliothek der Sportwissenschaften der Deutschen Sporthochschule Köln*

A 1928 ladies' handbook similarly encourages a workout on the
punching ball as a part of every modern woman's morning toilette. *Author's collection*

themselves "as physical exercise or as a competitive sport."[151] Leusch, however, did not envision this as a gentle workout in the manner of rhythmic gymnastics. In fact, he encouraged women to unleash their violent impulses on the punching bag: "Paint the face of your respective creditor on it and skillfully pummel him for three minutes." His admonition, moreover, assumed that women faced the same economic concerns as men and that they, too, would look to boxing for the skills and characteristics necessary for negotiating the social terrain.

Women's boxing gained further visibility, as well as a glamorous cachet, by attracting the rich, famous, and independent. The fashion journalist Helen Hessel had herself photographed sparring with her husband Franz, from whom she learned to box.[152] When the ex-fighter and boxing trainer Sabri Mahir opened a gym and "boxing salon" in the center of Berlin, he attracted almost as many female luminaries as he did male ones. There, prominent male prizefighters like Max Schmeling and Franz Diener crossed paths with actresses like Carola Neher and Marlene Dietrich. Neher regularly sparred with Mahir and sometimes even with Diener himself, and Neher approached these bouts with total focus. Schmeling recalled once seeing Neher and Diener hard at it: "I went quite casually up to the ring and made a couple of playful comments to Neher, but Diener sent me away. He took the entire thing just as seriously as his female pupil."[153] Both Neher and her sparring partner, quite clearly, saw nothing playful about it.

The best-selling author and screenwriter Vicki Baum trained at the gym, too, under the guidance of Mahir himself, who pushed her every bit as hard as he pushed his male boxers. Baum said of Mahir that he "was simply incapable of making a distinction during training between professionals and those who wanted solely to have an athletic workout. He was relentless."[154] This environment of equal expectations apparently paid off for Baum, who claimed to have once matched Diener's endurance at jumping rope.[155] Like so many others at the time, Baum built up her confidence as well as her muscles through boxing, and she developed an intimate self-awareness. "To overcome myself," she writes, "oh, yes, that was another matter. I failed on this account in Sabri Mahir's gym countless times, but also celebrated a few triumphs."[156] The parallels between Baum's remaking and that of a prizefighter extended to her strictly controlled post-workout lunch of a cucumber salad, which she shared with Mahir. Asceticism, it seems, marked female fighters, too.

To a much greater extent than her male counterpart, however, the female boxer symbolized independence in the postwar period. Women had only just begun to emerge from positions of social dependence in the early 1920s, and for many, the quality of "self-madeness" simply meant an ability to get by on one's own. The female boxer, even if she almost never earned a living from her sport, nevertheless possessed the fistic skills to protect herself and the aggressiveness to claim her share of social opportunities. Vicki Baum directly credited boxing for giving her a heightened assertiveness in her business dealings, enabling her to secure more favorable literary contracts and to take firmer charge of her professional life.[157] Because boxing fostered this sense of empowerment to a greater degree than other sports, many education reformers recommended its inclusion—and that of other combat sports like it—in the girls' curriculum. "It is easier to impart grace to powerful girls than power to graceful ones," advised the sports pedagogue Dr. Franz Kirchberg in 1923.[158] Kirchberg would have agreed with Baum that a well-trained body and a good pair of fists reaped benefits in every area of a woman's life.

Baum claimed that her boxing skills made her feel more secure as she moved about the bustling metropolis of Berlin. Although she never sparred with an opponent, even when training at Mahir's gym, Baum nevertheless insisted that she could defend herself with her fists if the situation demanded it, even against a man: "We learned a fairly mean straight left and a quick follow-up punch. As a woman, you never know if you might not have to defend yourself against an assailant, right?"[159] Annemarie Kopp made this point even more bluntly in 1927, when she wrote, "the woman wants and needs to fight the battle for survival....Weaklings cannot make it here."[160] Erik Schwabach's book *The Revolutionization of the Woman* made a similar argument the following year. Because the modern woman "wants to forego male protection," she now needed exactly the qualities that boxing and other intense athletic disciplines forged.[161] Boxing and an independent lifestyle went hand in hand.

The Sportpalast's boxing school exploited the sense of omnipresent danger by advertising its classes to potential male and female students with the slogan, "The times are unsafe! So learn boxing!!"[162] Self-defense programs catering to women who had moved to the city by themselves proliferated throughout the Weimar years. In addition to boxing, the popularity of jiu-jitsu had also taken off as a self-defense sport in the mid-1920s, thanks to a series of public demonstrations in which a female expert had ably thrown her male opponent to the ground.[163] In the face of rising numbers of attacks by Nazi brownshirts in the early 1930s, a Communist Party women's magazine urged its readers to learn jiu-jitsu so that they would not fall victim in the ever more volatile political climate.[164] Any woman wishing simply to navigate the urban landscape unaccompanied, these exhortations proclaimed, needed the ability to defend herself, whether she understood herself as leading an independent life or not.

The 1927 film *The Fighting Lady* drove that point home. Its opening intertitle announced that the film "demands universal attention because the woman appears here as her own defender...by means of powerful blows."[165] In the first scene, a shadowy figure mugs a woman as she walks alone in an urban park. The woman later complains to a friend of hers, a younger woman who boxes daily. In the next scene, she begins working out on the punching ball herself and improves rapidly. The times are unsafe, as the Sportpalast had so dramatically phrased it, and this woman was learning to box. Her fighting abilities improve rapidly, which threatens her fiancé's sense of himself as the protector in the relationship. Furthermore, the woman's daily gym workouts, in close proximity to dozens of fit male bodies, begin to arouse his jealousy. After a heated argument between the woman and her fiancé over her newfound athletic passion, the heroine takes a walk by herself in the very same park where the initial mugging had occurred. A mysterious assailant again leaps from the bushes to attack her, but, this time, the woman adeptly counters his assault with a wicked left and finishes him off with two more punches.

The woman's fiancé, who has tailed her the entire time because he suspects her of infidelity, then helps to drag the beaten criminal to the police station. The film cuts to rolling newspaper presses, on which the headlines scream the news of the heroine's remarkable crime-fighting achievement. The movie's final intertitle offers a glimpse many decades into the future and provides this revolutionary epilogue: "The lady in the year 2000, as she defends the men from perilous dangers with a mighty fist. How the times do change." Like so much of the Weimar discourse surrounding women's boxing, including coverage of the trial of Anita Wiznowski and Walter Rothenburg's 1921 review of the women's fights that he had seen on the Hamburg stage, this film presented the female fighter as a challenge to the man's social position and authority. For its female viewers, it additionally reinforced the perception of cities as places of danger, where a good left hook could keep one from becoming yet another crime statistic.

The film suggested, too, the highly fraught position of the self-made woman in the Weimar Republic. On the one hand, commentators recognized the single woman as a demographic fact and so wanted her to have the skills necessary to pursue a life without the protection and security of a husband. On the other hand, many men saw that self-sufficiency as a direct threat. A woman's capacity to fight for herself amplified and compounded the anxieties of men whose place in the world had already been shaken by the military defeat, their own declining status as economic breadwinners, and a radically restructured political and cultural order. When *The Fighting Lady* ended its story by marveling at "how the times do change," it explicitly positioned the boxing woman as a transforming force. In this, it anticipated by one year the caption to the 1928 cartoon on the revolutionary transformation in women's tennis at Wimbledon. The catalyzing power of sports in general, as the Weimar media regularly commented, bore a disproportionate responsibility for the new roles that men and women played in postwar society.

Sexy Sluggers: The Boxer as Object

In 1925, during a highly publicized European tour, the boxing superstar Jack Dempsey held a public training session in Berlin. In describing the event for the following issue of *Boxsport*, the journal's correspondent fell into a veritable swoon over the fighter's musculature and physical development. He lovingly detailed Dempsey's "outstanding and aesthetically developed body" from the bottom up. He began by praising the fighter's "highly developed, slim, and elegantly proportioned legs; a narrow, but agile waist; strong chest; broad, muscular back...[and] powerfully developed arms with good, defined musculature, appearing...elegantly proportioned and not the least bit 'bulky.'"[166] Dempsey represented much more than just a physical standard to which men aspired. Instead, this passage illustrated how the public's cool admiration of a boxer's body could slide seamlessly into sensuous longing.

In an era of mechanization, the male boxer reestablished the primacy of muscle power, but he also revealed that muscles owed at least part of their continuing economic value to their status as objects for show rather than means of production. The Weimar media had begun to eroticize the male body in general during the 1920s, and it concentrated with particular relish on that of the boxer. The technical distance so carefully maintained by statistical measurements and a clinical tone in some boxing reportage frequently gave way to more intimate descriptions that cast the fighter's body in a soft, erotic light. Fans and non-fans alike frankly expressed their appreciation of the prizefighter's lean, muscular form.[167] Boxers themselves encouraged this desire by marketing their own images in photographs, films, and—as Dempsey himself demonstrated above—in public training sessions at which unabashed ogling had a definite place on the agenda.

Indeed, the boxer emerged as something of a sex symbol in the postwar years. Not only did prizefighters cultivate admirably well-trained bodies, but they also exposed those bodies to a greater extent than any other athlete at the time, considering that even competitive swimmers still covered their torsos in the 1920s. Rumpelstilzchen applauded the fact that the prizefighter wore "only a loincloth," thanks to which "the muscles can be seen moving like steel bands over their thoroughly trained bodies."[168] The eroticization of the male boxer also stemmed from the emergence of women as sexual consumers in the Weimar Republic, who acknowledged their sexual desires and sought entertainments that catered to them. Dempsey felt at firsthand how these sexually self-aware women had begun to change men's boxing. As he admitted in a 1921 interview, "It's no longer enough to have speed and a good right arm to be the favorite. You have to be good-looking, too, now that ladies go to the fights."[169]

A 1922 article described female spectators as "excited to the tips of their fingers, lustful, inflamed for the slender one or the blond or the strong one. They are entirely absorbed and never take an eye off the fighters."[170] Three years later, Erwin Petzall spoke of the many female boxing fans, "who are moved by the athletic physiques of the protagonists."[171] In the postwar environment, women openly objectified men, and boxing matches provided them with the perfect venue for doing so. The physiologist Fritz Giese remarked in 1925 that women swarmed around prizefighters "like flies around a piece of sugar," an analogy that placed women in the active roles and the boxer as their quarry.[172] The most sought-after piece of sugar in the early years of the Weimar Republic was the heavyweight Hans Breitensträter, who possessed—in addition to his championship title—a trim body and blond hair. On the eve of one 1922 fight, a reporter underscored that the "main interest of the evening was palpably focused on the blond German heavyweight champion," especially by the "excited female fans," who lined the train platform to await his arrival.[173] This article made a fetish of Breitensträter's golden strands by referring to him repeatedly as "the blond Hans" or as "Schmidt's blond opponent," and by praising the fighter's "open, honest face with its crowning shock of hair." As the report made clear, Breitensträter's good looks fueled his popularity with female fans and, undoubtedly, some male ones, too.

According to a 1921 article in *Die Weltbühne*, Breitensträter "received fifty letters from women every day," and it added that everyone in Breitensträter's presence praised the boxer's "strong chest [and] his elegant legs" with wistful sighs.[174] Rumpelstilzchen joked that, thanks to "the blond Hans, the gold-crowned Breitensträter," Germans had caught up with southern Europeans when it came to unbridled displays of passion. Berlin's women, he claimed, awaited the boxer's next match "with flared nostrils."[175] In a 1932 article in *Der Querschnitt*, Breitensträter talked about his own status as a German heartthrob as well as the general tendency of fans to sexualize male fighters.[176] This could put on a strain on marriage, he warned: "A public boxer has a lot of male and female admirers. And it often comes about that he occasionally receives a kiss at a social function or celebration." Breitensträter did not go deeper into detail, but he made it clear that every prizefighter needed a wife who could accept these fans' attentions without jealousy.

Prizefighters found it even easier to market their bodies by the middle of the decade than Breitensträter had at the beginning, thanks to a vogue for photographs that took the boxer out of the ring and, often, out of his trunks. This genre built upon the practice in prewar Germany of celebrating bodybuilders' musculature, but it added several elements from female erotica, including the soft focus, averted gaze, and almost demure passivity of the models.[177] Max Schmeling described Weimar society as consumed by a "cult of the naked," with scores of coffee-table books featuring carefully posed shots of toned men in swim suits, posing straps, or nothing at all.[178] Some of these books purported to demonstrate an exercise regimen or advertise the benefits of healthy nudism, but others dropped that pretense altogether. Erwin Mehl, who reviewed one such book in 1926, revealed the unspoken premise of the genre, and his own desires, when he exasperatedly asked, "When will they finally get rid of those repulsive swim suits covering the male bodies?"[179]

The boxer's body became a magnet for such photographic studies, and it attracted some of the leading photographers of Weimar Germany. Frieda Riess, for one, found a muse in the compliant body of the light heavyweight Erich Brandl, which she immortalized in a series of consciously eroticized nudes in 1925. Max Schmeling provided another popular and much-sought-after subject for photographers. One much-circulated studio shot, for instance, pictured Schmeling from the waist up, as he gazes with intense self-satisfaction at his own flexed bicep. It first appeared on the cover of *Boxsport* in March 1927, after which *Sport und Sonne* picked it up for its August 1927 issue and, apparently liking it so much, ran the picture again in 1929.[180] Under the tantalizing subtitle "The champion boxer, secretly observed," *Sport und Gesundheit* published

UNSERE DEUTSCHEN MEISTER: I.

Max Schmeling
Europameister im Halbschwergewicht

This widely circulated 1927 photograph focuses attention on Max Schmeling's impressive physique. *Author's collection*

a nude snapshot of Schmeling washing off at the edge of a lake after a training practice during his 1929 tour of the United States. The caption referred to him by his pet name "Maxie," and it slyly noted that "only a very few people have seen the successful German champion boxer...like this," conveying a giddy delight in their own voyeurism.[181]

The leading sexologist and homosexual rights activist Magnus Hirschfeld even juxtaposed a picture of the famous statue of the Greek

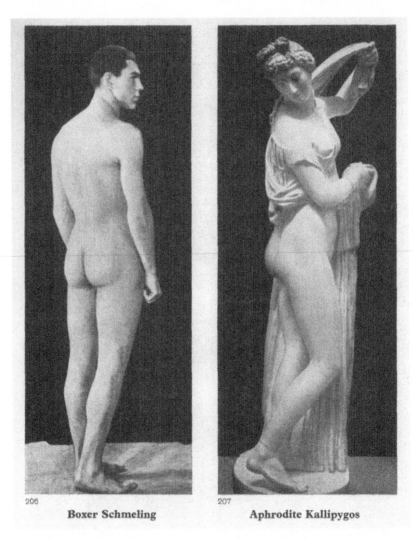

206   **Boxer Schmeling**   207   **Aphrodite Kallipygos**

The sexologist and gay-rights pioneer Magnus Hirschfeld chose Schmeling as the male physical ideal, and worthy counterpart of the female goddess Aphrodite, for his 1930 book *Science of Sex*. *Magnus-Hirschfeld-Gesellschaft*

goddess Aphrodite with a nude photograph of Max Schmeling from behind, in a pose almost identical to that of the statue. This pairing, which appeared in the 1930 book *Geschlechtskunde* (Science of Sex), invited an artistic and sensuous appreciation of Schmeling's body, whose own smooth and unblemished white skin mirrored that of the marble statue. This photographic pairing explicitly presented the boxer as the male physical ideal, a modern incarnation of classical perfection.[182] The journal *Der Querschnitt* contributed mightily to the idealization of the boxer's body as well. It published photographs of nude boxers with such regularity that the adoration of the pugilist's body seemed to have become a central part of its journalistic mandate. Dozens of top German prizefighters appeared in its pages throughout the Weimar years, including Erich Brandl, Helmuth Hartkopp, Emil Scholz, and Hein Müller.[183]

The boxer's erotic appeal extended, not surprisingly, to Weimar Germany's remarkably vibrant gay subculture. A 1921 personals ad in a gay magazine, for instance, used the sexual allure of boxing to entice potential sugardaddies: "Daredevil Sportsman, 19 years old, lean and lanky, champion in long-distance swimming, equestrian, and boxing, seeks manager or patron."[184] This man's self-description as "lean and lanky," and a pugilist, to boot, seemed perfectly pitched to readers' desires. Another notice from the previous month in the same magazine sought readers who would lend some boxing gloves to two young men.[185] Whether those two men intended the request as a pretext for meeting sexual partners or paying clients, or whether they truly needed two pairs of gloves and perhaps some coaching, they had incorporated pugilism prominently into their social self-presentation. A 1930 cover of the gay journal *Die Insel* (The Island) tapped into the boxer fantasy by featuring a young, blond model in the fighter's stance, with fists clenched—the incarnation of lean virility.[186]

The erotic desirability of the male boxer propelled the plots of countless pulp stories and films in the Weimar Republic as well, such that it constituted a distinct and consistently popular subgenre. The female protagonist in the 1922 short story "Mrs. Adi," for instance, bluntly explains to her suitor, "You know that I see in the athletic champion the essence of desirable manliness," a statement that he understands to mean: "Start boxing!"[187] Desperate to live up to his beloved's ideal, the man trains himself as a pugilist and eventually manages to win the Siberian flyweight championship. The 1926 short story "Inge and the Boxing Match" made female fantasy an even more central plot device.[188] Here, the protagonist falls in love with a boxer whom she has only seen in a painting, but whose appearance comes back to her again and again in feverish dreams. Acting on this fantasy, she attends her first bout and finds herself dazzled by both contenders, whom she refers to as her "two heroes." Once again, the sexual pursuit of a male boxer propels the narrative.

The 1926 film *The Boxer's Bride*, meanwhile, specifically presented the postwar woman's attraction to prizefighters as a radical departure from the prewar German norm.[189] The opening scene showed a nineteenth-cen-

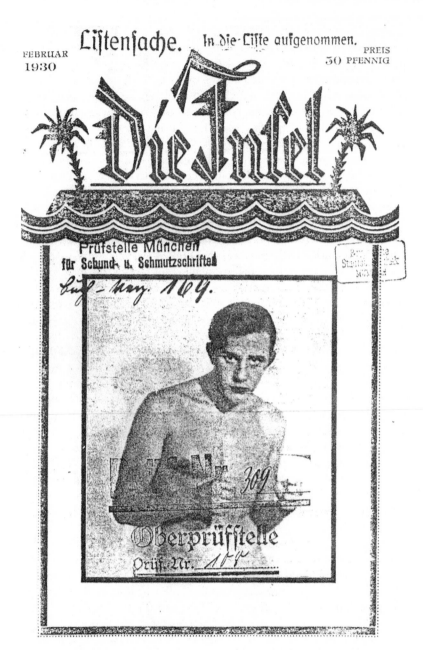

A 1930 cover of the gay magazine *Die Insel* positions its cover model in a classic boxing stance.
Bayerische Staatsbibliothek, München

tury lady's ideal suitor, a dapper romantic who dressed like a member of a barbershop quartet and made a show of bestowing upon his sweetheart a bouquet of flowers. The film juxtaposed that quaintly Wilhelmine gentleman with "the ideal of contemporary girls," a pugilist. Helen, the film's protagonist and the very embodiment of a contemporary girl, "especially swoons for boxing," much to the consternation of her boyfriend Fritz, a woefully un-athletic man who dresses and carries himself as if the *belle époque* had never ended. When the couple attends a boxing match, Helen takes the flowers that Fritz had just given to her and throws them to the victorious fighter. Adding insult to the injury, she later informs him that she refuses to marry anyone but a champion prizefighter.

Determined to have Helen, Fritz manages to convince her that he maintains a secret identity as the renowned black boxer "Fighting Bob," about whom he had recently read in the newspaper. He must fight in black face and under this pseudonym, Fritz lies to Helen, because his father finds the sport so disreputable that he would disinherit his son if he knew of Fritz's passion for pugilism. Fritz lends credibility to this absurd tale by hiring two men to allow him, in the presence of Helen, to knock them out. Helen, clearly impressed, marries Fritz shortly thereafter, but she quickly sours on the idea of having a boxer for a husband, in part because of her mounting jealousy of other female fans. In the end, the film reaffirmed the same dapper ideal that the opening scene had consigned to the history books. But it applied that ideal only to husbands. Helen may have discovered that boxers did not make the best spouses, but she still found their appeal irresistible. In fact, it was precisely that irresistibility to other women that made the prizefighter such a poor choice for a husband in the first place.

Whether husband material or not, the boxer in these Weimar-era stories readily gave in to women. In the 1928 film *Abwege*, for example, Irene, the female protagonist played by Brigitte Helm, attends a sparring session at the local gym with her friend Liana and immediately begins to flirt. While Liana sets her sights on a black boxer in one corner of the ring, Irene chats up another fighter, whom she had earlier seen at a nightclub. Irene changes her mind about the encounter after bringing the boxer back to her place, and only the unexpected entrance of her husband manages to prevent anything more from happening. Nevertheless, Irene had initiated that potential liaison and largely determined its trajectory.[190] In the subgenre of boxing fiction, the woman did the seducing and proved remarkably able to bend the boxer to her desire. A female commentator had this trope in mind when she referred in 1932 to prizefighters as "a collection of good-natured fools" who readily put themselves in others' hands.[191]

Max Schmeling described his film character in *Love in the Ring* as just such a fool, calling him an "inexperienced young man, who gets caught in the cleverly laid trap of the sinful beauty."[192] In that film, it takes the virtuous influence of a second female character to set him back on the path to a boxing title. The entire plot, in other words, revolved around a competition between two women, with the boxer as the trophy. In a 1930 review of the film, the magazine *Kinematograph* stressed that Schmeling's character depended entirely on the initiative and efforts of the second woman in order to bring about a satisfactory resolution: "She led him back to the path of training, made sure that he won in the decisive fight, and saved his career."[193] In Schmeling's second film, *Knockout*, his character falls once again under a woman's sway and proves even more compliant than he had in the previous film. In one scene, the woman, clearly enamored of the boxer's trained body, asks him if he would jump rope for her sometime. The film quickly cuts to the next scene, just a short time later, in which Schmeling's character—still dressed in his tuxedo, but now back at her apartment—dutifully complies with her wishes.[194]

Pugilists themselves worried about this vulnerability to women and tried to adhere to an age-old proscription against contact with the opposite sex during training. A line in *Love in the Ring* summarized the secrets to a successful fight as "Early to bed, no alcohol, no woman!"[195] Schmeling's character manages to stick to this regimen for a short time in the film *Knockout*. When a woman flirts with him by showing some leg, Schmeling's character deflects her advance by mimicking that same gesture: He rolls up his pants, crosses his legs, and gently rocks the top leg in a dismissive parody of her overt come-on. Ironically, it is precisely by rejecting a woman's sexual advances with his own display of feminine leg rocking that the boxer reaffirms his inner hardness, his ability to resist a temptation that would derail his career. Unlike the male tennis player, who pursued women at every opportunity, the ideal boxer deliberately, even proudly, avoided them. During training, he cloistered himself in an all-male environment. At the 1925 European amateur boxing championships, in fact, the German and English fighters reportedly danced with each other at the post-match celebrations, "where, naturally, the ladies were absent."[196]

The female boxer, not surprisingly, had a history of objectification that went back to her earliest participation in the sport. Before the war, audiences at carnivals and circuses enjoyed the occasional spectacle of women in skimpy outfits fighting one another, with the implicit promise that tugging and tearing would render those outfits skimpier still. Although the female boxer retained this erotic appeal in the Weimar Republic, it grew noticeably less tawdry over the course of the decade. By the mid-1920s, she even radiated a wholesome appeal—a woman building her fitness in a rigorous sport, with scarcely a hint of bawdiness. Male and female boxers found themselves on opposite trajectories when it came to their erotic appeal, in other words. Even as the public increasingly sexualized the former as the decade progressed, it seemed less inclined to do so with the latter.

The artist Anton Räderscheidt titled his 1930 painting of a female nude standing in a boxing ring *The Beauty Queen*, which suggested how thoroughly Weimar society had redefined standards of female beauty in a more athletic, muscular direction.[197] Räderscheidt used his own wife, a certified sports teacher, as the model in this and other sports-themed paintings, and her sturdy body and short hair defiantly flouted the conventional norm for female nudes, which tended to emphasize voluptuous curves and flowing hair. Done in the straightforward style of the "New Objectivity" movement, the painting's female boxer, moreover, stared matter-of-factly at the viewer, a pose that radiated self-confident frankness and served as a marked counterpoint to the coyly averted gaze that had become so standard in depictions of male boxers. She invited careful study, perhaps even admiration, but not desire.

The singer Claire Waldoff celebrated the pugilistic skills of the eponymous heroine of her popular cabaret song, "Hannelore," whose loveable appeal stemmed directly from her androgyny.[198] As Waldoff sings in the refrain, "no one can tell if you're a broad or a man," but that detail does not detract in the least from her desirability since, as the refrain's final line declares, everyone still considers her the "prettiest kid from Hallesches Tor," a working-class neighborhood in Berlin. Whereas the sexual appeal of the male boxer derived from his body's unmistakable maleness and the appeal of the prewar coquette from her unmistakable femaleness, the appeal of the female boxer seemed to depend, in part, on her ambiguity. In Hannelore's case, she donned ties and monocles, and, like Anita Wiznowski, also boxed avidly and engaged in petty theft. This renegade androgyny only enhanced her adorability, though, enabling her, as Waldoff sings at one point, to attract "a husband and a wife." Instead of appearing somewhat tawdry, in the tradition of burlesque, this female boxer appears simply vivacious and all the more attractive for it.

Perhaps in recognition of the clean-cut image of women's boxing that had emerged by mid-decade, the sports journal *Arena* anointed a "goddess of boxing," whom it praised in 1926 for having elevated pugilism from back-alley pursuit to reputable sport.[199] The choice of a female figure to represent the sport's emergent respectability illustrates the degree to which the image of the boxing woman had changed in just a few years. When *Sport und Sonne* needed a cover for its debut issue in January 1927, it chose a photograph of a pretty young boxer sweetly resting a gloved fist against a punching ball, an image that made her seem more wholesome than seductive.[200] The gloves and ball, along with her short haircut, presented this covergirl as both modern and irresistibly appealing. By carefully cropping the photograph above the shoulders, however, the magazine did not sexualize her in the same way that it did with male boxers, whose entire bodies, often nude, soon began to grace its pages. *Sport im Bild* portrayed two slender, young women sparring with one another in a 1928 issue as positively elegant. Apart from the boxing gloves, they seemed decked out for a fashionable night on the town, in skirts, tailored blouses, and even a turban.[201]

A brochure for the Hamburg-America Line in 1926 highlighted the way in which its oceanliners catered to the interests of the modern German traveler, and that included women who boxed. An illustration

A female boxer, simultaneously seductive and wholesome, graces the premier issue of the sports magazine *Sport und Sonne* in January 1927. *Sportbibliothek, Westfälische Wilhelms-Universität, Münster*

BOXEN

The Hamburg-America Line advertised its ocean liners' boxing rings to male and female passengers alike in this 1926 brochure. The faint line drawing on the *right* of the photograph shows two women sparring and, on the *left*, in an apparent post-match embrace. *Author's collection*

featured two women sparring in a ring, and the accompanying text promised passengers the opportunity to box in "a more or less expert match".[202] Like the illustration in *Sport im Bild* and the poem "Her Cares," this brochure presented female boxers as fashionably daring and assertively independent, but also clearly within the bounds of good taste. One could not have said that about women's boxing just six years earlier. The sport's featured place in a brochure aimed at upper-class trans-Atlantic travelers, though, showed how much women's boxing had changed from its notorious reputation in the hyperinflation years of the early 1920s. As with most avant-garde behavior, the attention given to the first female boxers helped to popularize the practice itself. It then moved from a fringe pursuit, whose shock value accounted for its initial stagings in burlesque theaters, to a practice that one might describe as mainstream trendy. Women's boxing had also left its earlier association with the lower-class milieu of carneval performers behind and gone decidedly upscale.

For this reason, a number of female celebrities cultivated their own image as pugilists, even if they had little to do with the actual sport. Here, too, we can chart the progression of the sport's public image over the course of the 1920s from disreputably lowbrow sensationalism to hip desirability. When the early silent-film star Henny Porten had herself photographed at the punching ball in 1918, she clearly played it more for outlandish, comedic effect than for fashionability.[203] Seven years later, women's boxing maintained only enough of its edginess to attract attention, not generate guffaws. A 1925 photograph of three women, identified in the caption as "film divas" who were engaged in a lighthearted sparring session on one of Berlin's popular lakeside beaches, linked the sport to healthy outdoor recreation. The commentator and sports physiologist Fritz Giese demurred, calling it "a denigration of sports" because of the women's lighthearted approach.[204] The photograph, however, simply showed three people enjoying the sport. The notion that boxing could bolster these women's career prospects in the movies, moreover, pointed to the shifting public perceptions of female pugilists.

As celebrities began to box, they, in turn, stoked the popularity of the sport among women even more. Actresses like Elizabeth Lennartz, Maria Bard, Marlene Dietrich, and Carola Neher glamorized women's boxing, and their formidable star power no doubt drew even more women to the practice. Photographs of celebrities working out on a punching ball, such as that of the Viennese stage star Lizzi Natzler in 1929, sent an implicit beauty and lifestyle tip to female fans: if you want to have a body like this, lace up the gloves.[205] Marlene Dietrich made a great advertisement for women's boxing, too, with her "long legs and very short hook," as Sabri Mahir put it, both on full display during her training sessions at Mahir's gym.[206] The 1930 short story "A Day in the Life of a Film Diva" made boxing a central component of any screen star's lifestyle, as the story's heroine wins both a boxing match and a beauty contest in the same afternoon.[207]

Like Brecht, Piscator, Flechtheim, and the other male cultural figures who similarly dedicated themselves to boxing, or at least affected such a dedication, these female stars also wished to project a masculine toughness. For Marlene Dietrich the sport contributed to her image as a powerful and independent woman, who did what she wanted and got what she wanted, not just because of her charms and beauty, but also because of her prowess. In the last years of the Weimar Republic, as depictions of female boxers proliferated in the German media, the sport marked women as modern, not outrageous. As early as 1926, in fact, the sports magazine *Arena* published a short story that actually treated women's boxing with a ho-hum, seen-it-before sigh. Titled "Miss Kiki is Bored," it tells the story of a young heiress who no longer felt that surge of adrenalin from boxing or ostrich races. In a desperate quest for the thrill and notoriety that boxing had once provided, Miss Kiki finally resorts to crocodile wrestling.[208]

The ubiquitous image of the boxer in films and songs, on theater stages and the covers of magazines, had a resonance in Weimar culture out of all proportion to the actual level of participation in the sport. Even men and women who would never have dreamed of stepping into the ring themselves still sought an association with the sport because it accorded status in a society that increasingly valued the lean, tough, and commercially successful. Boxers embodied a modern sensibility, and the physical and psychological qualities that they put so visibly on display transformed assumptions about male and female social roles, expectations, and possibilities.

The boxing man, who invited a close scrutiny of his meticulously trained body, established a new standard of physical fitness as well as male beauty. He also elevated blue-collar toughness and outright violence as admirable qualities in a man, prompting many intellectuals to flee their own effete reputations through pugilism. Furthermore, the prizefighter's financial success legitimized a self-interested—some might have said "shameless"—marketing of one's attributes for commercial gain. He emerged as a symbol of upward mobility, demonstrating the possibility in a postwar republic of transcending the class lines that had more sharply demarcated Imperial Germany.

At the same time, the prizefighter established flexible standards of masculinity for the new postwar man. He invited erotic objectification and exhibited a degree of passivity outside the ring that counteracted his aggressive activity inside it. In particular, the boxer appeared vulnerable to the controlling influence of a formidable woman, a tendency toward male submissiveness that film scholar Patrice Petro has described as a trope in Weimar films.[209] The fighter, like so many of his male peers, often looked more like someone under control than someone in control. Even prizefighters themselves, to borrow from Judith Butler, failed to live up to the image of "the prizefighter."[210]

Against a backdrop of profound social transformations in Germany since the war, the figure of the woman who knew how to throw a punch provided an appealing new model as well. Even the taboo against competitive women's boxing, all but ignored in the early years of the Weimar Republic, showed tentative signs of fading once again in the early 1930s. The organizers of Berlin's Museum of Physical Education, for instance, resolved in 1933 to dedicate a subsection of their permanent exhibition to "Women's boxing matches," in recognition both of their existence and of their relevance to the German public.[211]

The female boxer provided a remarkably masculine standard of self-sufficiency, free of reliance on male protection. She paralleled a key trend in Weimar cinema toward women who appeared, according to Petro's study, "aggressive, 'masculine,' even threatening."[212] The boxer took care of herself and her own interests, without sentimentality, whether in defending her right to walk through the city alone, as in the film *The Fighting Lady*, or negotiating a lucrative contract, as in the case of Vicki Baum. Just as important, she claimed a very public role for women, from stage performances to motion pictures to magazine covers. Even burlesque boxing provided women with a space in which to seize the spotlight, aggressively and without apology.

The National Socialists based many of their attacks against the Weimar Republic on that system's tolerance for such ostensibly licentious behavior, and the party singled out women's boxing for occasional criticism even after it seized power in 1933. The practice disappeared almost

entirely under the Nazi regime, at least publicly, but the government peri-
odically pointed to it as an example of the pernicious influence of the
United States. The illustrated sports and culture magazine *Koralle* featured cautionary pictures in 1936 of female boxers, purportedly American,
to highlight the sport's medical risks and the degeneracy of democratic
society.[213] One caption declared that the fighters "were gambling away
their health and female dignity in the interests of sensation."

Despite Nazi protests to the contrary, however, women's boxing had
clearly emerged from within German society rather than from influences
abroad. The men's boxing establishment in Germany drew far more from
the American example in the 1920s than women's boxing did. Even today,
a time when women's boxing has reemerged in Germany, it is largely a
homegrown phenomenon. A 2007 article in the newsweekly *Der Spiegel*
proclaimed Germany to be one of the hotbeds of the sport and a launching
pad for up-and-coming female pugilists from across Europe and Asia.[214] In
addition, the sport now finally affords women an opportunity for upward
mobility similar to what the men already had back in the 1920s. The
Armenian immigrant Susi Kentikian, for example, gained both her celebrity and her citizenship in Germany in large part due to her status as a
world-champion boxer, nicknamed the "Killer Queen." In terminology
that seemed straight out of a Weimar-era paean to the self-made prizefighter, *Der Spiegel* referred to the now-conventional wisdom within the
women's sport "that you can become someone as a female boxer in
Germany." Although the article did not seem aware of it, Germany's status
as a land of women's boxing has roots that stretch back to the Weimar
Republic.

3

German Engineering
Duty, Performance, and the Track and Field Athlete

When Georg Cornelius collapsed and died at the conclusion of the Olympic marathon race in the 1928 novel *Der Läufer von Marathon* (The Runner from Marathon), the author depicted his death as self-sacrificial heroism, with obvious parallels to the ancient Greek legend.[1] Werner Scheff, a remarkably prolific writer of sports fiction, set this story twelve years in the future, at the never-held 1940 Olympic Games. As the 26.2-mile competition entered its final laps at the end of the book, seven mysterious Chinese runners, all of them endowed with seemingly superhuman endurance, vied for the lead, followed by "a lone figure of a different color—Georg Cornelius, the German." In one final, all-consuming burst, Cornelius overtook all seven Chinese runners in the last few meters to capture the gold medal, before dropping to the ground.

All of Western civilization, Scheff exclaimed, joined the Germans in hailing this "savior of the white race." The American team even erected a memorial to commemorate his victory, and it bore an inscription of unambiguous racial-cultural solidarity: "We have triumphed!"[2] Georg Cornelius's fate, which he willingly suffered on behalf of his nation, paralleled that of the German soldiers who had ostensibly perished for the same cause on the battlefields of Verdun and the Somme just a dozen years earlier, and it offered an implicit rebuke to the wartime malingerers who had purportedly undermined the national war effort by pursuing their own interests over that of their fatherland. Motivated by a sense of patriotic duty alone, Cornelius's act illustrated an ideal of selfless, uncorrupted manhood that track and field claimed to instill in its athletes in the 1920s and which presented such a stark contrast to the more profit-motivated and even narcissistic examples proffered by the boxers and tennis players of the Weimar period. In men's track and field even fatal overexertion represented a virtue, since it served the greater glory of the nation.

Meanwhile, on August 2, 1928, in the same year that *Der Läufer von Marathon* hit bookstores across the country, the German middle-distance runner Lina Radke-Batschauer crossed the finish line of the Olympic 800-meter race with her arms raised in triumph, setting a new world record and winning Germany's only track and field gold medal of the Amsterdam Games. The press did not devote all of its post-race coverage to celebrating this historic national victory, however. It divided its attention instead between Radke-Batschauer's win and the image of two of her competitors lying on the ground in complete exhaustion. And no one in the media praised those two collapsed runners for their heroic self-sacrifice, either. Instead, commentators interpreted the post-race prostration as irrefutable proof that women lacked the requisite constitutions for middle-distance competition. Whereas the sight of a collapsed male athlete inspired admiration for his all-out effort, that of a collapsed female athlete prompted only anxious hand-wringing.

More so than any other branch of physical culture, postwar Germans criticized, promoted, and analyzed track and field explicitly within a context of perceived crisis and dizzying transformation. The military defeat in 1918 had led to exorbitant reparations payments, a humiliating war-guilt clause, and a strict limit on the size of the national army, but it had also ushered in greater political freedoms, a general atmosphere of social permissiveness, and an invigorated mass culture. The economy of the Weimar Republic, meanwhile, lunged violently from skyrocketing inflation to soaring unemployment, with five brief "golden years" of stability and relative prosperity in between. Against this backdrop of economic turbulence, ordinary employees confronted a reconfigured workspace that now demanded rising levels of productivity. Even relations between men and women, once viewed as comfortably stable, now seemed unexpectedly open for re-negotiation, a change that appeared all the more unsettling because it coincided with a sharp decline in the national birthrate.

Track and field athletes offered models for successfully maneuvering within and even mastering this unfamiliar new society. Their physical bodies were themselves products of that modern order, the results of a training regimen that drew on the same principles of the American industrial engineer F. W. Taylor that were simultaneously streamlining German industrial design in the 1920s. The Taylorized athlete thus provided a template for the physical efficiency that managers increasingly demanded of their secretaries and factory workers. His or her dedication to just one particular discipline—whether the sprint or the high jump— paralleled the broader trend of dividing production processes and realms of inquiry into ever more narrowly defined tasks and subfields. Whereas Wilhelmine Germany still valued well-rounded minds and bodies, postwar society increasingly demanded the type of highly proficient specialist that the track and field athlete represented.

This specialization extended to the distinct roles that postwar Germany expected its male and female athletes to perform—the male as a model of the patriotic and dutiful man, physically and mentally prepared to die for his country, and the female as a model of the patriotic and dutiful woman, physically and mentally prepared to give new life to her country. The track and field athlete, in other words, promoted new opportunities and radical transformation even as it simultaneously reinforced long-standing roles. The historian George Mosse has described this paradox as a hallmark of the nineteenth- and twentieth-century European gender order. "Masculinity," he writes, "was expected to stand both for unchanging values in a changing age and for the dynamic but orderly process of change itself, guided by an appropriate purpose."[3] This expectation extended to femininity as well, and the track and field athlete embodied its contradiction of dynamic possibility and reassuring stasis. Athletes' carefully engineered training and competitive pursuit of personal achievement reflected the era. At the same time, they adhered, at least rhetorically, to a centuries-old set of national obligations that Carl Diem, interwar Germany's leading sports official, neatly encapsulated in one statement: "For us the measure of sport is the extent to which it makes a man able to fight as a soldier and a woman able to bear children."[4]

The track and field athlete juggled a second pair of competing images as well: the selfish pursuit of glory and the selfless service of the collective. Even as they competed for individual laurels, officials and the media presented athletes as dedicating themselves to a much larger project of national rejuvenation, in contrast to the boxers and tennis players who unabashedly sought personal success and self-satisfaction. The women's 800-meter race at the 1928 Olympics threw these competing images of the athlete—modern and traditional, individualistic and collective-minded— into particularly sharp relief. As the debate unleashed by this race gradually ebbed, the consensus of opinion had shifted noticeably in Germany. Not only could women choose both motherhood and competitive athletics, but indeed they *should*. Track and field actually fostered healthy motherhood, according to most observers in the closing years of the Weimar Republic. In this regard, the female athlete had managed to reconcile the paradox after all, by creating an ideal of modern motherhood.

Next Year's Model: The Rationalization of the Track and Field Athlete

In the 1925 essay "The Discovery of the Female Body," Arnold Hahn heralded a new physical form for women, one that athletics had finally liberated from the "flabbiness and muscular atrophy" of an earlier era.[5] He wrote rhapsodically of the "slender, quick-as-an-arrow lope of taut-breasted girls" that suddenly seemed to populate postwar Germany. In Hahn's eyes, these women were nothing less than the sprinting, leaping harbingers of a new era. The men, too, had slimmed down and toned up. As the gentlemen's magazine *Der Herr* informed its fashion-conscious readers: "Slender clearly remains the ideal for the athletically trained man of today."[6] Weimar Germany had undergone a corporeal revolution. Where prewar society had promoted two separate ideals—brawny heft for the man and tightly corseted curves for the woman—postwar society now embraced a streamlined, androgynous body for men and women alike, and no one modeled this ideal better than the track and field athlete.

When Siegfried Kracauer sought an appropriate analogy to describe the sleek design of a brand-new housing complex in 1927, he chose that of an athlete's body, sex unspecified. The building's form, Kracauer wrote, gave the appearance of "a skeleton, thin and agile like a person in sports-hirt and sweat pants."[7] The following year Willi Baumeister composed a painting that featured a high jumper in action, her form ultimately identi-fiable as female only from the "taut-breasted" torso.[8] The painting's background depicted hallmarks of the industrial age, including an auto-mobile and two oil derricks, which presented the athletic body as consti-tutive of modernity itself. Like automotive engineers tinkering with the designs of engines, coaches and sports physiologists throughout the 1920s tried to reshape their high jumpers and sprinters for ever greater performance. The relentlessness with which the athletes themselves pur-sued peak performance, moreover, reflected the modern mentality of individual achievement.

The performance imperative in track and field marked a clear departure from the evolutionary trajectory of German physical culture up to the First World War. Throughout the imperial period, Germans had tended to satisfy their urge to exercise, to the extent that it existed, pri-marily through hiking or with an indigenous form of communal gymnas-tics known as *Turnen*. This latter practice had developed as a nationalist reaction to Napoleon's humiliating rout of the Prussian army at the Battle of Jena in 1806. Contemporaries interpreted this defeat as proof that German men had grown woefully effete and undisciplined. Friedrich Ludwig Jahn, known as the "father of *Turnen*," responded to this perceived degeneration of male bodies by modifying and propagating a system of gymnastics that he claimed would not only reinvigorate the physical self, but also infuse the spirit with a patriotic attachment to a German nation that did not yet exist in state form. Because *Turnen* conceived of itself as a force for unifying disparate members of a potential nation, it tended to downplay divisive competitiveness and individual achievement. Its explic-itly German identity also meant that the movement never attracted a siz-able following among non-Germans and generally insulated itself from the international sports movement at the end of the nineteenth century.

Competitive track and field, meanwhile, like its English cousins tennis and boxing, nurtured a far more cosmopolitan orientation from the beginning. The sport entered Germany via British expatriates in the late 1800s, and it wore these foreign origins on its sleeve. When the Berlin Cricket Club, whose moniker already indicated its Anglophile sensibility, organized one of Germany's earliest track meets in 1890, officials announced all events in English only and measured distances in yards, according to British practice, instead of in meters.[9] Not until 1898 did Germans assume a leading institutional role in their own budding track and field movement by founding a national federation to establish rules and sanction competitions. Even then, the sport attracted only a limited following prior to 1914, and Otto Peltzer, the country's middle-distance superstar of the 1920s, recalled having scarcely any awareness at all of competitive track and field during his prewar youth.[10]

Most *Turners*, not surprisingly, viewed competitive track and field as irredeemably foreign. As track and field began to attract more and more adherents after 1918, the tensions between these two branches of German physical culture only grew. Both recruited disproportionately from the middle classes, and both competed for the allegiances of the same finite pool of German bodies. It was their thoroughly opposing philosophies regarding the nature and purpose of physical culture, however, that raised tensions to a boil. Track and field, after all, did far more than simply challenge *Turnen*'s hitherto dominant share of the German exercise market. An entirely different value system animated competitive sports, one that sat uneasily with the generally conservative supporters of *Turnen*. The historian Christiane Eisenberg has gone so far as to call it a "culture clash between *Turnen* and sports," in which the latter's penchant for specialization, exact measurements, and the rewarding of individual performance ran entirely counter to *Turnen*'s communal, holistic approach to developing the body.[11]

The track and field athlete's pursuit of self-aggrandizement, in the eyes of many *Turnen* enthusiasts, exposed the sport's soulless, Anglo-American character. If, as the expressionist playwright Georg Kaiser declared in a 1929 manifesto, "The man of record achievements is the dominant type of this age," the track and field athlete expressed this type in its purest form.[12] The woman of record achievements enjoyed unprecedented prominence, too, as the 1929 novelty song "My Grandma Holds the World Record in the Pole Vault" suggested.[13] A credo that placed individual achievement above the collective good did not just alarm cultural conservatives. Critics on the political left joined the fray, too, as when some politicians opposed government subsidies for competitive sports like track and field on the grounds that they further eroded social consciousness. "Sport is the cultivation of individual interest," argued one Social Democratic member of parliament on the floor of the *Reichstag*, "which says: to hell with those in last place, as long as I'm first!"[14] Officials in the *Turnen* movement would have applauded heartily.

Track and field officials also pushed for a reintegration into the international sports community after the war, which the *Turnen* movement viewed as treasonous cozying up to the enemy. This chauvinist isolationism within the ranks of *Turnen*, in fact, made some Jewish members so uncomfortable that they decided to leave the movement in the 1920s and switch to the generally more tolerant and progressive-minded competitive sports associations.[15] The schism between *Turnen* and competitive sports over the question of international participation ran so deep that the national *Turnen* association formally withdrew from Germany's larger umbrella organization for physical culture in protest against that body's decision to participate in the 1928 Olympics. Carl Diem, the umbrella organization's general secretary, criticized *Turnen* for presuming to hold a monopoly on German patriotism. Sports clubs, too, Diem insisted, display "a strong leaning to 'black-white-red,'" by which he meant the conservative nationalism symbolized by the colors of the old imperial German flag.[16] Diem's attempt to claim revanchist expressions of national identity for track and field, too, illustrated the level of patriotic one-up-manship between *Turnen* and competitive sports. It also revealed the extent to which track and field allowed conservatives to set the discursive agenda, a circumstance that motivated that sport's efforts to create images of athletes as soldiers and mothers in the first place.

Turnen festivals, despite the heated rhetoric, actually included the very same running, jumping, and throwing events that track meets did, and like those meets, they distinguished the top finishers, too. Organizers claimed, however, to imbue such proceedings with a cooperative spirit that inoculated participants against the ruthless competitiveness that overshadowed track and field. The *Turnen* movement underscored the opposing philosophies in 1923. Track and field meets, began an article in *Turnen*'s national journal, represented a pure reflection of modern society—atomized, self-absorbed, and strictly business—all "hustle and bustle...scarcely a heartfelt handshake, no personal warmth or feeling of unity."[17] A *Turnen* festival, on the other hand, exuded a cozy feeling of community, in which participants supported one another, each one "buoyed by the consciousness of being a full-fledged citizen of this proud gathering." Four years later, Edmund Neuendorff, *Turnen*'s national leader, lashed out against the postwar idolization of track and field champions.[18] Just replace the heads on statues of Bismarck with those of Germany's top male sprinters, Neuendorff sneered, since "the Bismarck memorials are out of date anyway." Here, track and field appeared as a bulldozer of modernity, clearing away the storied traditions and storied figures that had made the country great.

The *Turnen* movement saw itself, on the other hand, as perpetuating a distinctly German sensibility that had clear parallels to the rustic craftsmen of traditional small towns, whose owner-operated cobblers, brewers, and bakers enjoyed iconic status among cultural conservatives. Like a handworker who possessed all of the component skills that went into producing a shoe or a loaf of bread, the *Turner* cultivated a well-rounded physical fitness. The track and field athlete, by contrast, more closely resembled an assembly-line worker who performed just one task in the production process, with speed and efficiency.

The training of athletes, too, mirrored the rationalization of the postwar workplace, in which telephone operators, factory workers, and even homemakers sought to maximize their output. As the historian Frank Becker has argued, the fact that competitive athletes had so visibly and successfully adopted components of rationalization made its imposition in other areas of postwar society both more comprehensible to Germans and less threatening.[19] Indeed, athletes played a similar role in many parts of the world in the 1920s. China—which, like Germany, had recently lost a military conflict, shed its imperial system, and adopted a republican government—also saw competitive sports as a means of rationalizing its citizenry, and leading Chinese modernizers, like their German counterparts, made a point of discrediting the dominant forms of physical culture from the imperial period as inherently obsolete.[20] An athlete, like a modern business, placed a premium on staying ahead of the competition. Whereas rationalization in the business world had an unsettling effect on many Germans, though, even the casual observer could see how it benefited the victorious athlete.

Track and field athletes did not just popularize rationalization in the 1920s. They also promoted a larger set of attitudes that postwar Germans subsumed under the rubric of "Americanization," including individualism, commercialization, and cutthroat competition, all of which provoked positive and negative reactions alike.[21] Beate Bartels, writing in the women's journal of the right-wing German National People's Party, raised an alarm against creeping American influence on Weimar society via competitive sports. Athletic instruction in the schools, she argued, did nothing to build character and only promoted an unhealthy "American striving for records."[22] Carl Diem, on the other hand, saw a need to promote exactly this sort of striving. Impressed by the U.S. performances in the 1912 Olympics, Diem lured the American team's track and field trainer to Germany in order to impart the same successful techniques. Not until 1925 did a German, Josef Waitzer, take charge of the national team, and he incorporated most of the same methods as his American predecessor.[23] That same year, *Der Leichtathlet* delivered an ode to those methods: "That's another thing that we still have to learn from the Americans—this athletic discipline, this voluntary…submission to the sure leadership…of an absolutely competent man."[24] Here, even discipline and obedience—those two most stereotypical of German character traits—could take on a New World hue when discussed in the context of the Americans' superior approach to athletics.

"American methods" meant, above all, Taylorism; and Taylorism meant the minute study of isolated body movements, using stop-action photography and precise scientific measurement to eliminate wasted motions and maximize productivity. The French physiologist Etienne-Jules Marey had already used photography in his late-nineteenth-century research on athletic movement, but it was the American F. W. Taylor who got the credit, or blame, for the wave of rationalization that took German society, including its sports culture, by storm in the 1920s. Taylor, whose theories for boosting efficiency also emerged in the late nineteenth century, focused specifically on factory productivity, but everyone from architects to coaches devised applications for his system after the war. The increasing status of the athletic coach in the first place reflected an aspect of Taylorism, which involved not just the study of movement but also the shift in decision-making from the workers on the shop floor to the managers monitoring them from above. In much the same way, coaches increasingly made the decisions for their athletes on everything from diet to training to pre-race strategy.

The physiologist Wilhelm Knoll pioneered the filming of hurdlers and sprinters in the 1920s to look for physical inefficiencies.[25] A German sports journal praised such uses of stop-action photography in 1926 for enabling the analysis "of a start, a baton exchange, or a [javelin] throw in all its details."[26] Another article that same year demanded "More technical training!...systematic and strict," in order to ensure that "the athlete has rid himself of all sorts of bad little habits and adopted the detailed new improvements."[27] In a 1927 article in *Die Leibesübungen*, Richard Honisch declared, "Today, the technique of all of our track and field drills are based upon ongoing motion studies."[28] In presenting Taylorism as the sine qua non of peak performance, sports reports promoted the same philosophy that was simultaneously reconfiguring the working lives of so many Germans. Businessmen even drew an explicit connection between rationalized athletic training and higher economic productivity overall, including Ernst Poensgen, the deputy chairman of United Steel Works, who preached the gospel of company sports in interwar Germany specifically as a way to boost his employees' performance.[29]

The body that resulted from this training also signaled a caesura between postwar Germany and the preceding era. Streamlined, toned, and androgynous, the athlete presented a functional and explicitly modern alternative to the stouter figures of Imperial Germany. This modern body, moreover, demanded continual improvement. No matter how impressively it performed, it never achieved completion. Instead, athletes and trainers tinkered restlessly with diet, equipment, and regimen in the pursuit of an even better performance at the next meet. Athletes embodied Karl Marx's notion of modernity as a state of perpetual becoming, in which, to paraphrase *The Communist Manifesto*, portions of the solid body melt into air, making it sleeker, lighter, and swifter. Sebastian Haffner recalled his own relentless athletic striving in the 1920s: "For two years, my intellectual life stood almost still, and I trained fiercely in middle- and long-distance running and would have sold my soul to the devil without a second thought to run the 800 meters under two minutes just one time."[30]

This striving drove the development of sports science in the 1920s and fueled the growing belief that one could engineer better athletes. "The era of the natural runner is gone," sighed Richard Harbott in 1926, now that "running has intensified into a scientifically taught procedure, whose training alternatives and tactical and technical modifications grow daily."[31]

Physical culture had entered an "Age of Calibration," and Germany quickly established itself as a leading center for the scientific study of the athlete.[32] The Institute for Exercise in Hamburg and the German College of Physical Exercise in Berlin, among others, meticulously studied the body's physiological response to a workout. Dynamometers measured muscle strength; sphygmographs recorded the pulse; pneumatometers calculated how much air one exhaled; and ergographs figured out how much actual muscle work the athlete performed. An ambitious sportsman or woman had either to stay abreast of the latest techniques or live with being an also-ran. Track and field did not provide a respite from the pressures of society, it intensified them.

The *Berliner Illustrierte Zeitung* drew arresting visual attention to the rationalized athlete in 1931 when it showed a runner harnessed to a complex battery of monitors.[33] The headline read simply, "The Sportsman as Guinea Pig." The middle-distance champion Otto Peltzer saw his fellow athletes in a similar manner, as specimens for scientific study, including the Olympic 400-meter champion Ray Barbuti. "After the race I appeared in his changing room right away," Peltzer recalled proudly in 1928, in order "to bring him immediately to the medical examination laboratory, so that he could be observed there and the doctors could see...the sorts of splendid figures that athletic training produces."[34] The same laboratory mentality spawned early forays into doping, as athletes experimented with everything from alcohol, caffeine, kola nuts, and chocolate to phosphates, cocaine, strychnine, arsenic, testicular extracts, and ultraviolet radiation in their quest to boost performance.[35] This tinkering with the human body further widened the philosophical gulf between track and field and *Turnen*, given the latter's claims to natural self-development.

Rationalized athletic training did indeed produce a number of "splendid figures," to borrow Peltzer's term. The physiologist Fritz Giese praised the athlete's streamlined frame in his 1925 book *Geist im Sport* (Spirit in Sports), in which he juxtaposed the photograph of a lithe gravity-defying runner with that of a bodybuilder, whose colossal *Gestalt* seemed to render him immobile. This latter figure exhibited the "unaesthetic effect of muscular hypertrophy," Giese sneered, whereas the runner's build represented the "ideal man's body."[36] On the eve of the 1928 Olympic Games, *Sport und Sonne* declared an end to Germany's status as the "land of strongmen," whose bulky physical form advertised excessive consumption and obsolescence.[37] "The new era has created the strongly slender, swift athlete-type," it concluded, whose body illustrated efficient, disciplined self-management.

The sports commentator Willy Meisl enthusiastically concurred. In a book on the 1928 Olympiad, Meisl pointed to the oversized physiques of Germany's 1912 Olympic team as indicative of an outdated physical form. In an almost perfect echo of Giese, he dismissed that earlier generation of athletes as "colossal figures, giant, massive musclemen," suggesting elephants, rather than cheetahs.[38] Since the war, Meisl continued, even shot putters had "slender athletic frames, certainly not weak or diminutive chaps, but just as clearly not muscled hulks and by no means avalanches of flesh." The new physical form had established its hegemony, he concluded: "The era of the fat guys is over, the era of the harmoniously strong athletes has begun." As a model of the modern body, no one surpassed the track and field athlete.

This held every bit as true for the female as for the male. Rumpelstilzchen found the lithe body of the female runner absolutely captivating in 1924, while watching the German women set a new record in the 400-meter relay in Berlin. He admitted to having spent more time watching their legs than the stop clock. "Your heart leaps with joy when you admire such elegant proportions, loveliness, and youth," the usually cynical columnist gushed.[39] A 1929 essay by Käte Bruns praised the "muscle-packed legs" of female sprinters, which she far preferred to those of ballerinas.[40] *Sport und Sonne* admired the powerful legs of female runners, too, contending in 1930 that "the musculature unquestionably becomes more pronounced, but, upon closer examination, one has to admit that the body is lovelier."[41]

The new female body derived from the very same dedicated, serious training that had created the new male body. As early as 1919 Walter Ball, the director of a Munich athletics association, underscored the commitment that he expected from members of both sexes and took a swipe at the rival *Turnen* movement at the same time. "We are not some social club like...the female *Turners*," he told the women's sports magazine *Damen-Sport und Damen-Turnen*. "We are a serious organization. Every lady who comes to us must have the determination to work seriously to achieve her personal best."[42] By focusing more on performance than appearance, more on internal self-development than external self-presentation, women in competitive track and field presented an important alternative to the surface-oriented New Woman, who tended to view thinness as a fashionable end in itself, rather than as a means to better performance.[43]

Within just a few years of the end of the war, a whole cohort of German women had achieved international recognition in their disciplines. Wally Wittmann, for instance, won the national javelin championship as a nineteen-year-old in 1924 and went on to set a world record in the 100 meters. Her success, along with that of her countrywomen, made the 1920s an unprecedented era for female athletes in Germany, who garnered acclaim for their physical abilities rather than their physical appearances. At a time when Weimar cultural critics like Siegfried Kracauer were describing the serialization of female bodies in revues and fashion magazines, the track and field champion presented herself as a recognizable individual with a singular ability. Unlike a member of the Tiller Girls, who carefully synchronized her movements to the rest of the kickline, the athlete fought hard to stand out from her rivals. She was not like the rest of them; she was better. Her body was not interchangeable with others; it was swifter, stronger, more productive. The champion gained fame through her achievements, pushing her way into a public sphere that had hitherto remained the exclusive domain of men.

Athletes provided important role models to postwar women for how to develop themselves in accord with modern society. In 1924, the Berlin Sports Club published a commentary in Germany's leading sports magazine that underscored how track and field benefited the growing legions of women in the workforce. Modern life demanded more of the woman than ever, the article stated, since they "are forced into a career and don't know how to refresh the spent nerves and low energy that result from long hours of office work and, on top of that, the housekeeping concerns."[44] Track and field fostered the necessary strength and endurance to meet these challenges. A 1925 article echoed this sentiment: "We do not want to exclude the female sex in sports from competition. The woman is more than ever in competitive life. She has to compete...for her living, [and] for her rights."[45] The opportunities, demands, and sheer tempo of postwar German society dwarfed that of the Wilhelmine era, and the country needed entirely new bodies if it hoped to keep pace.

Sport im Bild, meanwhile, emphasized the increasing convergence between male and female abilities when it characterized the sportswoman in 1926 as a "modern girl who trains like her comrade of the other sex."[46] Under the 1927 headline "Become Beautiful," Fritz Kniese argued that women and men now strove toward the same corporeal ideal: "slender, strong, and sleek."[47] By the early 1930s, as the National Socialist Party registered dramatic gains on a platform of racial purity, some articles advanced the claim that postwar female athletes were actually repopularizing an ancient Germanic tradition of robust and self-sufficient women, of which the legends provided ample evidence. As one poet exclaimed in his 1930 paean to female javelin throwers: "you can have the delicate, fine-as-silk ladies; you can have the girls who doll themselves up; I sing the praises of these daughters of the Valkyries."[48] This invocation of the Valkyries bestowed upon the athlete an indigenous gloss that moderated her reputation as a conduit for American ideas.

When Werner Scheff presented his vision in 1928 of what the German women's track and field team would look like twelve years in the future, he foresaw "very few ladies, but all that many more representatives of what this time was literally the strong sex," whose bodies possessed the speed, the power, and, most importantly, the form of the men's.[49] Carmol, a brand of liniment, featured a female shot-putter, rather than a male, in a 1931 ad, which promised that it would soothe the "muscle aches following strenuous exercise."[50] The advertisement assumed that its audience would view women as athletes who trained just as hard—and understood the nature of muscle soreness just as well—as men. The advertisement's appearance in Germany's leading track and field magazine, as opposed to one that targeted an exclusively female readership, moreover, suggested that product endorsements by female athletes carried weight with male consumers, too.

In terms of dedication, commentators in the 1920s frequently contended that female athletes, like their counterparts in women's tennis, exhibited far greater dedication and ambition than male athletes. Alexander Abraham, writing in 1927, admired how women adhered to their training regimen "without force from outside."[51] "Their ambition makes it easy for them to live perfectly within the spirit of sports," he asserted, whereas men required constant nagging and supervision. Furthermore, Abraham continued, "the elasticity and agility of the female body" made it innately suited for the high jump, long jump, or hurdles. A *Sport und Sonne* article two months earlier purported that women took to the throwing events, like javelin, more easily than the men, which made their competitions "perhaps even more beautiful" than the latter's.[52] A 1930 article similarly concluded that women possessed a superior form to men when it came to the shot put. Three of the instructional photographs that accompanied the piece used women to illustrate proper form in the discipline, while the lone depiction of a male shot-putter showed readers what not to do.[53]

The level of women's athletic performance took off in the 1920s, reaching and even surpassing many of the men's records of the prewar period. As *Der Leichtathlet* noted in 1926, after an athlete set a new record in the women's discus, "It would have meant a new record for men [just] 20 years ago."[54] Such performances testified to the potential of the female

Der Wettlauf der Geschlechter von 1926

A female runner races her male counterpart to a dead heat in this 1927 illustration in the popular magazine *Uhu.* The caption reads, "The contest between the sexes of 1926." *Ullstein Bild/The Granger Collection, New York*

body, and they called into question some basic assumptions about the "natural" differences between the sexes. Heinrich Mann, in an essay the following year, described a young woman who "performed an exercise that, in an earlier army, only a few officers could do." An accompanying illustration, over the caption "The contest between the sexes of 1926," depicted a male and female runner with identically sinewy physiques crossing the finish line in a dead heat.[55] The male runner, however, threw his head back in anguished effort, whereas his female rival bore such a serene look that she might gladly have completed another few laps. An onlooking couple, dressed in Wilhelmine fashions to symbolize the prewar generation, registered shocked disbelief at the modern woman's remarkable performance and muscled body, fully visible in the identical short pants and shirt that the man wore.

That match-up was not entirely a product of Mann's imagination. Men and women did compete against one another in certain contexts during the Weimar period, and commentators even more frequently compared the performances of male and female athletes. A 10-kilometer race in 1929, for instance, grouped the female runners in the same heat as male runners over forty, which the women won.[56] These women had not defeated men in their own age cohort, to be sure, but their top finishes highlighted the fact that only the best male runners could expect to outperform a well-trained female athlete. A 1932 commemorative book on the Los Angeles Olympics made much the same point by drawing attention to the surprisingly narrow margins that separated the winning times and distances in some of the men's events from those in the women's and by noting that the female champions had outperformed many of the male Olympic qualifiers.[57] "How many men are incapable, in spite of all their training, of jumping higher than 1.65 meters! How many lack the ability to cover 100 meters in 11.9 [seconds]!" the author asked rhetorically as he praised the female gold medalists. His statement hinted that male champions might not maintain that edge forever.

The stunning performance and androgynous appearance of the female athlete led, not surprisingly, to her discursive masculinization. *Der Leichtathlet* may have resisted this trend in 1925, when it wrote that the female sprinter "gave no cause at all for the claims of all-too timid contemporaries [that she is a] 'mannish woman,'" but by 1926 the same journal exhibited no such reservations about commenting that the women's 100-meter champion "runs like a man."[58] Another sports journal that same year quoted former decathlon champion Karl Ritter von Halt, who insisted that competitive practices in women's track and field would take "our German girls and make hard, manly bodies out of them."[59] Halt cast a decidedly critical eye on this trend, as did Rudolph Stratz in his sports novel *Lill*, in which he described the female discus champion Emilie Kneuper as having "the figure of Venus de Milo [but] a chest like a man." In case readers had failed to note her manliness this first time, Stratz later referred to Kneuper as "the Germanic powerhouse with a measured, deep voice" and dubbed her "der starke Emil" (the strong Emil), a term that deliberately employed both the masculine article "der" and the male equivalent of the female name Emilie.[60]

Rumpelstilzchen referred to the muscles on the champion German hurdler Eva von Bredow in 1927 as "bands of steel," to which he added, "I can well imagine that she would be a good partner on an elephant hunt in East Africa." Rumpelstilzchen then invoked Norse legend, when he asked rhetorically, "Where is a King Gunther who would want to marry such a Brunhilde?," a reference to the famous Valkyrie who would only marry a man capable of defeating her in three track-and-field-like contests.[61] By repeatedly using Bredow's physical prowess to question her womanhood, the columnist revealed an anxiety that her masculinity surpassed his own. When *Sport und Gesundheit* called a female shot-putter a "modern Amazon" in 1930, on the other hand, it intended this as high praise.[62] The recurrent comparison of female athletes to mythological figures may also have stemmed from her trailblazing role. Without a contemporary analogy for these women's achievements, commentators could turn nowhere else but to legend.

As the products of carefully calibrated workouts and disciplinary specialization, track and field athletes inspired a host of critics as well, and not just from the *Turnen* camp. Sports commentators like Rudolf Hartung saw in the modern athlete precisely those catalysts of postwar social transformation that he most opposed: Taylorism and Americanization. In a 1927 article, Hartung condemned the soulless "materialism" of competitive track and field, with its focus on "motion studies, mechanics, technique, [and] measurement," which he contrasted to the athletic "idealism" of indigenous German physical culture.[63] Even Carl Diem, the man who had personally recruited an American to modernize German training before the war, expressed his yearning for a "liberation from exclusively technical objectives for the body" by mid-decade.[64] Joseph Waitzer, another generally pro- rationalization official, praised one of his sprinters in 1927 for training "simply and naturally—[with] none of the daily American forced labor that turns the body into a mighty machine but deprives it of the fine sense of improvement."[65] Here, Waitzer waxed nostalgic for an era before the engineered body, an era that his own coaching techniques had, in fact, helped to end.

The opening scene of Fritz Lang's monumental 1926 motion picture *Metropolis* reflected this same romanticized longing for the organic athlete who remained free from the constrictions of rationalized training.[66] The film opens with a running competition that Freder, the laughing, rosy-cheeked protagonist, wins. The following scene highlights Freder's natural, un-rationalized essence by directly contrasting him to the workers below ground, who labor under strictly disciplined, precisely timed, and slave-like conditions. This contrast, of course, entirely elided the fact that the same clock that precisely measured the workers' lives below ground also measured the race that Freder had just won. His victory, moreover, relied on a training program whose slavish demands bore at least some similarities to the workday below. Even though *Metropolis* carefully sought to obscure the fact, Freder's victory derived from the same aspects of modernity that the film so vigorously criticized in the very next scene.

Waitzer and his fellow critics of the new methods understood that those methods had enabled the nation's interwar athletic success, and none of them would have advocated a genuine return to the "natural" runner. *Der Leichtathlet* may well have admired a Kenyan in 1925 for having equaled a world record without the benefit of "any specialized training and scarcely possess[ing] the most elementary technical knowledge of running," but the magazine never suggested that German runners adopt a similar approach.[67] On the contrary, it insisted that the Kenyan would have run even faster if he had submitted himself to precisely that "specialized training." A commemorative book on the 1932 Olympics also engaged in a bit of misty-eyed nostalgia when it lauded the uncoached runners from developing countries as "certainly healthier and stronger than us."[68] The book even asserted that Germans "would do themselves a favor by taking such ruggedness and lack of corruption as an example." Nevertheless, it concluded, these "primitive peoples" almost always finished last, an outcome that would only change once they had began modern training. As Paul Landau pithily observed in 1927, "yearning for the primitive is a trait of our culture," but hardly anyone wished to turn that yearning into practice.[69]

The track and field movement did worry seriously, though, that the modern methods had produced one-sided individuals. The middle-distance runner Otto Peltzer, whose 1926 victory over Paavo Nurmi in a 1,500-meter race in Berlin had made him into a national hero overnight, often appeared in journalistic profiles as a man unhealthily obsessed with his training. "Peltzer lives only for sport," began Heinz Cavalier, in a 1931 piece for *Der Leichtathlet*. "He avoids [even] the common pleasures and comforts of life, which are...not conducive to achievement."[70] Unlike a boxer, whose monasticism in the weeks leading up to a fight inspired a certain amount of awe and admiration, Peltzer's did not. The boxer relied heavily on the parent-like supervision of a coach to enforce his discipline, and many boxers publicly succumbed to their hedonistic impulses, which lent them a sympathetic degree of humanity. Track and field athletes, on the other hand, policed themselves, which occasionally lent them a stern and slightly inhuman air and made the athlete-as-machine metaphor seem all the more apt.

The 1929 essay "The Olympic Type" referred disparagingly to the "skinny, nervous builds" of elite runners, an assessment echoed by the track and field journal *Start und Ziel* that same year, when it called middle-distance champions "small, nervous types."[71] Even Paavo Nurmi, the legendary Finnish runner, received a scathing critique in 1930 from *Die Leibesübungen*, which found his legs impressive enough, but not his "truly withered, narrow, clearly unathletic upper body, [with] a small, emaciated head."[72] By the close of the 1920s then, even some sports journals had begun to question the physical consequences of disciplinary specialization and to wonder if track and field had lost sight of the somatic whole. Dr. Helmut Kost, writing in the pages of *Die Leibesübungen* in 1930, called for scrapping women's competitions altogether and substituting a holistic regime of gentle gymnastics instead.[73]

The perception of an athlete's training-induced fragility, in both men and women alike, had circulated widely enough by 1931 that *Der Leichtathlet* engaged in a bit of damage control. The track and field journal explicitly addressed the medical concerns, conceding that a record-breaking run invariably required post-race recuperation. "However," the journal added vehemently, "it is simply not true that the record athlete is not of any use for mental or physical work!"[74] Coming two years after the onset of the Depression, this statement spoke directly to the nation's economic concerns. The implosion that began in November 1929, just after the New York Stock Market crashed, prompted Germans to reassess the entire direction that postwar society had taken, particularly its adoption of the U.S. model. This crisis in the business world had a ripple effect in the sports world, thanks to the athletic body's close association with that U.S. model, and that crisis heightened the scrutiny of Taylorized bodies as well as the glowing praise of "natural" ones. It also signaled a resurgent cultural conservatism in Germany in the 1930s that manifested itself in growing support for the National Socialists and a backlash against some of the most pioneering aspects of Weimar culture.

Criticisms of the modern athlete in the 1920s, which repeatedly deployed terms like "excessive" and "one-sided," revived a prewar debate over how best to maintain a body's productivity over its lifetime. On one side, as Anson Rabinbach explains in his seminal study of the debate, a "science of work" paradigm assumed the existence of a finite supply of energy in the human body, which one needed to parcel out with care, in order to optimize its use over a lifetime. On the other side, the Taylorist paradigm did not assume a limited energy supply and gave little thought to the long-term consequences of its expenditure. It focused only on maximizing productivity to achieve short-term goals.[75] Track and field had generally embraced the Taylorist paradigm, but with an added twist: it also presented the sport as a rejuvenating pursuit that would actually increase a body's energy and strength for future labors. Some critics at the close of the decade, however, called this claim into question and drew on the "science of work" paradigm in so doing. As the lesbian magazine *Garçonne* warned its readers in 1931, "Ladies' sport is not about closing in on Peltzer's and Nurmi's records. It should mean rejuvenation, not create weariness."[76] As the following section shows, the track and field establishment had a tremendous investment in the notion that competitive athletes rejuvenated the German nation.

The People's Body: Militarism, Maternity, and the National Project

Since at least the early nineteenth century, German leaders had paid a great deal of attention to the physical bodies of their populations. When Napoleon defeated the Prussian army in 1806, Friedrich Ludwig Jahn argued that all German men had a duty to harden their bodies for future fights, and he developed *Turnen* to help them do just that. Over the course of the next century, the national community increasingly placed demands on the bodies of its members, in terms of how they developed those bodies and what they did with them. As Germany once again confronted defeat in 1918, a number of leaders drew the same instinctive conclusion that Jahn had reached a century earlier: the nation had grown soft and needed deliverance from its corporeal malaise.[77] This time, however, *Turnen* faced competition from other branches of physical culture, and from none more so than track and field.

Track and field claimed not only to strengthen and discipline German men but also to prepare German women for their roles as productive and, above all, reproductive members of the national community. It thereby emphasized a physical difference between male and female bodies that seemed so shockingly erased in the streamlined forms of the athletes themselves. If the female athlete often appeared un-maternal and the male athlete one-sided, this reassertion of gender-specific roles provided a certain measure of reassurance about the extent of the corporeal revolution taking place. Track and field stood to gain more than just a soothed public, of course. By successfully selling itself as critical to the nation's postwar recovery, track and field secured valuable support from the state. A patriotic self-presentation also counteracted the sport's hitherto alien image by anchoring it within a specifically German project. Furthermore, it stoked the sport's growing popularity among the middle classes, for whom patriotism remained a defining value. Finally, apart from any larger strategic aim, the claim also reflected the genuine convictions of most track and field officials and athletes, who generally saw themselves as contributing directly to national rejuvenation.

The majority of sports observers, notwithstanding the vocal skeptics of Taylorized training, concurred, especially with regard to track and field's claim to build future soldiers. The assertion, after all, simply reiterated a widely held belief since the nineteenth century that physical fitness equaled fighting force, the same belief that had inspired Pierre de Coubertin to revive the Olympic Games after France's defeat in 1871. It also appealed to a demand within Germany for a "hardened masculinity" that emphasized toughness, endurance, service, and duty, all of which track and field promised to develop in spades. This demand had already emerged in the aftermath of the prewar Eulenburg scandal (see chap. 1), and it grew dramatically in response to the humiliation of 1918.[78] Because the Versailles

Treaty had so drastically reduced the size of the German army and, hence, of the number of men who would receive their physical training through military service, postwar leaders anxiously sought alternative means to maintain a basic level of fitness in the male population. Track and field promoted itself as just such an *Ersatzwehrdienst*, a substitute for military service. The German Federation of Physical Culture, in a letter to the war minister, boldly claimed that athletes constituted the "voluntary core of a future army."[79] The fact that Article 177 of the Versailles Treaty explicitly forbade such contact between German sports organizations and the war ministry showed that the rest of Europe shared Germany's assumptions regarding sport's military applications, as well as the ineffectualness of treaty enforcement.

The press repeatedly called attention to track and field's martial utility and deployed a surprisingly wide array of military metaphors in their sports reportage. As *Illustrierter Sport* reminded its readers in April 1919, two months before the signing of the Versailles Peace Treaty had even taken place, "a sportsman is always a good soldier."[80] A 1925 report in *Der Leichtathlet* referred to the discus and javelin thrower Hans Hoffmeister as the country's "most formidable weapon" for the Amsterdam Olympics three years hence. In 1927, the same journal invoked the notion of wartime mobilization by writing that "Germany is arming [itself] for the Olympic Games of 1928." *Der Leichtathlet* continued this motif in a 1928 report that labeled the track and field squad "die deutsche Streitmacht" (the German armed forces). *B.Z. am Mittag* promised its readers that sports officials had done everything in their power "to send Germany's representatives fully armed into battle in Amsterdam." In a similar flourish, a 1928 guide to the Amsterdam Games referred to the millions of German fans "behind the lines," who would eagerly "await the news from the Olympic front."[81]

Heinz Cavalier, the editor of *Der Leichtathlet*, picked up on this notion of an "Olympic front" in 1927 when he called on fans to do their duty in ensuring a German victory at the upcoming Olympics. "Each should give, as far as it is in his powers," he implored. "Without sacrifices, we cannot expect success....Be fighters on the homefront and support the front!"[82] With his explicit use of the terms "front," "sacrifice," and "duty," Cavalier's plea could have come straight from a war bond rally during the Great War itself. When Germany's track and field team fared worse at the Games than expected, Cavalier upped the rhetorical ante by propagating an Olympic version of the infamous "stab-in-the-back myth," which had attributed the nation's defeat in 1918 to traitors at home, especially Jews and socialists. Cavalier blamed the poor showing of track and field athletes on the treacherous apathy of the German public. "This mood on the homefront," Cavalier reprimanded his readers in 1928, with reference to the lack of fan support, "called to mind...the November days of the year 1918, when Germany had lost a war."[83] A nation's athletic success, in Cavalier's estimation, necessitated the same collective effort as a military one and held a similar importance. Only the total mobilization of athletes and fans alike would ensure victory.

Carl Diem referred to track and field athletes in 1928 as "an army of 100,000 men and women, boys and girls," a number that, not coincidentally, exactly equaled the size limit imposed upon the postwar German army.[84] Unlike the actual army, though, Diem's athlete-army included women and girls as well. *Der Leichtathlet* even proposed in 1929 that the government take the money that it would otherwise have spent on an unrestricted army and invest those funds directly in track and field, since both promoted the same outcome.[85] Berlin's urban planner, Martin Wagner, adopted this same rationale to justify a dramatic expansion of the city's athletic fields under his tenure. Prior to the war, Wagner wrote in 1929, "each Prussian had to squeeze a lifetime's worth of exercise into his two-year army service."[86] By encouraging exercise throughout one's life, Wagner believed, Germany would actually enjoy an even higher level of preparedness than it had before 1914.

Track and field associations reinforced the connection still further by organizing competitions that had unambiguously warlike overtones. Many of these had already gained popularity during the war, such as the steeplechase in full battle gear, the sprint with gas mask, and the hand grenade toss for distance and accuracy, some of which the army adapted for use in helping wounded soldiers return more quickly to combat.[87] A 1920 drawing in *Illustrierter Sport* depicted a track meet as trench warfare, in which competitors clambered over steeplechase barriers, sloshed through water hazards the size of artillery craters, and hurdled over barriers the height of barbed-wire entanglements.[88] At the same time, the press highlighted the military service of track and field athletes. When Karl Ritter von Halt won the 1921 German decathlon title, *Sport im Bild* published a photo of him in his army uniform, rather than his athletic one. The caption then went out of its way to explain that Halt had received a knighthood for his "bold resolve as a company commander in the face of the enemy" during the war.[89] A 1928 photograph of the shot-putter Emil Hirschfeld featured him without a shirt, but nevertheless wearing his sergeant's helmet.[90] This composition simultaneously encouraged viewers to admire Hirschfeld's chiseled torso and make a visual connection between fitness and combat readiness, an approach that prefigured the hypermuscular statuary that would soon adorn so much Nazi-era architecture.

Otto Peltzer, although not a member of the German army, did present himself as a dutiful servant of the national interest and thus consciously set himself apart from champions in other sports. When Peltzer's stunning 1,500-meter victory over Paavo Nurmi in 1926 led to a flood of commercial offers, including one from a Hollywood studio that reportedly promised $50,000 over four years, he seemed have it made.[91] Peltzer declined it, however. As the press later reported, "he would rather remain a poor schoolteacher...and serve his fatherland than betray it for 50,000 dollars." This dramatic gesture distinguished him from the prizefighter, who eagerly

This 1920 drawing, published less than two years after the end of the war, depicts a men's track meet in images reminiscent of trench warfare. *Freie Universität Berlin, Bereichsbibliothek Erziehungswissenschaft, Fachdidaktik und Psychologie*

cashed in on his success and would have all too gladly signed the first Hollywood contract to come his way. Peltzer, by contrast, performed a masculinity that placed patriotic duty at its center, just as Georg Cornelius did and just as the public increasingly expected all track and field athletes to do. When Peltzer recounted in his memoir, "I dreamed of becoming a genuine sports hero," he understood that to mean someone who competed for his country and not just for himself.[92]

Although the militarization of the sport generally met with widespread support over the course of the 1920s, a few voices expressed opposition. On the political left, a number of figures sharply criticized the manner in which competitive track and field had stoked national rivalries and martial impulses. On the eve of the 1928 Amsterdam Olympics, Hamburg's socialist daily juxtaposed a drawing of soldiers storming the trenches with one of sprinters crossing the finish line. The caption reinforced the suggestion that athletic competition did not foster peaceful coexistence after all.[93] Some on the political right, meanwhile, echoed the *Turnen* movement in their suspicion that track and field provided a poor foundation for a future army, since its excessive individualism undermined hierarchical obedience. Rumpelstilzchen cautioned in 1923, "sports are good, sports are healthy, sports are necessary, but we've won our great wars not with sports but with discipline."[94] Competitive sports, moreover, clearly lacked firm ideological underpinnings. "Today, even the Communists participate in sports," Rumpelstilzchen sniffed, and thereby implied that the same athletic skills that might defend a nation could just as easily overthrow it.

Rumpelstilzchen touched once again upon the suspicion of cultural conservatives that the inherently cosmopolitan sensibility of modern sports would never allow them to become truly German. Track and field journals tried to counteract this by infusing the sport with an ethnic nationalism similar to that in *Turnen*. Articles regularly highlighted those American champions who traced their genealogy to central Europe, as when *Sport und Sonne* wrote in 1928 that Jonny Kuck, the American-born shot-put champion, was, "like most of the strong American throwers, of German descent" and then went on to admire his blond hair and "Frisian" features.[95] In a 1930 profile of America's four best shot-putters, the same magazine declared with proprietary glee that "three belong, in the terminology of racial science, to the fair Nordic race and one to the dark Alpine race that is more common in the south of Germany."[96] It added that statistics "confirm the fact that German-Americans, of all the nationalities in the U.S., produce the greatest percentage of 'Olympic physical builds.'"

Der Leichtathlet even published an occasional appeal to German-Americans to return to their "homeland." When the American-born Paul de Bruyn won a 1931 marathon in Germany, the journal first gushed over his blond hair and then expressed its wish "that he may resist the allure of the 'New World' and remain what he is—a good German!"[97] A 1932 album of trading cards, meanwhile, made a point of stating that the Olympic gold medal won by a German-American decathlete "rightly belongs to the United States" alone, by which it meant to suggest, of course, exactly the opposite.[98] This ethnic chauvinism scarcely narrowed the ideological distance between competitive track and field and *Turnen*, but it did feed into the vibrant discourse on "race hygiene" in Weimar Germany, a subject on which Peltzer himself wrote a PhD dissertation in 1925. Georg Cornelius's redemption of the Nordic race by defeating the Chinese runners at the conclusion of *Der Läufer von Marathon* reflected this chauvinism in the extreme, but it found a nonfiction echo in *Der Leichtathlet*'s coverage of the 1932 Olympic Games. When the German sprinter Arthur Jonath won the bronze medal in the 100 meters, behind two black American sprinters, the journal proudly anointed Jonath "the fastest man of the white race over 100 meters."[99] This statement offered a mild foretaste of the far more extreme racist rhetoric and politics of the National Socialist Regime that came to power less than six months later.

The contention that track and field prepared women to fulfill their physical obligation to the nation sparked a far more heated debate in the Weimar Republic than that for men. Especially in the early postwar years, medical authorities and even sports officials worried that intense training and competition would permanently damage a woman's reproductive organs, and countless commentators recommended nothing more strenuous than gentle stretching and light gymnastics.[100] Even by the middle of the decade, the opening sequence of the 1926 film *Metropolis* still reflected this sensibility. It begins with an exclusively male running competition inside a massive stadium, not a woman in sight. The audience caught its first glimpse of female characters in a following scene, as they flirtatiously played a game of blind man's bluff in an idyllic garden far removed from the stadium. The juxtaposition of a strenuously masculine race with gently feminine play echoed the dominant discourse on athletic competition immediately after the war, in which women's races appeared as incursions into an intrinsically male domain. Over the course of the Weimar Republic, however, this view shifted markedly toward one that actively encouraged women to compete in track and field.

This increased acceptance of female athleticism nevertheless remained stubbornly predicated upon the same set of assumptions that framed the debate all along—that track and field's worth lay solely in the extent to which it promoted reproduction. Germany's birthrate had plummeted from 25.9 per thousand inhabitants in 1920 to 14.7 in 1933, the lowest in Europe, and the fitness of postwar children seemed to have worsened, too.[101] For those active in the eugenics movement, track and field athletes had a particularly important duty to raise families since they came disproportionately from the middle classes, precisely the social group that ostensibly produced the best children and, at the same time, appeared so worrisomely reluctant to do so. The *Reichstag* responded with a hodgepodge of initiatives to address the perceived crisis, from introducing Mother's Day in 1922 to supporting family welfare programs to restricting the advertisement of contraceptives. This social and political climate placed tremendous pressure on women's track and field to justify its own contribution to the national birthrate.

The sport had to negotiate a precarious balance in the Weimar Republic. It dramatically transformed the social opportunities for women by reshaping their bodies, altering perceptions of their physical capabilities, and normalizing their competitiveness. Already by January 1919, just two months after the end of the Great War, the head of the German Sports Federation called on local sports clubs to remove the remaining barriers to women's athletic participation. Before the year was out, "scarcely a single sports festival failed to have ladies' competitions," as *Illustrierter Sport* triumphantly reported.[102] At the same time, though, track and field reaffirmed the woman's traditional role as mother, and those first women's competitions after the war restricted themselves almost exclusively to the short sprints, which purportedly did not overtax the system. As late as 1925, a meet in Dresden featured sixteen events for men and just four for women: the 100 meters, the 100-meter relay, the javelin, and the long jump.[103]

As officials and the female athletes themselves gradually expanded the number of women's events in the mid-1920s, they sparked a passionate debate over acceptable activities for women and the physical limits of the female body. Some commentators opposed the expansion of competitive track and field for women simply because the sport, by its very nature, emphasized self-development and personal achievement. This inherent me-centeredness clashed with the ideal of the domestic angel, who denied her own ambitions and dedicated herself entirely to the nurturing of husband and family. The dilemma of the female athlete, as the historian Ann Taylor Allen writes, lay precisely in the fact that "ambition, lauded in elite males as a sign of superior fitness, was deplored in females of the same class as a selfish pretext for the avoidance of motherhood."[104]

Indeed, most critics of women's track and field based their attacks on the fear that running and jumping competitions would make women less maternal in both an emotional and a physical sense. These fears surfaced clearly at Germany's first conference on women's physical culture in 1925. One attendee categorically declared, "excessive training and overly intensive exercise or a one-sided training regimen damages women in their fitness for childbearing."[105] The speaker conceded knowing of no studies to justify her concerns, but her description of the "excessive," "overly intensive," and "one-sided" training of female athletes managed to consolidate almost every criticism leveled against competitive athletics since before the war. These criticisms, significantly, did not assume that the female body could not train rigorously, but only that doing so would jeopardize its reproductive capacity.

A 1926 article proposed opening track and field to girls, but not to women who had reached childbearing age and needed to devote themselves to raising a family.[106] On the physiological question of whether exercise ultimately built up or depleted a body's strength, this article hedged. Girlhood athletics, it implied, would increase the female body's capacity for future labors, but those same activities resulted in a net loss when performed by adult women. Charlotte Deppe worried that even girlhood sports went too far. The woman, Deppe argued at a 1929 conference on women's sports, "must not squander her energies in competitions during her youth, at a time when she should be saving them in order to be able to create anew later!"[107] For Deppe, track and field sapped necessary reproductive energy no matter when women engaged in it.

A medical journal in 1931 worried far less about energy reserves than about the reproductive organs themselves. "The woman's body is made directly more masculine through those excessive sports that mimic the men," it asserted. "The female abdominal organs fade away and the artificially bred, mannish woman is complete."[108] Again, the article never suggested that a woman lacked the ability to compete at an elite level, only that her doing so would lead to sterility and the erasure of her biological sex. Helmut Kost, on the other hand, suspected that some women had an inherent masculinity that made them ill suited to motherhood anyway. Rather than eliminating women's competitions altogether, therefore, Kost advocated their restriction to these "Amazon types" who would almost certainly never raise families and so might just as well pursue athletic honors.[109] As for the majority of German women, though, Kost felt it imperative that they save their strength for the task of rearing the next generation.

These arguments against women's track and field did not go unchallenged. As early as May 1919, Hermann Fromme informed readers of a leading women's sports magazine that they not only had a right to exercise, but a patriotic duty to do so, because "the natural profession of the woman as mother requires physical training, too."[110] Unlike Kost and Deppe, Fromme believed that sports replenished a female body's energy. On the question of what women should do with that energy, however, Fromme agreed with the other two completely. They should make babies. Seven years after Fromme's article, *Der Leichtathlet* called on sports officials to evaluate all women's sports exclusively in terms of their effect on the birthrate, a position that entirely subsumed women's individual desires to those of the national demographers.[111] Fromme's outspoken advocacy of women's track and field nevertheless represented an early voice on behalf of the sport that grew over the course of the 1920s and revised assumptions about the capabilities of women.

Advocates of women's track and field concentrated much of their public-relations efforts in the 1920s on deflecting the accusations that competitive athletics rendered women infertile. One gynecologist at the 1925 women's sports conference took examples from her own practice, including one patient who trained throughout all eight of her pregnancies, had always resumed competition immediately after giving birth, and yet "had such a perfectly lovely body that I couldn't believe her story of eight children."[112] Others shifted the emphasis from fertility to parenting skills. Grete Gräber argued in 1928 that athletic mothers raised superior children, not just more of them. "We have plainly recognized, contrary to the earlier point of view, that our married women, in particular, need sports in order to meet the challenges that are placed on the wife and especially on the mother," she wrote in the pages of *Der Leichtathlet*.[113] Her notion that German society as a whole had "plainly recognized" the social value of women's track and field may have been premature, but it did indicate the emerging trend.

In a 1929 essay in *Sport und Sonne* with the urgent title "Mothers, Do Sports!" Hildegard Fritsch contended that female athletes had more energy, not less, for raising a family.[114] She declared sports to be an "obligatory extension of household duties," since the athlete-mother "will always be a cheerier, more youthfully in-touch parent, well-disposed to ball-playing, small running races, and all sorts of high jinks, [and] more than that, a good companion!" Fritsch, like so many of her fellow advocates for female athletics, ascribed to women the exclusive responsibility for bringing up the next generation. Helmut Buchholz argued on precisely these grounds that female sports should receive far more attention, encouragement, and underwriting than male sports, since "girls and women will be the carriers of our future more than the boys and young men."[115] Because women played the more important role in Germany's rejuvenation, Buchholz argued, they merited the greater support. Track and field magazines like *Der Leichtathlet* and *Sport und Sonne* never discussed men's track and field within the context of familial obligations, and terms like "fatherhood" and "paternal fitness" remained conspicuously absent from the Weimar German discourse.

Just as track and field meets incorporated martial elements to underscore the male athlete's duty as a soldier, they also promoted events to highlight the female's duty as a mother. In the *Paarlauf*, for instance, a man and a woman raced in tandem, either hand-in-hand, with one leg tied together, or wheelbarrow-style. Because these races generally involved only newlyweds or single members of marriageable age, they re-created on the running track exactly the sort of heterosexual coupling on which Germany pinned its hopes for a rising birthrate.[116] Unlike mixed doubles in tennis, which had a reputation for unrestrained sexuality and outright infidelity, the *Paarlauf* affirmed committed, monogamous unions and implied procreative rather than recreational sex. Egg-and-spoon races, which also restricted themselves to newlywed or marriageable women, had the appearance of modern-day fertility rituals.[117] If nothing else, the spectacle of female runners carefully trying to convey their eggs across the finish line intact provided an aptly visual metaphor for precisely the anxiety of so many track and field critics. If the egg-and-spoon race still proved too subtle a message, Berlin's premier athletics club, SC Charlottenburg, sponsored a women's relay in 1927 in which competitors transferred a baby carriage from runner to runner, instead of a baton.[118]

The Motherliness of a Middle-Distance Runner:
Victory and Defeat in the Women's 800 Meters

I want to return now to the image with which this chapter opened: Lina Radke-Batschauer crossing the finish line of the women's 800-meter competition in triumph at the 1928 Amsterdam Olympic Games. Not only had Radke-Batschauer won the Olympic debut of this women's event, but she also gave Germany its only track and field gold medal of the Games, a bright spot in an otherwise disappointing finish for a country that had entered with such high expectations. Along with celebration, however, the race also brought to a boil the debate that had swirled around the women's sport since its inception, and it channeled a decade's worth of anxiety about declining birthrates, changing gender roles, and the consequences of modernity.[119] Radke-Batschauer's world-record-setting performance itself did not provoke alarm, but the sight of two of her competitors collapsing in exhaustion at the end of the race definitely did.

The avalanche of post-race commentary crystallized the central tension over women's track and field and women's roles in general since the end of the war. On the one hand, the performance imperative demanded everything of the athlete, even to the point of collapse, in pursuit of faster, stronger, and better. On the other hand, the rhetoric of traditional motherhood sought to calmly reassure the public that track and field fortified rather than exhausted its participants and prepared them for their true roles as mothers. The debate also illustrated the double standard for male and female athletes, still anchored in place throughout the Weimar period. No commentator dreamed of describing the collapsed female athletes as "heroic," in the manner of a Georg Cornelius.

Despite the sharp attacks against female athleticism that immediately followed the Olympic 800 meters in some newspapers, the general reaction of the German press proved generally supportive of both the event and of female athletes, especially when compared to the official reaction of the sport's international governing bodies. By the mid-1920s, Germany had actually established itself as something of a powerhouse in women's track and field, a country in which, despite lingering opposition, female athletes could train and compete with comparatively strong support and undeniable success. Already at their first international competition in 1926, Germany's women had taken home half of the first-place medals and outperformed both the British and the French.[120] At a time when, as the *New York Times* reported in 1928, American coaches confined their female athletes to the sprints, the German women were busily amassing middle-distance titles.[121] The *Times* spoke of a more conducive atmosphere for women's sports in central Europe that "has supplied vast numbers of European women with a strong physique, which they can take with them into competitive events," and it rightly predicted that a German would win the Olympic 800-meter race. Back in Germany, patriotic fans eagerly

DER LEICHTATHLET

Olympiade 1928

Die einzige
Goldmedaille
errang in der Leicht-
athletik Frau Radtke-
Batschauer

für Deutschland
durch ihren
Olympischen 800-m-
Weltrekordsieg

Germany's leading track and field journal celebrates Lina Radke-Batschauer on its cover after her historic gold medal in the 1928 Olympic première of the women's 800 meters.
Universitätsbibliothek, Freie Universität Berlin

anticipated just this outcome. Given that the Amsterdam Games marked Germany's first appearance in an Olympiad since the war, a successful performance here would symbolize the country's resurgence, ready to reclaim its central place in the international arena.

Track and field journals in the Weimar Republic, meanwhile, had worked hard to build support for women's middle-distance running. *Der Leichtathlet* assured readers in 1926 that the 800 meters had the backing of "a whole series of medical testimonials and evaluations," all of which testified to its positive effects on a woman's physical development.[122] The following year, *Sport und Sonne* castigated the opponents of this event as completely out of touch by pointing out that physicians had voiced the very same reservations with regard to male athletes just ten years earlier. "During the war," it snickered, "one doctor was still warning men against running more than 200 meters."[123] Future generations, the article implied, would one day shake their heads in similar disbelief that anyone could hold such views on women's middle-distance events. In fact, that very same issue reported that Lina Batschauer, soon to be Radke-Batschauer, had just set a world record in the 800 meters, which may have seemed at the time to put the entire issue conclusively to rest. *Sport und Sonne* wrote that "athletics has rarely appeared more beautiful anywhere."[124]

When Radke-Batschauer repeated her success at the Olympics with another record-setting triumph, *Der Leichtathlet* proudly featured her on its August 7, 1928, cover.[125] The lead article praised Radke-Batschauer as "brilliantly trained" and commented that after examining her post-race condition, "there are no longer any indications of the incredible exertion." It devoted the rest of the article, however, to damage control, as it labored to reduce the alarm over the two women who had collapsed after the finish. This "does not necessarily say anything against the distance," the journal argued, "for even men are no longer able to stay on their feet after their races."

This defensiveness stemmed from the newspaper coverage of those two runners lying on the ground and from the commentaries that interpreted this as irrefutable proof that women should not compete in an 800-meter race. The *Vossische Zeitung* offered its blunt assessment on the day after the race: "The 800 meters is clearly not a suitable distance for the female sex."[126] The lead sports article of the *Berliner Tageblatt*, after trumpeting the fact that Germany had finally won gold in track and field and even describing the patriotic euphoria among the German spectators, nevertheless labeled the event a terrible mistake.[127] "Hopefully, the 800-meter women will have recovered by now," the reporter wrote with hyperventilated concern. "For the time being, they are lying entirely collapsed on the grass, a pitiful sight. Why are ladies allowed to run 800 meters...anyway?" This newspaper had, significantly, arrived at a completely different conclusion just three weeks before, when the German sprinter Helmut Körnig collapsed at the conclusion of his Olympic qualifying race.[128] "That's how a runner must be able to fight, if he wants to achieve success in the Olympic Games," the article wrote approvingly. Whether a collapse indicated a heroic effort or "much too long of a stretch" plainly depended on the sex of the competitor.

Olympic officials as well as the International Amateur Athletic Federation seemed to employ exactly this logic. At the quadrennial meeting of the International Olympic Committee immediately following the Amsterdam Games, delegates voted 13 to 9 to eliminate the event from future Olympiads. Women would not compete in an Olympic 800-meter race again until 1960. In late fall 1928, Willy Meisl, one of Weimar Germany's best-known sports analysts, defended this decision on the part of the Olympic Committee to discontinue the event.[129] "Almost all of the participants had so exhausted themselves," Meisl wrote, that officials had no choice. "Women's sports are, after all, still so young," he concluded, "that it is quite unlikely that they are fully up to the most difficult tasks yet."

Meisl hardly spoke for all Germans, however. In fact, scores of officials and commentators quickly spoke in favor of women's middle-distance running. Eugen Wagener, a leader in Weimar Germany's track and field movement, exalted in Radke-Batschauer's success in the pages of *B.Z. am Mittag* on the day after the race.[130] He made no more than an oblique reference to her two collapsed competitors and instead called for even greater support for Germany's women so that they could further widen their existing lead over rival countries. A poem in the same paper on the following day expressed awe at Radke-Batschauer's "lightning-fast footfalls," along with a prediction that her win would inspire her country-women to assert themselves more fully at home and in public, to the detriment of husbands who kept suspiciously late hours.[131] "With bulging biceps, [and a] taut waist," the last stanza went, "so she stands before you, in victor's laurels—in front of you, the unathletic scoundrel [who has just snuck into the house]!" "That is the flip side of [Radke's] medal," the poem warned its male readers, "not all that glitters is gold!" Female athleticism spelled the end of extra-marital dalliances, the poet feared, thereby testifying both to the formidability of women runners and to the middle-class virtues of track and field, which stood in such stark contrast to the reputation of tennis.

Fred Hildenbrandt actually heaved an immense sigh of relief at the sight of the two female runners lying exhausted on the ground because, after a decade of stunning advances in women's track and field, it provided reassuring proof that these athletes were not superhuman after all.[132] In a front-page article in the *Berliner Tageblatt*'s sports section one week after the race, Hildenbrandt contended that many men had enjoyed a secret moment of *Schadenfreude*, "because these girls, with their broad shoulders, firm upper arms, hard calf muscles and powerful feet, iron necks and steel fists...ultimately cannot quite push us to the wall." Hildenbrandt readily conceded that men collapsed after races, too, and he entertained no delusions that the two athletes' exhaustion had exposed an inherent female weakness. Instead, he simply welcomed any sign of these sportswomen's limits. Indeed, popular images of female athletes seem to have suffered little in the German media after the Olympic race. Within three weeks, an ad for Kola Dallmann energy tablets chose the image a woman triumphantly breaking the finish-line tape to sell its product, and it appeared in the *Berliner Tageblatt*, the same newspaper that had called for discontinuing the women's 800-meter race. The tagline claimed that Kola Dallmann bestowed the "will power, stamina, [and] unshakable courage" that the female runner exemplified.[133]

Der Leichtathlet embarked on its own campaign to defend women's middle-distance running. In its August 14 issue, the editor Heinz Cavalier delivered a sharp rebuke to those "few newspapers" that had blown the story entirely out of proportion by "writing that the exhaustion of the female runners had been so frightfully great that…they had all passed out."[134] Radke-Batschauer, he added, "was no more worn-out than other Olympic winners," male or female. Two weeks later, another commentator exclaimed with exasperation, "Even Nurmi lay on the ground for a moment after the 5,000 meters in Amsterdam!" without prompting calls for the elimination of that event.[135] "Years of investigation by sports physicians at the German College of Physical Exercise as well as private examinations have revealed that women are more capable of feats requiring stamina than those requiring short, intense bursts of energy," the commentator added, with a clear implication that old-fashioned stereotypes had once again trumped rational science when it came to the popular press coverage of women's sports.

In a November 1928 essay in the sports magazine *Die Leibesübungen*, Erich Harte returned to the male comparison: "We all know that the contest in the 800 meters is perhaps the hardest running event of all…. Have you ever watched the behavior of the men after this competition?"[136] Where earlier commentators had only alluded to chauvinism as the decisive factor in the event's Olympic cancellation, Harte made his accusation crystal clear. Men, he argued, simply did not want to see their conception of delicate womanhood so radically contradicted "by the strained contortions" of female competitors. Harte also questioned whether men had the standing to rule on the matter at all. He concluded his essay by stating, "The International Women's Track and Field Association, in which women make the decisions, will once again hold [the 800 meters] at its 1930 meet in Prague."

Dr. Lina Müller-Passavant used *Der Leichtathlet* in November 1928 to rebut a report on the women's 800-meter race that had appeared in the daily *Berliner Morgenpost*.[137] The newspaper had derided the runners' red faces in particular, to which Müller-Passavant retorted, "In the future, spare us the account of men's reactions to the sight of an athletically competing woman." She appealed to officials to base their decisions regarding women's middle-distance running on careful monitoring, not reflexive impulse. In doing so, Müller-Passavant reasserted the very same rationalizing sensibilities that had hitherto dominated discussions of track and field during the Weimar Republic. Milly Reuter, a champion discus thrower, placed the women's 800-meter race in a long line of impressive female accomplishments that year. Since female aviators had recently proven themselves capable of flying "thousands of kilometers from South Africa to London," Reuter asked rhetorically, "why should we have considered it overtaxing when the young girls ran 800 meters at the Olympic Games?"[138]

In a 1928 commemorative book on the Olympic Games, the physician Friedrich Messerli placed his own conservative spin on the women's 800-meter race by emphasizing Radke-Batschauer's ability to reconcile her competitive running with her domestic obligations.[139] Messerli praised her as "an outstanding housewife [who] looks after her household all by herself," and he insisted that every female athlete could achieve this same proper balance, "as long as [she] seeks to reach her level of performance through rational training." Once again, female athletics had value only in so far as it reaffirmed domesticity, which, in Messerli's view, "rational training" would help to maximize.

When the issues surrounding the race surfaced yet again at the 1929 Berlin conference on women's sports, the consensus had tipped in favor of the women's 800 meters. Some remained unconvinced, such as Dr. Mallwitz, who maintained that track and field competitors "do not correspond at all physiologically to the standards that the medical expert would apply to a normal woman."[140] Most attendees passionately defended the event, though, including Dr. Hede Bergmann, who had attended to the collapsed runners right after the race and spoke from personal experience.[141] Bergmann explained that one of the collapsed runners had entered the 800 meters only in order to serve as a pacesetter for a teammate and had never trained in the distance herself, while the second runner had felt ill on the day of the event. "By the way," Bergmann continued, "both of them started on Canada's 4x100-meter relay team the following day and won it in a new world record."

Alice Profé, who coached the German track and field team at the 1930 Women's Olympic Games in Prague, at which the 800 meters remained a fully sanctioned event, told *Start und Ziel* at the conclusion of the competitions that everything had gone off without a hitch, and the "first-aid workers had nothing to do."[142] With implicit reference to the 1928 Olympics, Profé then criticized the tendency to propagate "horror stories" about women's competitions, which, she argued, simply reflected prejudices and preconceptions. Profé ended with a call for ongoing physical and spiritual emancipation: "Life is a struggle. One has to fight to overcome obstinacy, lethargy, and narrow-mindedness. Nothing is of value just because it was of value yesterday.... Let youth find its own new ideals, let young people live their own lives, whatever the risks." By the time that an international commission on women's health published the results of its study on the long term consequences of sports in 1932, in which it concluded that they had no detrimental effects on women whatsoever, it seemed only to confirm what most German observers had already concluded for themselves.[143] This study by no means ended the debate in Germany, but it did signal just how far the pendulum of opinion had swung in favor of female athleticism by the end of the Weimar Republic.

The real-life Olympic track and field champion Lina Radke-Batschauer shared a number of traits in common with the fictional Olympic track and field champion Georg Cornelius. Both had won their respective races thanks to a specialized focus on that single event, careful training, and a fierce desire to finish first. The two runners shared another important similarity as well: both struck a tenuous balance between modernity and tradition. On the one hand, they embodied a world of individual achievement, maximum output, and a physical convergence of the sexes that the media habitually subsumed under the term "Americanization." On the other hand, they stood for tradition, a world in which men and women served their nation in ostensibly "natural" and gender-specific ways. The male athlete generally had a much easier time maintaining this balance than the female, but as we have seen, commentators criticized the Taylorized man in the 1920s, too, for producing an unharmonious and ultimately dysfunctional body. Male and female athletes thus embodied modernity in its many aspects—its highly productive ideal state and its potentially self-destructive underside. The discourse surrounding these athletes not only shaped German thinking about sports and the human body but also German attitudes toward social change as a whole during the Weimar Republic.

The respective races of Cornelius and Radke-Batschauer highlighted key differences in how German society understood and valued men and women as well. When Cornelius expended every ounce of energy to win the race, ultimately giving his life in the process, he inspired unqualified awe. His act of sheer will brought glory to the entire German people, and his self-sacrifice thus represented the pinnacle of duty-bound German manhood. When the two female runners collapsed at the end of the Olympic 800-meter race, by contrast, the act generated only shocked outrage or anxious defensiveness in the German press. In this case, the expenditure of every ounce of energy represented only physiological failing, a woman's inherent unsuitability for middle-distance competition. Even the track and field journals, which otherwise saw themselves as the chief lobby for women's track and field, never once praised the two runners for their effort and certainly never suggested that they had brought credit to their nation. At best, the press portrayed the incident as an unavoidable and unfortunate part of female competition, no reason to eliminate the event, but no reason to valorize the two competitors, either. At worst, some demanded the event's immediate elimination, and this despite Radke-Batschauer's own hearty post-race condition, despite her contribution of

Germany's only track and field gold medal, and despite a German dominance in this event that promised many more medals in the years to come.

The tale of these two collapses, then—Cornelius's and that of the two women—highlighted the limits of Weimar Germany's, and indeed the postwar West's, remarkable revolution in gender roles. Despite the modernization of the male athlete in a direction that emphasized his economically productive role, he still represented first and foremost a future soldier, with the expectation that he give his life for his country. Cornelius's death at the end of the marathon evoked a warrior's death on the battlefield, in that both deaths preserved the nation's honor. The repeated examples of real-life male athletes who fell to the ground at the finish of their races, even when none died as a result, likewise conjured an association with the infantryman's placement of his physical self at risk.

Germany expected the female athlete to preserve her physical life and strength in order to give life to others. Her sacrifice was a spiritual one, a duty to focus not on her own development, but on that of her husband and children. A collapsed female runner represented the irresponsible placement of that life-giving life in jeopardy; "giving her all" indicated selfishness. By pursuing personal glory at a time when the nation needed her to save her physical strength for a higher purpose, she conducted the exact opposite of a selfless act on behalf of the national honor. This double standard for men and women also suggested that F. W. Taylor's imperative to achieve maximum output applied more to the former than to the latter. The female athlete, many commentators believed, should seek an optimum output, a level of performance that exercised the body without tiring it and that focused more on long-term health than on setting records. In this regard, women's track and field fit much more easily within the Science of Work paradigm that offered an alternative model for employing physical energy to that of the Taylorists. Competitive track and field's insistence that the athlete continually push herself to the limits of her potential ran head-on against society's insistence that she forsake that goal on behalf of familial duty.

As the consensus of opinion gradually tipped toward a belief that athletic competition could coexist with motherhood—that it might, in fact, even promote it—the attacks against female athleticism declined significantly. By the early 1930s, the female runner faced fewer difficulties in balancing competition and family than she had just one decade earlier. She achieved this balance in part by modernizing motherhood. Society still expected her to raise a family, but it seemed increasingly willing to accept the fact that she could pursue individual goals and self-development while doing so. Moreover, the definition of healthy motherhood had changed dramatically and so had the assumptions about what a woman could physically do. Furthermore, society seemed to ascribe a greater role to women in educating, developing, and encouraging their children, rather than relegating mothers to a largely caregiver role.

The debate surrounding the limits of women's track and field continued to percolate for decades to come, but the image of maternal athleticism that officials had carefully cultivated over the course of the 1920s enjoyed a broad acceptance in German society even after the Nazi regime came to power in 1933. Following the women's 80-meter hurdles at the German championships that very year, the head of the national track and field association praised the event's three medalists as "carriers of our race" and "future mothers of the next generation."[144] A 1936 article titled "Women's sports, but properly!" juxtaposed a picture of a smiling female hurdler with that of two female boxers, purportedly taken in the United States. The caption under the hurdler enthused, "Girls on the track. That is healthy sport that makes one fit for life without the least negative consequences."[145] This picture of wholesome womanhood stood in explicit opposition to the boxers, of course, who, according to the article, "placed their health and dignity as women in jeopardy for the sake of creating a sensation." The same article proclaimed the sprinter Inge Braumüller-Beetz "a symbol of our times: mother and athlete!"

The relatively strong support that Germany provided its female athletes in the 1930s paid off in the international track and field competitions, where the women's contingent contributed disproportionately to the country's success. Gisela Mauermayer, for instance, held the world record in the shot put, discuss, and pentathlon at various points in the decade and captured the gold medal in discuss at the 1936 Olympic Games. When Germany finished those Games at the top of the medal standings, the *New York Times* commented on the irony, "This masculine Third Reich owes much of its success to its women athletes."[146] It might have done even better had it not purged Jewish athletes from the national roster, including Gretel Bergmann, who had equaled the German national record in the women's high jump and would have stood a good chance at the gold medal in 1936.[147] In a regime that otherwise tended to view extrafamilial activities on the part of women with hostility and in which the birthrate assumed an even higher priority than it had during the 1920s, the support for female athleticism in the 1930s underscored just how significantly German attitudes had changed since the end of the First World War. The postwar East German government built even further on this national strength in women's track and field to establish itself as a medal-winning juggernaut in the 1970s and 1980s.

Not only did the National Socialists continue the Weimar Republic's practice of promoting track and field as an investment in motherhood, but they also—not surprisingly—continued to tout the sport's martial benefits for German men. Adolf Hitler had lauded the self-sacrificing patriotism of the marathon runner as early as *Mein Kampf* in 1925, in which he wrote, "The laurel wreath of the present rests upon the brow of the dying hero."[148] At the same time, however, the rhetorical attacks against the Taylorized athlete, already present in the Weimar discourse, increased in Nazi Germany as well. An essay that appeared just weeks after the National Socialists had come to power in 1933 wrote scathingly, "Many an athlete is so highly trained that he is, despite unprecedented achievements in his event, in every other respect a pathetic cripple."[149] The effort to maximize performance in one discipline, the author concluded, came only at the expense of the body as a whole. In that same year, a group of Berlin students dug up the running track in the Berlin Stadium and planted oak trees in its place, a symbol of *Turnvater* Jahn and of the students' hopes that the new regime would end the "terror of the measuring tape."[150]

The discourse within German physical culture in the 1930s certainly did shift away from an admiration for the rationalized body, which had characterized much of the prominent commentary in the Weimar Republic, and toward a glorification of the holistic and ostensibly organic physical form that fit more harmoniously into the *völkisch* worldview of the Nazi movement. As in so many areas, though, the National Socialist rhetoric did not necessarily conform to practice. Although Leni Riefenstahl's famous documentary of the 1936 Olympic Games sought to present elite athletes as organic ideals, that year's German team had trained in every bit as rationalized a way as its Weimar predecessors. The track and field athlete in Nazi Germany faced the very same pressure to reconcile modernity with tradition, to present a carefully engineered body as, at the very same time, reassuringly "natural." The changes initiated by the track and field athlete in the early 1920s continued apace long after the demise of the Weimar Republic but, just as in the 1920s, all the while maintaining an impression of not changing things that drastically at all.

Conclusion
Body beyond Weimar: Germany's Athletic Legacy

In a 1928 essay, the commentator Willy Meisl imagined himself looking back on contemporary German society from the vantage point of the year 4000. "It was sports that cleared the way for the emancipation of the woman," Meisl wrote, in mock retrospection. "It made her more similar to man and also enabled her to make man more similar to her, until ultimately they met on that middle ground where humankind truly becomes one."[1] More than any other single group in German society, Meisl argued, athletes had done the work of bringing the sexes closer together in the 1920s. By appropriating the tactics, competitiveness, and training habits of the men's sports, female athletes had gone beyond simply promoting a new feminine ideal. They had claimed masculine ideals for women and thereby sparked a fundamental reassessment of the similarities and differences between the two sexes.

Meisl gave the female athlete a great deal of credit for having created a new man, too, arguing that sports "enabled her to make man more similar to her." Indeed, male athletes—whether prompted by female counterparts, by the demands of a new society, or by their own individual initiative—reshaped what it meant to be a man after the First World War. The Wilhelmine gender order, after all, had applied to men and women alike. Although only those men who openly displayed non-normative behavior received the crushing sanctions of their peers, all men felt the constraints of society's physical and emotional expectations. Male athletes in the 1920s challenged some of these constraints. They emancipated men from many of the cultural conventions that had circumscribed male behavior for generations just as surely as female athletes had emancipated women. When the male tennis player cultivated an aesthetic game rather than an aggressive one, or when the male boxer consciously marketed himself as an erotic object, he blurred the distinction between male characteristics and female ones to the same degree as the female tennis player who attacked the net or the female boxer who sent her opponent to the canvas.

The Germans who had expected competitive sports to shore up eroding male authority after the war found themselves confronted with an unexpected outcome: athleticism, like any other form of cultural expression, proved remarkably adept at subversion. Whereas the word "Weimar" today primarily conjures visions of political and economic paralysis, Meisl's radical prophecy reminds us that German society after 1918 gave rise to a remarkably exuberant creativity as well. The Weimar Republic inspired innovative architecture and visual arts, sexual liberation, and social welfare programs, and it supported a trailblazing physical culture, as well. Unlike the pioneering collage artists, birth-control advocates, and policy reformers, though, champion athletes were household names. Thanks to the devoted attention of a vibrant and varied media industry, sportswomen and men had the power to establish new standards of behavior and physical development.

Between 1918 and 1933, German athletes did just that. The long-standing expectation of manly stoicism held little sway over male tennis players, while their female counterparts thoroughly undermined beliefs in a woman's inherent delicacy. The top male boxers, meanwhile, mingled toughness with an almost coquettish self-presentation, while women seized upon pugilism as a means to greater self-sufficiency and as a platform for uninhibited performance, in which one could earn a small income by acting in ways that no other venue would have tolerated. In track and field, athletes of both sexes applied the methods of industrial engineering in an effort to realize the physical body's full potential. Their rationalized physiques presented the logical corporeal extensions of the modern business climate. All of these athletes, moreover, from doubles players to light heavyweights to javelin throwers, reaffirmed the body's place in a mechanized world. Even as muscle power declined in the economic sector, it still mattered in athletic competition, as the newspapers' bulging sports sections reminded Germans on a daily basis.

Competitive athletes did more than just reaffirm the body, though. They reinvented it. By the end of the 1920s, a trim, taut, and efficient muscularity had come to define the modern ideal for both women and men. As Wolfgang Graeser remarked in 1927 with regard to the athletic model, "There appears to be only one ideal type: the thin, sinewy, tall, and boyish body."[2] According to Graeser, Meisl's vision of an androgynous future had already arrived, and its physical form reflected the shared pressures, demands, and ambitions of postwar men and women.

Athletes crafted new, distinctively modern sensibilities to go along with their new bodies—more individualistic and more willing to assert oneself both within and against society. The athlete's emphasis on competition captured, in the eyes of many observers, the essence of modern business practice and democratic self-interest. In this regard, the sportswoman or man stood decidedly at odds with the communal spirit of most other forms of German physical culture and with the regimented conformity of the nation's military tradition. For the female athlete in particular, this individualism also clashed head-on with the traditional expectation that a woman, especially a middle-class one, stay at home and devote herself to her family's development, rather than to her own. The female champion represented a direct challenge to this maternal and familial imperative, since her very success indicated the attention that she had devoted exclusively to her own athletic development. That championship success, moreover, drew her even farther out of the home and into the public spotlight. This held true, albeit to a lesser extent, for nonchampions, too, since all female athletes demanded attention for themselves, whether from spectators, from officials, or simply from their opponents.

The athlete's pursuit of self-interest opened up a new set of postwar aspirations to previously marginalized groups in German society. For working-class men as well as for single women of any class background, becoming a sports champion meant moving up the social ladder, at least in terms of cultural access, if not directly in terms of income. Some enjoyed both, of course. Male boxers and female tennis players pioneered professional opportunities in their respective sports at a time when strictly enforced amateurism remained the rule almost everywhere, and the financial fortunes of top champions became an integral part of their public images. The successful prizefighter symbolized the attainment of an upper-class lifestyle to his blue-collar fans, even as—conversely—he inspired a sort of blue-collar posturing among his upper-class admirers. Even when athletes lacked direct professional opportunities, as in the case of most track and field competitors, the champion still possessed a level of renown that reaped dividends in terms of future opportunities.

This pursuit of individual self-interest extended to the satisfaction of sexual desire. Tennis players, in particular, cultivated a reputation for blithely disregarding conventional morality. On the one hand, this attitude fit neatly into postwar society's generally tolerant and permissive atmosphere, particularly in the metropolitan centers. On the other hand, it still struck many Germans as conduct unbecoming of a proper lady or gentleman. The male player's tendency to act on sexual impulses completely ignored the Wilhelmine admonition that men exercise self-control at all times. The female player's sexuality appeared doubly subversive by combining a bold willingness to pursue and initiate affairs with a clear disinclination to make them long-term and monogamous, let alone marital and reproductive.

This climate of relative sexual openness extended to many sports fans as well. Women's magazines and handbooks encouraged readers to sit ringside for better views of the muscled pugilists, for example, and an entire literary and cinematic subgenre featured female fans in hot pursuit of their favorite fighters. As in tennis, women seized the active role here, and boxers did not take long to understand the opportunities presented by this eroticization of the male form. They paid more attention to their appearance, and they posed for pictures that were designed to induce double takes. By consciously inviting fans to admire their bodies in films and photographs, as well as in the ring, male fighters turned the accustomed position of the man-as-viewing-subject into that of the man-as-viewed-object.

On this count, the male boxer represented only the most prominent example of a much larger trend. A certain level of voyeurism suffused the entire sports culture of the Weimar Republic, a reflection of the era's sexual openness and a factor in its continuation. Hans Gragün, in his tellingly titled 1921 article "Sports Exhibitionism," described how a 400-meter runner took off his shirt after the race with the full knowledge "that here at the finish a few hundred to a thousand eyes will ogle his sweat-dampened skin," before slowly roaming "down to his beautiful thighs."[3] The sexual openness of Germany's sports culture did have its limits, however. Athletes may have gotten away with occasional and circumspect expressions of same-sex desire, but they knew better than to acknowledge these feelings publicly.[4] Despite the relative strength of the Weimar Republic's homosexual-rights movement, the most visible and organized in the world at the time, same-sex attraction remained a taboo in the nation's sporting culture.

Even in matters of heterosexual desire, tennis players were exceptional in their reputation for uninhibited sexuality. In fact, most athletes devoted their efforts to suppressing or redirecting sexual impulses rather than releasing them. The boxer's training camp, to take the best example, assumed a monastic air, and the female track and field athlete, too, tempered her focus on personal achievement with a commensurate dedication to traditionally respectable sexual behavior, meaning marriage and motherhood. The debate over how and if female athletes could reconcile rigorous training and personal ambition with the expectations of family underscored the challenge that women in competitive sports inherently posed to the social order, especially in a place of plummeting birthrates like Weimar Germany. This debate reached a crescendo in the aftermath of the women's 800-meter race at the 1928 Olympic Games, which ultimately revealed strong German support for competitive women's track and field, but only after replaying a number of the most stubborn stereotypes and misconceptions. By the early 1930s, female athletes had redefined motherhood to accommodate physical training and the pursuit of personal goals, even if the more fundamental social imperative, that a woman must become a mother, remained firmly in place.

The tentative consensus in favor of competitive women's sports did not come to an end with the establishment of the Nazi regime in 1933. Nazi officials did, predictably, caricature the Weimar Republic as a haven for female degeneracy, and the 1934 *N.S. Frauenbuch* (National Socialist Women's Book) specifically blamed "excessive sports" in the 1920s for having "ruined the health of German women."[5] The regime's media criticized female participation in especially masculine sports, like boxing, but such rhetoric reflected propaganda more than policy. The National Socialists actively promoted competitive women's sports, and they continued and accelerated most of the athletic trends that had begun under the Weimar

Republic. The Weimar body, in other words, and with it some of the Weimar sensibilities, outlived the Weimar Republic.

The manual for the *Bund deutscher Mädel*, Nazi Germany's counterpart to the Hitler Youth, for instance, insisted that "the modern girl is an athlete," a statement that could just as easily have come straight from any number of Weimar-era publications.[6] The manual then listed the physical requirements for a ten-year-old to advance to the next level of the organization, which included an ability to sprint 60 meters in fourteen seconds and to long-jump two meters. The regime's glorification of female athleticism did not stop at puberty, either. In a 1937 article titled "A word to women," one SS officer wrote, "For promoting good health, the javelin and the pole vault are of far more value than lipstick."[7] The officer encouraged every woman to earn the Reich Sport Medal, a designation of physical fitness that would make her good material for marrying a member of the SS and, more importantly, for producing a brood of healthy children.

The nation's leading sports magazine, *Sport im Bild*, increased the percentage of space devoted to images of female athletes throughout the 1930s. According to a recent study by Christine Walther, dozens of photographs in each issue celebrated female sports champions, and many managed to present these women simultaneously as champions and as mothers or homemakers.[8] This promotion of female athleticism with the explicit goal of producing healthy, fit mothers represented the implementation, in a more systematic manner, of the same aim that so many Weimar officials and commentators had advanced prior to 1933. This veneration of women's physical achievement extended to the highest echelons of the regime. After Tilly Fleischer won the gold medal in the javelin competition at the 1936 Berlin Olympics, Hitler publicly received her in his loge and later sat her at his table during the closing banquet. The female athlete, having first attained insider status under the Weimar Republic, cemented it under the Nazi regime.

The National Socialists co-opted Weimar impulses in the realm of men's sports, too. The 1936 law mandating military service gave to the state the authority to "reconstruct" the recruit's body, "against his will if necessary, as to extract from it its maximum fitness."[9] This policy built directly on two developments from the previous decade—the linkage of sports to military preparation and the unmistakably Taylorist goal of extracting "maximum" fitness from the physical body. The regime built upon a Weimar aesthetic of the male form, too, in the muscular torsos of Arno Breker's and Josef Thorak's monumental sculptures, which graced so many of the Nazis' prestige building projects.[10] The Nazi effort to increase Germany's presence in international sporting events after 1933 similarly continued along a trajectory that republican predecessors had launched in the mid-1920s, and this despite Hitler's decidedly anti-internationalist foreign policy, and in the face of continued opposition from the *Turnen* movement.

For both men and women, the meritocracy that the Weimar Republic officially promised, and that its athletes perhaps best exemplified, continued to establish itself under the Nazi regime. As the historian Götz Aly has recently argued, Hitler "promulgated the idea that his government would guarantee gifted individuals the opportunity to better their lot, no matter how poor and uneducated they had grown up."[11] This guarantee targeted members of the working class in particular, the very same group to which the lure of a lucrative career in prizefighting during the Weimar Republic had appealed.

Many aspects of the Weimar body and sensibility did not survive the rupture of 1933, of course, at least not in Germany. Above all, the Nazi regime prohibited Jewish athletes from belonging to the nation's leading sports clubs and drove many of the best to seek asylum in other countries, including the tennis player Daniel Prenn and the high jumper Gretel Bergmann. The Jewish outsider who had managed to become a Weimar insider, at least in part through athletic accomplishment, now found her- or himself on the outside once again. In some respects, though, just as many exiled German writers, artists, and filmmakers continued to produce innovative works from their havens abroad, these athletes, too, represented a "Weimar in exile." Many of them still competed, set records, and helped to popularize their own successful techniques and strategies in their newly adopted countries.

Following the Second World War, East Germany carried on a number of the important athletic legacies of the Weimar Republic as well. Not only did the GDR nurture sports as a means to speed the country's recovery and to foster a still-tentative national attachment, but it also made the cultivation of women's sports and female champions a top priority. The resulting dominance in international women's competitions from the 1960s to the 1980s unquestionably owed much to the systematic use of performance-enhancing drugs, but it also stemmed from the fact that East Germany treated women's sports more seriously than most other countries. Taking a cue from the late-Weimar discourse on female athletes, moreover, East Germany made a consistent and explicit case for the compatibility of athletic success and motherhood.[12]

We can still see signs of the Weimar legacy in sports today, and nowhere more directly than in the resurgence of women's boxing since the 1990s as a fitness program and a competitive sport. Not only has Germany reestablished itself as a hotbed of women's boxing, but its commentators again view the sport as a marker of emancipation and unprecedented possibility. Alice Schwarzer, one of Germany's leading feminist voices for the past four decades, points specifically to pugilism as a sign that women have overcome barriers that had hitherto seemed insurmountable. "Women travel into space, women box, women are chancellor. What is a man anymore?" she asked rhetorically in a recent interview.[13] The younger generation sees these fighters as figures of empowerment, too. In the words of one German teenage girl, boxing allowed women to "show that they can do something that only men typically do."[14] Female boxers today enjoy even greater opportunities than their Weimar-era predecessors. Fikriye Selen, a highly ranked and photogenic Turkish-German boxer in the late 1990s, hired a sports manager to juggle all of her endorsements, fashion shoots, and talk-show spots. Selen's 1998 advertisement for Levi's jeans projected a blend of power, aggression, and sex appeal that defines the female ideal at the turn of the millennium, showing her smiling sweetly for the camera after having punched a fist-sized curve into a wrought-iron lamppost.[15]

Sports continue to emancipate men from certain social and cultural constraints, too. Just as it did in the Weimar Republic, boxing enables outsiders in Germany today to become insiders, especially recent immigrants and their children. In an even more direct example of Weimar's long reach, Luan Krasniqi, a boxer from Kosovo who attained German citizenship in 1994, listed Max Schmeling in 2005 as his biggest role model. Krasniqi admired Schmeling's financial acumen, as well as his skills in the ring, and on the occasion of their only meeting, Schmeling offered a piece of advice aimed at the newly minted self-made man: "Take care of yourself, young man, and keep your money together."[16] The top-ranked German tennis player Tommy Haas, meanwhile, has explicitly challenged the relative restrictiveness of male fashions as compared to the more revealing clothes that the women wear. "You see Serena and some of the ladies wearing tight stuff," he said. "It's interesting. It looks good. It brings something else to the game." Haas struck an additional blow for greater male self-display in 2000 by posing nude with his girlfriend.[17]

Finally, anyone who has seen or read an "up close and personal" profile of an elite athlete in recent years will immediately recognize the most important legacy of the Weimar sports culture in the accelerating rationalization of the athlete's body. Hundreds of recent examples aptly illustrate this point, but a 2008 article on the German soccer player Thomas Hitzlsperger summarizes the current philosophy of physical development in terms that could have come straight out of *Der Leichtathlet*, circa 1928: "[There is] no weakness of the body that cannot be improved through training, no fiber whose function cannot be optimized."[18] The modern body's restless quest for faster, stronger, and more efficient shows no sign today of letting up.

Our contemporary world of sports traces a direct line to the athletic culture of the interwar years, and no place crystallized this culture with greater clarity or analyzed it more extensively and insightfully than the Weimar Republic. Sports and its leading athletes comprised important and long-overlooked elements of that society's legendary cultural modernism. To Germans after the First World War, competitive sports offered a physical expression of the rapidly modernizing, increasingly permissive, and socially unstable society in which they lived, just as cinema, architecture, fiction, and music did. Through sports, men and women articulated a response to the changes around them and presented new standards of manhood and womanhood. Above all, the elite athlete, whose every move received widespread media attention and almost instant trend-setting status, changed the behaviors and attitudes of men and women and reshaped the physical body itself to better fit the demands and expectations of the modern age.

Notes

Introduction

1. Harry Kessler, *Harry Graf Kessler Tagebücher, 1918–1937*, ed. Wolfgang Pfeiffer-Belli (Frankfurt/M: Insel, 1996), 200. The issue of *Berliner Illustrirte* is dated August 24, but the publishers released advance copies in order to coincide with the inauguration. Our contemporary media have proven equally conscious of somatic symbolism. When the *New York Post* ran a cover photograph of then-president-elect Barack Obama in his swimsuit, the headline trumpeted his impressive physique as indicative of his capacity to lead. See "Fit for Office: Buff Bam is Hawaii hunk," *New York Post*, Dec. 23, 2008, cover. The visible love handles of a topless French president Nicolas Sarkozy, meanwhile, prompted the magazine *Paris Match* in 2007 to airbrush the offending bulges away. See "Magazine retouches Sarkozy photo," BBC News (Aug. 22, 2007), http://news.bbc.co.uk.

2. For a discussion of how that magazine cover and its satirical knockoffs rippled through the political discourse of Weimar Germany, see H. M. Albrecht, *Die Macht einer Verleumdungskampagne: Antidemokratische Agitationen der Presse und Justiz gegen die Weimarer Republik unter ihren ersten Reichspräsidenten Friedrich Ebert vom "Badebild" bis zum Magdeburger Prozeß* (PhD diss., Universität Bremen, 2002); and Otto May, *Vom Wachsen lassen zum Führen: Die Ansichtskarte als Zeuge einer versäumten Erziehung zur Demokratie in der Weimarer Republik* (Hildesheim: Brücke-Verlag Kurt Schmersow, 2003). Perhaps in an effort to live down this unfortunate image, President Ebert later appeared at the 1920 dedication of the Deutsche Hochschule für Leibesübungen (German College of Physical Exercise).

3. "An unsere Leser!," a message from the journal's editorial staff, *Illustrierter Sport* 7, no. 1, Apr. 29, 1919, 2.

4. J. Trygve Has-Ellison, "A Baedecker of the European Aristocracy," review of *Aristocracy in the Modern World*, by Ellis Wasson, H-Net Book Review (H-German), May 2007.

5. Modris Eksteins, *Rites of Spring: The Great War and the Birth of the Modern Age* (New York: Houghton Mifflin, 1989), 125.

6. Kurt Doerry, "Der Sport als Zeitsymbol," *Sport im Bild* 32, no. 24, Nov. 26, 1926, 1077.

7. Peter Gay, *Weimar Culture: The Outsider as Insider* (New York: Harper and Row, 1970).

8. Siegfried Kracauer, "Sie sporten" (1927), repr. in *Sportgeschichten*, ed. Bernd Goldmann and Bernhardt Schwank, 12 (Frankfurt/M: Insel, 1993).

9. George Mosse emphasized the anti-modern sensibilities of interwar German body culture in his seminal book *Nationalism and Sexuality: Respectability and Abnormal Sexuality in Modern Europe* (New York: Howard Fertig, 1985). Two recent and important works on the nudist movement have explicitly avoided framing nudism as anti-modern, but they do see the movement as arising from a desire to counteract the purported ill-effects of an urbanizing, rationalizing, mechanizing, accelerating society. See Michael Hau, *The Cult of Health and Beauty in Germany: A Social History, 1890 to 1930* (Chicago: University of Chicago Press, 2003); and Chad Ross, *Naked Germany: Health, Race and the Nation* (New York: Berg, 2005).

10. *Tennis* (Ufa, 1925, from an American film by Stoll Pictures), based on the censor's cards in the Bundesarchiv-Filmarchiv, Microfiche 394, Prüfung 11541.

11. A rich body of scholarship has explored this impulse to measure and calibrate the human body in Germany. For a comprehensive discussion, see Anson Rabinbach, *The Human Motor: Energy, Fatigue, and the Origins of Modernity* (Berkeley: University of California Press, 1992). For two articles that explicitly connect the tendency in German labor management to that in sports, see Michael Hau, "Sports in the Human Economy: 'Leibesübungen,' Medicine, Psychology, and Performance Enhancement during the Weimar Republic," *Central European History* 41 (2008): 381–412; and Michael Mackenzie, "The Athlete as Machine: A Figure of Modernity in Weimar Germany," in *Leibhaftige Moderne: Körper in Kunst und Massenmedien 1918 bis 1933*, ed. Michael Cowan and Kai Marcel Sicks, 48–62 (Bielefeld: transcript, 2005).

12. Hans Fallada, *Little Man, What Now?* trans. Eric Sutton (Chicago: Academy Chicago, 2001 [orig. 1933]), 138.

13. Heinz Landmann, "Heroenkult," in *Der Sport am Scheidewege*, ed. Willy Meisl, 149 (Heidelberg: Iris, 1928).

14. Carla Verständig, "Rhythmik, Leibesübungen und freie Frau," *Die Leibesübungen* 12, June 20, 1927, 282.

15. Walter Schönbrunn, "Körperliche Ertüchtigung," *Die Leibesübungen* 14, July 20, 1930, 415.

16. For comprehensive membership figures, see Christiane Eisenberg, "Massensport in der Weimarer Republik. Ein statistischer Überblick," *Archiv für Sozialgeschichte* 33 (1993): 137–77.

17. Reinhard Koselleck, "'Erfahrungsraum' und 'Erwartungshorizont'—zwei historische Begriffe," in *Vergangene Zukunft: Zur Semantik geschichtlicher Zeiten* (Frankfurt/M: Suhrkamp, 1989), 349–75. Americans today would almost unanimously consider athletes, fashion models, and movie stars to be the physical ideals, for instance, even as Americans themselves grow steadily more overweight.

18. Michael Ott, review of *"English Sports" und deutsche Bürger: Eine Gesellschaftsgeschichte 1800–1939*, by Christiane Eisenberg, *IASLonline* (May 14, 2002): http://iasl.uni-muenchen.de/rezensio/liste/ott.html. The numerous studies of the German workers' sports movement offer a partial exception to the general reluctance of social historians to acknowledge the important role of sports. Even here, though, the most important works have come from sports historians, and these, unfortunately, tilt decidedly toward more narrowly focused institutional studies. For the classic overview of this movement, see Horst Ueberhorst, *Frisch, frei, stark,*

treu: Die Arbeitersportbewegung in Deutschland 1893–1933 (Düsseldorf: Droste, 1973).

19. Michael B. Poliakoff, *Combat Sports in the Ancient World: Competition, Violence, and Culture* (New Haven, CT: Yale University Press, 1987), 1.

20. Institutional factors have helped to create this situation. A number of German universities maintain separate institutes or departments of sports history, which has given a valuable boost to the study of sports, but has also had the effect of isolating sports historians from the history departments that might foster a more synthetic or holistic approach. Arnd Krüger, a pioneer in sports history, for instance, held his position in the University of Göttingen's Institute for Sports Sciences rather than in the history department. For an example of his work, see his pathbreaking *Sport und Politik: Von Turnvater Jahn zum Staatsamateur* (Hannover: Fackelträger, 1975). As recently as November 2008, a remarkably heated debate erupted at the sports history conference "A Whole New Game," sponsored by the German Historical Institute in Washington, D.C., over the extent to which sports historians can and should weave athletic developments into larger historical narratives.

21. In particular, the works of Frank Becker, Christiane Eisenberg, Gertrud Pfister, and Bernd Wedemeyer-Kolwe have situated sports in its wider social context in nineteenth- and twentieth-century Germany. Becker argues that sports symbols helped to make the new economic and political institutions of the Weimar Republic both understandable and acceptable to German citizens in *Amerikanismus in Weimar: Sportsymbole und politische Kultur 1918–1933* (Wiesbaden: Deutscher Universitäts-Verlag, 1993); he pointed to the ways in which female athleticism idealized a new physical form in "Die Sportlerin als Vorbild der 'neuen Frau': Versuche zur Umwertung der Geschlechterrollen in der Weimarer Republik," *Sozial- und Zeitgeschichte des Sports* 8, no. 3 (Nov. 1994): 34–55. Eisenberg describes sports as a "motor of modernization" and shows how athletic competitions shaped German middle-class identity in *"English Sports" und deutsche Bürger: Eine Gesellschaftsgeschichte 1800–1939* (Paderborn: Schoningh, 1999). Gertrud Pfister, meanwhile, has pioneered the history of women in sports. See, for example, *Goldmädel, Rennmiezen und Turnküken: Die Frau in der Berichterstattung der Bild-Zeitung*, which she co-wrote with Marie-Luise Klein (Berlin: Bartels u. Wernitz, 1985). Wedemeyer-Kolwe has connected physical culture, particularly body building, to larger social discourses. See his *"Der neue Mensch": Körperkultur im Kaiserreich und in der Weimarer Republik* (Würzburg: Königshausen u. Neumann, 2004). Perhaps in a sign of historians' growing recognition of the important role that sports has played in the past two centuries, the College Board's 2006 AP European History exam posed the following question: "How did Europeans perceive the role of organized sports in Europe during the period from 1860 to 1940?" See www.collegeboard.com. Thank you to my honors student Kyle Fields for bringing this to my attention.

22. Jim McKay, Michael A. Messner, and Don Sabo lament this divide in the introduction to *Masculinities, Gender Relations and Sport*, ed. McKay, Messner, and Sabo (Thousand Oaks, CA: Sage, 2000), 4–5.

23. Christine Walther, *Siegertypen: Zur fotografischen Vermittlung eines gesellschaftlichen Selbstbildes um 1900* (Würzburg: Königshausen u. Neumann, 2007), 27.

24. Figures come from *The Weimar Republic Sourcebook*, ed. Anton Kaes, Martin Jay, and Edward Dimendberg (Berkeley: University of California Press,

1994), 5. In Irmgard Keun's 1932 novel, *Das Kunstseidene Mädchen*, for example, the protagonist Doris provides companionship and a certain level of care for Brenner, a veteran blinded during the war, for whom she acts as a pair of eyes by describing to him all of the sights and sounds of the metropolis on their daily outings.

25. Robert Musil, "Die Frau gestern und morgen," in *Die Frau von morgen: Wie wir sie wünschen*, ed. Friedrich M. Huebner, 91 (Leipzig: E.A. Seemann, 1929).

26. Karla Mayburg, "Männlich–Weiblich," *Garçonne. Junggesellin*, 19, 1931, 1–2.

27. Entry for Oct. 31, 1932, *Harry Graf Kessler Tagebücher, 1918–1937*, ed. Wolfgang Pfeiffer-Belli (Frankfurt/M: Insel, 1996), 735.

28. Joseph Roth, "Konferenz-Athletik: Körpertraining am Grünen Tisch," originally in *Neue Berliner Zeitung—12-Uhr-Blatt*, Mar. 23, 1921, repr. in *Berliner Saisonbericht: Unbekannte Reportagen und journalistische Arbeiten 1920–39*, ed. Klaus Westermann, 135 (Cologne: Kiepenheuer u. Witsch, 1984).

29. "Der Sport der Minister und Generaldirektoren," *B.Z. am Mittag*, July 18, 1928, 3. The same imperative exists for leaders to this day, as shown in a recent article on Hillary Clinton's search for the "right" sport to represent her character and candidacy. See Patrick Healy, "Hillary Clinton Searches for Her Inner Jock," Week in Review, *New York Times*, June 10, 2007.

30. Sindbad, "'Heimkehr des Olympiasiegers': Ein psychologischer und sportwissenschaftlicher Kommentar, geschrieben für Publikum, Sportleute, Theaterdirektoren und Schauspieler," in *Der Scheinwerfer* (1932), repr. in *Der Scheinwerfer: Ein Forum der Neuen Sachlichkeit, 1927–1933*, ed. Erhard Schütz and Jochen Voigt (Essen: Klartext, 1986), 37.

Chapter 1

1. Dr. Walter Bing, "Hans Moldenhauer zum Gedächtnis," *Tennis und Golf* 7, no. 1, Jan. 3, 1930, 4.

2. Dr. Bill Fuchs, "Die deutschen Ranglistenspieler," in *Tennis-Handbuch: Zum 25jährigen Jubiläum 1902–1927, Amtliches Jahrbuch des Deutschen Tennis-Bundes* (yearbook of the German Tennis Federation), ed. Ferdinand Gruber, 183 (Heidelberg: Hermann Meister, 1927).

3. Dr. Paul Liebmann, "Tennis," in *Frankfurter Sport-Almanach 1925–26*, ed. Deutscher Reichsausschuß für Leibesübungen, 187 (Frankfurt/M: Wilh. Hemp, 1926).

4. "Tennissport in Badeorten," *Sport im Bild* 27, no. 29, July 22, 1921, 1074.

5. W. A. Lamprecht, "Die Bedeutung des Tennis," *Illustrierter Sport* 7, no. 3, May 13, 1919, 49. The historian Christiane Eisenberg estimates that women comprised 40 percent of the German Tennis Federation membership in the 1920s, a higher percentage than in any other sport except golf and ice skating. In fact, the sports of tennis, hockey, and golf together accounted for 25 percent of all female athletes in 1930, even though they comprised only 4 percent of the total sports membership for both sexes, and Eisenberg's figures include only those women who joined the association, not the even greater numbers who played casually. See table 5 in Christiane Eisenberg, "Massensport in der Weimarer Republik: Ein statistischer Überblick," *Archiv für Sozialgeschichte* 33 (1993): 160–61.

6. I borrow this term from R. W. Connell's influential notion of "hegemonic masculinity." See Connell, *Masculinities* (Berkeley: University of California Press, 1995).

7. Eisenberg, "Massensport in der Weimarer Republik," 163. The precursor to lawn tennis originated as an aristocratic sport in the Middle Ages, and servants and laborers were prohibited from playing the game. As the sports historian Allen Guttmann writes, "In this instance, class clearly mattered more than sex, for women were not excluded and a certain Margot de Hainault was mentioned in 1427 as superior to the best male tennis-players of Paris." Guttmann, *From Ritual to Record: The Nature of Modern Sports* (New York: Columbia University Press, 1978 [revised and updated 2004]), 30. According to Guttmann, Walter Wingate invented modern lawn tennis in England in 1873, and it had already spread to Germany within five years of that date (60).

8. Christiane Eisenberg, *"English Sports" und Deutsche Bürger: Eine Gesellschaftsgeschichte 1800–1939* (Paderborn: Ferdinand Schöningh, 1999), 195.

9. Leni Riefenstahl, for example, recalled her stay at the German tennis resort of Bad Nauheim in the early 1920s, where she flirted with both an heir to a Chilean silver mine and a Spanish aristocrat. See Leni Riefenstahl, *Leni Riefenstahl: Memoiren* (Munich: Albrecht Knaus, 1987), 40.

10. Dr. Max Ostrop, "Der Sport als Sprachschöpfer," *Die Leibesübungen*, no. 2, Jan. 20, 1931, 43. Irene Guenther charts a similar Germanicization of fashion-related words from their French variants to more German-sounding (and -looking) words during the First World War. See Guenther, *Nazi Chic? Fashioning Women in the Third Reich* (New York: Berg, 2004), 29. In a related vein, some Germans today express concern about the incursion of foreign words more generally into the language. See the *Spiegel* cover story, "Rettet dem Deutsch! Die Verlotterung der Sprache," *Der Spiegel* 40, Oct. 2, 2006, 182–98. German boxing launched a similar campaign in the 1920s to replace English terms with German ones. A front-page article in a 1925 issue of the boxing magazine *Boxsport* offered a glossary of German equivalents for English terms, including "Umklammerung" for "clinch" and "Niederschlag" for "knockout." Just three weeks later, apparently after further reflection, a follow-up article extended the list by nearly a dozen more. See Friedrich Burger, "Deutsch, meine Herren, Deutsch!" *Boxsport* 5, no. 223, Jan. 3, 1925, 1; and Burger's follow-up, "Deutsch auch im Boxen," *Boxsport* 5, no. 226, Jan. 23, 1925, 1–2. For an even earlier example of this effort to anglicize German boxing, see Kurt Severin, "Mehr Deutsch im deutschen Boxsport," *Boxsport*, Oct. 6, 1921, 12.

11. As J. Trygve Has-Ellison notes, all nobles were aristocrats, but not all aristocrats were nobles. According to Has-Ellison, the aristocracy comprised the most elite subset of the nobility (he estimates 1–2 percent of it). See "A Baedeker of the European Aristocracy," review of *Aristocracy in the Modern World*, by Ellis Wasson (2006), in H-Net Book Review (H-German) May 2007. For stylistic reasons, I use the terms "aristocratic" and "noble" interchangeably and intend *both* terms in the broader sense of "pertaining to the nobility." Also, many people married into the nobility—and into a noble surname—as the tennis player Paula von Reznicek did, and others simply adopted the "von" as an affectation. My larger point, however, is that the "von," and the noble surname, signified a particular lifestyle to the larger German public, regardless of whether the individual bearing that moniker actually grew up "noble."

12. Ferdinand Gruber, "Wiederaufbau des Tennissports," *Illustrierter Sport* 7, no. 2, May 6, 1919, 37.

13. "Deutschlands erste Damen-Klasse im Tennis," *Sport im Bild* 30, no. 7, Apr. 4, 1924, 343.

14. F. W. Esser, "Moment-Aufnahmen vom Swinemünder und Heringsdorfer Tennis-Turnier," *Illustrierter Sport* 8, no. 36, Sept. 7, 1920, 697.

15. *Sport-Chronik am Sonnabend* 3, no. 13, Dec. 24, 1926, cover.

16. On the reevaluation of labor since the seventeenth century and the image of European nobility as "unproductive labor," see Anson Rabinbach, *The Human Motor: Energy, Fatigue, and the Origins of Modernity* (Berkeley: University of California Press, 1990), 7.

17. George L. Mosse, *The Image of Man: The Creation of Modern Masculinity* (New York: Oxford University Press, 1996). Marcus Funck, "Ready for War? Conceptions of Military Manliness in the Prusso-German Officer Corps before the First World War," in *Home/Front: The Military, War and Gender in Twentieth-Century Germany*, ed. Karen Hagemann and Stefanie Schüler-Springorum, 57 (New York: Berg, 2002).

18. "Aus Bädern und Sommerfrischen," *B.Z. am Mittag*, July 18, 1928, 8.

19. Richard Goerring, "Besseres Tennis in Spielfilmen," *Tennis und Golf*, no. 1, Jan. 6, 1928, 9. Precisely because of this intimate connection between tennis and afternoon coffee in the minds of the public, though, coffee companies often used illustrations of elegant, male tennis players to sell their product. See, for example, the advertisement for Kaffee Hag, *Sport im Bild* 30, no. 17, 1924, 1021.

20. Sebastian Haffner, *Geschichte eines Deutschen: Erinnerungen 1914–1933* (Munich: Deutscher Taschenbuch Verlag, 2004 [orig. 1939]), 80.

21. Marcus Funck, "Ready for War? Conceptions of Military Manliness in the Prusso-German Officer Corps before the First World War," in *Home/Front: The Military, War and Gender in Twentieth-Century Germany*, ed. Karen Hagemann and Stefanie Schüler-Springorum, 48–49 (New York: Berg, 2002).

22. For another discussion of this, see Kirsten O. Frieling, *Ausdruck macht Eindruck: Bürgerliche Körperpraktiken in sozialer Kommunikation um 1800*, Europäische Hochschulschriften, Bd. 970 (Frankfurt/M: Peter Lang, 2003).

23. Quoted in Eisenberg, *"English Sports" und Deutsche Bürger*, 199.

24. Hans Egon Holthusen, "'...Joe, mach die Musik von damals nach!,'" in *Alltag in der Weimarer Republik: Erinnerungen an eine unruhige Zeit*, ed. Rudolf Pörtner, 444 (Düsseldorf: ECON, 1990).

25. Burghard von Reznicek, *Tennis: Das Spiel der Völker* (Marburg/Lahn: Johann Grüneberg, 1932), 6.

26. Paula von Reznicek, *Auferstehung der Dame* (Stuttgart: Dieck and Co., 1928), 143.

27. P. von Reznicek, "Nichts ist schwerer zu ertragen..." *Der Querschnitt* 8, no. 8 (1928): 548.

28. The historians Kirsten Frieling and Thomas Kleinspehn have focused attention on comportment as central to middle-class identity in nineteenth-century Germany. Frieling describes an effort at the time to "de-physicalize" the physical body by repressing its impulses. Men instead modeled themselves according to the military notions of self-discipline, will power, dignity, and moral strength. See Frieling, *Ausdruck macht Eindruck*, 81; and Kleinspehn, *Der flüchtige Blick: Sehen und Identität in der Kultur der Neuzeit* (Reinbek bei Hamburg: Rowohlt, 1989). See also Mosse, *Image of Man*.

29. Petr Roubal, "Politics of Gymnastics: Mass Gymnastic Displays under Communism in Central and Eastern Europe," *Body and Society* 9, no. 2, 2003, 5.

30. See David Winner, *Those Feet: A Sensual History of English Football* (London: Bloomsbury, 2005).

31. Riefenstahl was later engaged to Froitzheim for a time. Riefenstahl, *Leni Riefenstahl: A Memoir* (New York: Picador/St. Martin's Press, 1992), 20, 33.

32. "Der illustrierte Tennisbericht," *Tennis und Golf* 10, no. 4, Feb. 15, 1933, 84.

33. Vicki Baum, *Pariser Platz 13* (1930), in *Eine Komödie aus dem Schönheitssalon und andere Texte über Kosmetik, Alter, und Mode,* ed. Julia Bertschik (Berlin: Aviva, 2006).

34. Personals ad, *Die Freundschaft* 12, Mar. 27–Apr. 2, 1920, 6.

35. Werner Scheff, *Das weiße Spiel* (Bremen: Carl Schünemann Verlag, 1928), 151.

36. Hedda Westenberger, "Der Partner," *Sport im Bild* 36, no. 18, Sept. 9, 1930, 1324.

37. Dr. Volkmar Iro, "Winke für mondaine Sommer-Reisen," *Sport im Bild* 32, no. 12, June 11, 1926, 523.

38. Scheff, *Das weiße Spiel*, 105.

39. *Sport und Gesundheit*, no. 42, 1929, 669.

40. Werner Scheff, "Gemischtes Doppelspiel. Eine Tennisnovelle," *Sport im Bild* 31, no. 19, Sept. 11, 1925, 1201. Scheff was the same author who later penned *Das weiße Spiel*, and he made a specialty of writing works of pulp fiction that combined romance with athletic competitions, including *Der Läufer von Marathon* (see chap. 3).

41. Eisenberg, *"English Sports" und Deutsche Bürger*, 202.

42. Norbert Elias, *The Civilizing Process: The History of Manners*, vol. 1, trans. Edmund Jephcott (New York: Urizen Books, 1978), 187.

43. See Ben B. Lindsey and Wainwright Evans, *The Companionate Marriage* (Garden City, NY: Garden City Publishing, 1927).

44. Erik Ernst Schwabach, *Die Revolutionierung der Frau* (Leipzig: Der Neue Geistverlag, 1928), 86. For a scholarly analysis of the discourse of sports as a companionate model, see Frank Becker, "Die Sportlerin als Vorbild der 'neuen Frau': Versuche zur Umwertung der Geschlechterrollen in der Weimarer Republik," *Sozial- und Zeitgeschichte des Sports* 8, no. 3 (Nov. 1994): 40.

45. Heikki Lempa, "Men Dancing, Men Walking: Defining Male Habitus in Early Nineteenth-century Germany," paper presented at the Annual Meeting of the German Studies Association, Oct. 2003.

46. Scheff, *Das weiße Spiel*, 13.

47. "Dame und Herr beim Sommersport," *Sport im Bild* 32, no. 10, May 14, 1926, 438.

48. Bernd Wedemeyer-Kolwe, *"Der neue Mensch": Körperkultur im Kaiserreich und in der Weimarer Republik* (Würzburg: Königshausen und Neumann, 2004), 287.

49. Ilse Friedleben, "Eindrücke vom Territet-Turnier," *Sport im Bild* 32, no. 11, May 28, 1926, 468.

50. On the identification of a category of consumer-oriented "new men" in the United States and Britain in the 1980s, see Bill Osgerby, "A pedigree of the consuming male: Masculinity, consumption and the American 'leisure class,'" in *Masculinity and Men's Lifestyle Magazines*, ed. Bethan Benwell, 60 (Malden, MA: Blackwell, 2003).

51. Mosse, *Image of Man: The Creation of Modern Masculinity*, 139.

52. Günther von Diergandt, "Continuous Play," in *Tennis und Golf*, no. 13, May 23, 1930, 359.

53. Conrad Weiss, "In Memorium Hans Moldenhauer," *Tennis und Golf* 7, no. 2, Jan. 17, 1930, 27.

54. *Sport und Sonne*, no. 1, Jan. 1928, 43.

55. Dr. Bill Fuchs, "Die deutschen Ranglistenspieler," 141.

56. Ibid., 149.

57. "Von der Schönheit und dem Rhythmus der Tennisschläge," *Sport und Sonne*, no. 28, Aug. 1928, 481.

58. Kasimir Edschmid, *Sport um Gagaly* (Berlin: Peter Zsolnay, 1928), 67–68.

59. Scheff, *Das weiße Spiel*, 240.

60. Wilhelm Schomburgh, "Eindrücke von Wimbledon," *Tennis und Golf*, no. 21, July 20, 1928, 587.

61. Hans Kreitner, "Finale. Stars und Stile der Saison," *Sport im Bild* 35, no. 19, Sept. 19, 1929, 1513.

62. Gertrud Dagen-Höfer, "Wenn die weißen Bälle fliegen: Vom Siegeszug des Tennisspiels," *Sport und Sonne* 6, no. 3, Mar.–Apr. 1930, 97.

63. "Australiens Tennisspieler bei 'Rot-Weiss,'" *Illustriertes Sportblatt: Sport-Spiegel des Berliner Tageblatts*, July 20, 1928, 2.

64. Conrad Weiss, "In Memorium Hans Moldenhauer," 24–29.

65. Dr. Hermann Rau, "In Memorium Hans Moldenhauer II," *Tennis und Golf* 7, no. 3, Jan. 30, 1930, 72.

66. Polizei-Leutnant W. K., "Sport bei der Polizei—Polizei beim Sport," *Der Querschnitt* 8, no. 8 (1928): 540.

67. Kurt Doerry, "Sport der Alten Herren," *Der Leichtathlet* 6, no. 1, Jan. 3, 1929, 4.

68. Janice Taylor, "Die Herren Athleten," *Der Querschnitt* 12, no. 6 (1932): 400–402.

69. Osbert Sitwell, "Der Unfug des Sports," *Der Querschnitt* 9, no. 4 (Apr. 1931): 254.

70. Fritz Giese, *Geist im Sport: Probleme und Forderungen* (Munich: Delphin-Verlag, 1925), 41.

71. Volkmar Iro, "Winke für mondaine Sommer-Reisen," *Sport im Bild* 32, no. 12, June 11, 1926, 522.

72. Advertisement for Elida skin cream, *Berliner Illustrirte Zeitung* 40, no. 27, July 5, 1931, 1120.

73. Advertisement for Odol mouthwash, *Vossische Zeitung*, Aug. 7, 1928, 4.

74. Gerald Patterson, "Patterson erzählt...," interview by M. F. Micheler, *Sport im Bild* 34, no. 17, Aug. 17, 1928, 1238.

75. *Der Weltspiegel: Illustrierte Zeitung* 31, no. 27, insert with the *Berliner Tageblatt*, July 5, 1931, 16.

76. Hans Kreitner, "Finale: Stars und Stile der Saison," *Sport im Bild* 35, no. 19, Sept. 19, 1929, 1513.

77. Quoted in Wolfgang Hofer, *Ein Jahrhundert Tennis in Berlin: 100 Jahre Lawn-Tennis-Turnier-Club Rot-Weiss Berlin* (Berlin: Nicolai, 1986), 43.

78. George F. Salmony, "Sport in den 'Goldenen Zwanzigern': Aus den Memoiren eines Amateur-Zuschauers," in *Das grosse Spiel: Aspekte des Sports in unserer Zeit*, ed. Uwe Schultz, 109–10 (Frankfurt/M: Fischer, 1965).

79. "'Rot-Weiss'-Berlin 'Berea' Johannesburg," *Berliner Tageblatt*, July 10, 1931, 3. Beiblatt, 1.

80. "Rot-Weiss/Südafrika 2:1," *B.Z. am Mittag*, July 11, 1931, "Beilage zum Sport."

81. Prenn grew up in Vilnius, Lithuania, but his parents had moved to St. Petersburg during the First World War.

82. I borrow the idea of insiders and outsiders from Peter Gay, *Weimar Culture: The Outsider as Insider* (New York: Harper and Row, 1970).

83. Interview with the *C.V. Zeitung*, July 26, 1929, 391. Quoted in Gideon Reuveni, "Sports and the Militarization of Jewish Society," in *Emancipation through Muscles: Jews and Sports in Europe*, ed. Michael Brenner and Gideon Reuveni, 54 (Lincoln, NE: University of Nebraska Press, 2006).

84. Recounted in Bella Fromm, *Blood and Banquets: A Berlin Social Diary* (New York: Harper and Brothers, 1942), 18.

85. *Israelitisches Familienblatt* 34, no. 29, July 21, 1932, 10; quoted in Jacob Borut, "Jews in German Sports during the Weimar Republic," in Brenner and Reuveni, *Emancipation through Muscles*, 78 (Lincoln, NE: University of Nebraska Press, 2006).

86. Dr. Hermann Rau, "Die deutschen Erfolge im Davispokal," *Tennis und Golf* 9, no. 23, Aug. 12, 1932, 508.

87. It was the match against Don Budge in the Davis Cup final in July 1937. Egon Steinkamp, *Gottfried von Cramm: Der Tennisbaron* (Munich: F. A. Herbig, 1990), 12. Cramm could play winning tennis, of course, and until the 2004 French Open, Cramm held the distinction of being the most recent man to have saved a match point in the French Open final and then gone on to win the match and title, which Cramm did in 1934 against Jack Crawford of Australia. This historical footnote was mentioned in Christopher Clarey, "Gaudio Wins French Open Roller Coaster," *New York Times*, June 7, 2004, D2.

88. The lives of Prenn and Cramm paralleled one another in a particularly tragic way after 1933, when both faced persecution by the National Socialist regime. In April 1933, the Nazis forced the German Tennis Federation to remove Prenn from the national Davis Cup team as part of its blanket expulsion of Jewish players from its ranks. Shortly thereafter, he fled to England. Cramm, because of his impeccable "Aryan" background, continued to play for the next five years, but he ran afoul of the Nazi regime in 1938 when authorities sentenced him for a violation of Paragraph 175a, the law that criminalized even the appearance of homosexual solicitation. The authorities accused Cramm of having an affair from 1934 to 1936 with Manasse Herbst, a Galician Jew, who then allegedly blackmailed money from Cramm in order to flee Germany. Family connections helped to secure Cramm's release from prison seven months later, but he never returned to elite competitive tennis. Cramm, who in 1937 had divorced Lisa von Dobeneck after seven years of marriage, never admitted to the affair and may have freely given the money to Herbst, since the two met again after the war. Cramm served in the army during the war and later married Barbara Hutton, the Woolworth heiress. See Egon Steinkamp, *Gottfried von Cramm*, 121–26.

89. Dr. F. W. Esser, "Moment-Aufnahmen vom Swinemünder und Heringsdorfer Tennis-Turnier," *Illustrierter Sport* 8, no. 36, Sept. 7, 1920, 698.

90. George F. Salmony, "Sport in den 'Goldenen Zwanzigern': Aus den Memoiren eines Amateur-Zuschauers," in Schultz, *Das grosse Spiel*, 109 (Frankfurt/M: Fischer, 1965).

91. Dr. H. Rau, "Deutsches Tennis 1929," *Die Leibesübungen*, no. 4, Feb. 20, 1930, 93.

92. *Damen-Sport und Damen-Turnen* 2, no. 15/16, Aug. 1919, 178.

93. Heinrich Mann, "Der Bubikopf" (1926), in *Sieben Jahre: Chronik der Gedanken und Vorgänge* (Berlin: Paul Zsolnay, 1929), 304.

94. Georg Lehmann, "Der dritte Stand der Tennisspieler," *B.Z. am Mittag*, repr. in *Sport-Chronik am Sonnabend* 3, no. 3, Oct. 16, 1926, 15.

95. Suzanne Lenglen, quoted in Jacques Mortane, "Suzanne Lenglens Erinnerungen," *Sport und Sonne*, no. 3, Mar. 1928, 152.

96. "Was Berufssportler verdienen können," *Die Leibesübungen*, no. 5/6, Mar. 20, 1927, 132.

97. Dr. Willy Meisl, "Das Problem des Amateurismus," *Die Leibesübungen*, no. 5/6, Mar. 20, 1927, 129.

98. Emil Lenk, *Frauentypen: Heilige, Mütter, Dirnen* (Berlin: Dr. Madaus u. Co., 1928), 297–98.

99. See, for example, the advertisements, guidebooks, and paintings of Berlin's lesbian scene in Mel Gordon, *Voluptuous Panic: The Erotic World of Weimar Berlin* (Venice, CA: Feral House, 2000).

100. For a succinct discussion of the important economic and diplomatic reforms, see Detlev J. K. Peukert, *The Weimar Republic: The Crisis of Classical Modernity*, trans. Richard Deveson (New York: Hill and Wang, 1989 [orig. 1987]). For an in-depth discussion of the inflation, see Gerald Feldman, *The Great Disorder: Politics, Economics, and Society in the German Inflation, 1914–1924* (New York: Oxford University Press, 1993).

101. Eisenberg, *"English Sports" und Deutsche Bürger*, 219–20. In September 1926, 700 clubs operated in Germany, with a total of 75,000 players. Three years later, these figures had climbed to 978 clubs, with a total of 97,431 members. "Deutsches Tennis 1929," *Die Leibesübungen*, no. 4, Feb. 20, 1930, 94.

102. Lenk, *Frauentypen. Heilige, Mütter, Dirnen*, 298.

103. B. von Reznicek, *Tennis*, 202.

104. P. von Reznicek, *Auferstehung der Dame*, 146.

105. Elsa Hermann, *This is the New Woman* (Hellerau: Avalon, 1929), 32–43, reprinted in *The Weimar Republic Sourcebook*, ed. Anton Kaes, Martin Jay, and Edward Dimendberg (Berkeley: University of California Press, 1994), 207.

106. Heinz Lorenz, "Frauenanmut und Sport," *Sport und Sonne*, no. 3, Mar. 1927, 134. The second quotation comes from the article "Schönheit der sportlichen Bewegung. Anmut im Tennisspiel," *Sport und Sonne*, no. 11, Nov. 1927, 691.

107. Ken Montague, "The Aesthetics of Hygiene: Aesthetic Dress, Modernity, and the Body as Sign," in *Journal of Design History* 7, no. 2 (1994): 108.

108. Scheff, *Das weiße Spiel*, 161.

109. "Sport-Gotha," *Der Querschnitt* 12, no. 6 (Jan. 1932): 428.

110. For a great discussion of the relationship between the discourses of rationalization and of sports, see Frank Becker, *Amerikanismus in Weimar: Sportsymbole und politische Kultur 1918–1933* (Wiesbaden: Deutscher Universitäts-Verlag, 1993); as well as Becker, "Sport bei Ford: Rationalisierung und Symbolpolitik in der Weimarer Republik," *Stadion* 17, no. 2 (1991): 207–29.

111. Rudolph Stratz, *Lill: Der Roman eines Sportmädchens* (Berlin: August Scherl, 1929), 31.

112. Ibid., 82. Over the course of the novel, however, Lill outgrows her ostensible self-absorption and realizes her "natural" desire to care for a male companion, a discovery that Stratz no doubt hoped would serve as a lesson to his female readers.

113. "Die Wienerin und der Weisse Sport," *Almanach der Dame*, no. 2 (Spring 1930): 37.

114. Annemarie Kopp, "Wettkampf und Weiblichkeit" (1927), in *Frau und Sport*, ed. Gertrud Pfister (Frankfurt/M: Fischer Taschenbuch, 1980), 130.

115. *Sport und Sonne*, no. 8, Aug. 1927, 458.

116. Ilse Friedleben, "Deutsches Damentennis. Spaziergang unter Meisterinnen," *Sport und Sonne*, no. 2, Feb. 1928, 83.

117. Rafael Schermann, "Die Schrift des Champions," in B. von Reznicek, *Tennis*, 302.

118. Ferdinand Gruber, "Der Deutsche Tennissport," in *Die Olympischen Spiele Paris 1924 und der Deutsche Sport*, ed. Julius Wagner and Guido Eichenberger (Zürich: Julius Wagner, 1924), 92.

119. B. von Reznicek, *Tennis*, 192.

120. Richard Goerring, "Das deutsche Damen-Tennis wird aufgewertet: Randglossen zum Alvarez-Gastspiel," *Tennis und Golf* 5, no. 12, May 18, 1928, 320.

121. Alfred Kremer, "Mädchen im Tempel. Eine Wertung olympischer Frauen," *Der Leichtathlet* 5, no. 51/52, Dec. 18, 1928, 28.

122. Horst M. Wagner, "Lehren einer Tennis-Spielzeit," *Die Leibesübungen*, no. 9, May 5, 1931, 242.

123. Burcu Dogramaci has emphasized the omnipresence of athletic women in the fashion magazines of the 1920s, and he argues that the readership viewed the designation "Amazon" positively, not pejoratively. See Dogramaci, "Mode-Körper. Zur Inszenierung von Weiblichkeit in Modegrafik und -fotografie der Weimarer Republik," in *Leibhaftige Moderne: Körper in Kunst und Massenmedien 1918 bis 1933*, ed. Michael Cowan and Kai Marcel Sicks (Bielefeld: transcript Verlag, 2005), 122. Burghard von Reznicek dubbed California "the birthplace of the tennis Amazons," in his article "Kommende Cracks?" *Sport im Bild* 36, no. 10, May 20, 1930, 726. Two years later, he called the legendary 1926 match between Suzanne Lenglen and Helen Wills "The Battle of the Amazons at Carlton Beach." See B. von Reznicek, *Tennis*, 130.

124. Dr. Paul Weeks, "Wandlung im Tennis," *Sport und Sonne* 6, no. 6, June/July 1930, 204.

125. Stratz, *Lill*, 35.

126. Ibid., 124.

127. Ibid., 45.

128. One of six panels, collectively titled "Tennis-Meteorologie," by the illustrator Rolf Peter Bauer, *Tennis und Golf* 9, no. 9, May 1, 1932, 213.

129. Advertisement for "4711" cologne, *Sport im Bild* 33, no. 15, July 22, 1927, 885.

130. *Der Lawn-Tennis-Sport* 4, no. 29, Nov. 7, 1907, 621.

131. "Deutsche Tennisspielerinnen," *Damen-Sport und Damen-Turnen* 1, no. 3, Nov. 1918, 32.

132. Horst Wagner and M. Ziegler, "Tennis im Rahmen der Körpererziehung," *Die Leibesübungen*, no. 11, June 5, 1928, 278.

133. "Die internationalen Meisterschaften von Deutschland," *Tennis und Golf*, no. 25, Aug. 17, 1928, 701.

134. Heinrich Mann, "Der Bubikopf" (1926), in *Sieben Jahre*, 304.

135. Dr. Fr. Messerli, "Die Wettkämpfe der Damen," in *Die Olympischen Spiele 1928. St. Moritz–Amsterdam*, ed. Julius Wagner, Fritz Klipstein, and Dr. F. Messerli, 65 (Zürich/Stuttgart: Julius Wagner, 1928).

136. Dr. Rau, "Tennis-Ereignisse," *Sport und Sonne*, no. 9 (Sept. 1928): 534. This comment motivated Rau to write a longer piece in the December issue of *Sport*

und Sonne in defense of men's tennis. See Dr. Rau, "Tennis-Ereignisse," *Sport und Sonne*, no. 12, Dec. 1928, 720.

137. Advertisement for N. G.-Busch eyeglasses, *Sport im Bild* 33, no. 10, May 13, 1927, 551.

138. Advertisement for Kaffee Hag, *Sport im Bild* 35, no. 20, Oct. 3, 1929, 1623.

139. Arthur Schnitzler, *Fräulein Else* (Berlin: Paul Zsolnay, 1924), 39.

140. M. F. Micheler, "Deutscher Tennis-Nachwuchs," *Sport und Sonne*, no. 7, July 1927, 434.

141. "Kölner Hallen-Schaukämpfe," *Tennis und Golf* 7, no. 1, Jan. 3, 1930, 10; and "Von Woche zu Woche," *Tennis und Golf* 7, no. 23, Aug. 1, 1930, 621.

142. Dr. Hermann Rau, "Weltereigniße im Tennis," *Die Leibesübungen*, no. 7, Apr. 5, 1931, 175.

143. Dr. Walter Bing, "Tennis. Die Ewige Olympiade," in *Welt-Olympia 1928 in Wort und Bild*, ed. Josef Waitzer and Wilhelm Dörr, 138 (Berlin: Conzett und Huber, 1928).

144. Rumpelstilzchen (a.k.a. Adolph Stein), feuilleton from July 16, 1931, in *Nu wenn schon!*, collected essays, vol. 12, 1931/32 (Berlin: Brunnen-Verlag, 1932), 360. Cilly Aussem still contributes to German national identity today. The German rail network named the intercity express train between Berlin and Bonn after Aussem, and its printed schedule remembers her as having "contributed decisively to helping German women's tennis to an international reputation." Travel itinerary for the ICE #940 (the "Cilly Aussem"), Berlin Ostbahnhof to Bonn Hauptbahnhof (Deutsche Bahn, 1999).

145. The fact that Schmeling had won on a technicality also contributed to the muted response to his win.

146. Carla Verständig, "Ein Plädoyer für den Wettkampfsport" (1930), in Pfister, *Frau und Sport*, 128.

147. "Deutsche Tennisspielerinnen," *Damen-Sport und Damen-Turnen* 1, no. 3, Nov. 1918, 31.

148. Schnitzler, *Fräulein Else*, 11–12.

149. "Drei Frauen stehen vor uns. Die Drei Typen: Gretchen, Girl, Garçonne," *8-Uhr Abendblatt*, June 4, 1927, quoted in Lynne Frame, "Gretchen, Girl, Garçonne? Weimar Science and Popular Culture in Search of the Ideal New Woman," in *Women in the Metropolis: Gender and Modernity in Weimar Culture*, ed. Katharina von Ankum (Berkeley: University of California Press, 1997), 12.

150. P. von Reznicek, *Auferstehung der Dame*, 148.

151. Stefan Zweig, "Zutrauen zur Zukunft," in *Die Frau von Morgen: Wie wir sie wünschen*, ed. Friedrich M. Huebner (Leipzig: E.A. Seemann, 1929), 12. The historian Ute Frevert writes, "To say openly that women as well as men had sexual desires and wished to fulfill them, inside or outside marriage, was to break irreversibly with the 'genteel' society which kept such libertarian tendencies at arm's length." See *Women in German History: From Bourgeois Emancipation to Sexual Liberation*, trans. Stuart McKinnon-Evans (New York: Berg, 1988), 131.

152. Billy Wilder describes his experiences in "Herr Ober, bitte einen Tänzer!' Aus dem Leben eines Eintänzers," in *Der Prinz von Wales geht auf Urlaub: Berliner Reportagen, Feuilletons und Kritiken der zwanziger Jahre*, ed. Klaus Siebenhaar (Munich: Diana Verlag, 2000). Astrid Eichstadt describes the phenomenon of the "berufsmäßigen Frauenhelden" in "Irgendeinen trifft die Wahl," in *Neuen Frauen:*

Die Zwanziger Jahre, ed. Kristine von Soden and Maruta Schmidt, 13 (West Berlin: Elefanten Press, 1988).

153. Atina Grossmann, *Reforming Sex: The German Movement for Birth Control and Abortion Reform, 1920–1950* (New York: Oxford University Press, 1995), 69. See also Paul Weindling, who notes that "sexual reform was stigmatized as promiscuity." Weindling, *Health, Race and German Politics Between National Unification and Nazism, 1870–1945* (New York: Cambridge University Press, 1989), 368.

154. Elsbeth Killmer, "Die Siegerin," *Die Freundin* 3, no. 6, Apr. 4, 1927, 3.

155. Operetta *Eine Frau, die weiß, was sie will* (Oscar Straus, debuted in Berlin's Metropol Theater in August 1932).

156. Scheff, *Das weiße Spiel*, 258.

157. Stratz, *Lill*, 62–63.

158. P. von Reznicek, *Auferstehung der Dame*, 124.

159. Beverley Nichols, "Señorita de Alvarez oder Tennis ohne Tränen," *Der Querschnitt* 8, no. 8 (1928): 567.

160. Rumpelstilzchen (a.k.a. Adolf Stein), feuilleton from July 3, 1924 in *Bei mir—Berlin!*, collected columns, vol. 4 (Berlin: Brunnen-Verlag, 1924): 343.

161. F. P. Weidemann, *European Sporting Activities: Amsterdam—Cologne*, ed. Karl Kiesel and Walter Hulek (Bremen: The University Travel Department of the North German Lloyd, 1928), 136.

162. "Deutschlands erste Damen-Klasse im Tennis," *Sport im Bild* 30, no. 7, Apr. 4, 1924, 343.

163. Mr. Buchgeister, "Ueber Frauensport," *Der Leichtathlet* 3, no. 34, Aug. 24, 1926, 22.

164. Beverley Nichols, "Señorita de Alvarez oder Tennis ohne Tränen," *Der Querschnitt* 8. n. 8 (1928): 566.

165. Sander Gilman, *Making the Body Beautiful: A Cultural History of Aesthetic Surgery* (Princeton, NJ: Princeton University Press, 1999), 229–30.

166. *Die Literarische Welt*, quoted in John Willett, *Art and Politics in the Weimar Period: The New Sobriety, 1917–1933* (New York: De Capo, 1996 [orig. 1978]), 103.

167. P. von Reznicek, "Unsere Tenniskinder," *Sport im Bild* 32, no. 17, Aug. 20, 1926, 734.

168. Greg Demasius, "Ein Wochenende in Paris," *Tennis und Golf*, no. 5, Feb. 28, 1930, 131.

169. Dr. Hermann Rau, "In memorium Hans Moldenhauer II," 72.

170. Tennis courts were not the only venues for striking up affairs in Reznicek's universe. She also published a story in Germany's national automobile magazine, for instance, in which a male and a female driver engage in a spontaneous automobile race, before striking up a conversation and deciding to drive to a nearby seaside hotel. P. von Reznicek, "Die ver'herrlichte' Nebenbuhlerin," *Allgemeine Automobil Zeitung* 29, no. 26, June 30, 1928, 17. Eric Roubinek brought this article to my attention, in his paper "Social Mobility or Bourgeois Stability? The New Woman, Sexuality, and the Automobile," German Studies Association conference, Oct. 2007.

171. Greg Demasius, "Ein Wochenende in Paris," *Tennis und Golf*, no. 5, Feb. 28, 1930, 131.

172. "Sport-Gotha," *Der Querschnitt* 12, no. 6 (June 1932): 431.

173. In addition, both male tennis players and Jews were, according to stereotype, cosmopolitan and effete. I am indebted to Claudia Koonz for pointing out to me the repeated depictions of Jews as tennis players in the cartoons of the Nazi newspaper *Der Stürmer*. Conversation with the author at the conference "Impossible

Citizens: Engendering Politics in a Comparative World Perspective," University of Minnesota, May 2002.

Chapter 2

1. Bertolt Brecht, *Das Renommee—Ein Boxerroman*, in *Werke: Große kommentierte Berliner und Frankfurter Ausgabe*, vol. 17 (Frankfurt/M: Suhrkamp, 1989), 423.

2. Ibid. 424.

3. David Bathrick famously described the male boxer as an icon of Weimar culture, and he also discusses Bertolt Brecht's fascination with the sport and its champions. See "Max Schmeling on the Canvas: Boxing as an Icon of Weimar Culture," in *New German Critique*, no. 51 (1990): 113–36.

4. Kurt Doerry, "Carpentier im Film," *Sport im Bild* 27, no. 8, Feb. 25, 1921, 254.

5. Walter Rothenburg, "Zwölf bildschöne junge Damen...," *Boxsport*, Nov. 10, 1921, 1.

6. Susan K. Cahn describes this implicit male opponent as a common motif in media coverage of female athletes throughout the twentieth century. See *Coming on Strong: Gender and Sexuality in 20th-century Women's Sports* (Cambridge. MA: Harvard University Press, 1994), 209–10. Cahn notes that the American sports commentator Grantland Rice anxiously viewed women's sports in the 1920s as the means by which women would overtake men and reduce the latter to dependency.

7. Vicki Baum, *Es war alles ganz anders: Erinnerungen* (Frankfurt/M: Ullstein, 1962).

8. Peter Jelavich, *Berlin Cabaret* (Cambridge, MA: Harvard University Press, 1993), 22. The film was, most likely, the 1896 British short *Boxing Kangaroo*, directed by Burt Acres, which also ranks as the very first known boxing film. See *Sports Films: A Complete Reference*, compiled by Harvey Marc Zucker and Lawrence J. Babich (Jefferson, NC: McFarland, 1987), 67.

9. For a full treatment of the history of professional boxing in Germany, see Knud Kohr and Martin Krauß, *Kampftage: Die Geschichte des deutschen Berufsboxens* (Göttingen: Die Werkstatt Verlag, 2000). For a sense of how the history of boxing appeared to a contemporary just after the war, see Leonhard Mandlár, "Entwicklung des modernen Boxsports in Deutschland und seine Organisation," *Boxsport*, Oct. 13, 1921, 1–3.

10. Bernd Wedemeyer, *Starke Männer, starke Frauen: Eine Kulturgeschichte des Bodybuildings* (Munich: C. H. Beck, 1996), 31.

11. Max Schmeling, "Wie kamen Sie zu Ihrem Schicksal?" *Das elegante Köln*, Dec. 1, 1929, 20.

12. Rolf Jäger, "Die Boxer," pt. 1, *Das Tage-Buch* 3, no. 16, Apr. 22, 1922, 619.

13. Modris Eksteins, *Rites of Spring: The Great War and the Birth of the Modern Age* (Boston: Mariner, 1989, 2000), 16.

14. Otto Friedrich, *Before the Deluge: A Portrait of Berlin in the 1920s* (New York: Harper Collins, 1972, 1995), 257.

15. Otto Friedrich claims that the man's real name was Sally Mayer and the entire "Sabri Mahir" moniker and backstory was nothing but an elaborate fiction. Mahir's true identity and past, in keeping with boxing's role as a vehicle for self-reinvention, remains murky. See *Before the Deluge*, 257.

16. Bertolt Brecht, "Der Kinnhaken" (1926), repr. in *Der Kinnhaken und andere Box- und Sportgeschichten*, ed. Günter Berg, 8 (Frankfurt/M: Suhrkamp, 1998).

17. Christopher Isherwood, "Goodbye to Berlin," in *The Berlin Stories* (New York: New Directions Books, 1963 [orig. 1939]), 190.

18. Bruno Manuel, "Der stärkste Mann Berlins," *Berliner Tageblatt*, July 17, 1931. 1 (supplement).

19. *Spione*, directed by Fritz Lang (Germany: Ufa Production, 1927/28). Bernd Ruland similarly remembers boxing as a fixture of interwar Berlin nightlife. See Ruland, *Das war Berlin: Erinnerungen an die Reichshauptstadt* (Bayreuth: Hestia, 1972), 183.

20. For a more extensive discussion of the efforts on the part of the German boxing establishment to groom "proper" spectators, see Erik Jensen, "Crowd Control: Boxing Spectatorship and Social Order in Weimar Germany," in *Histories of Leisure*, ed. Rudy Koshar, 79–101 (New York: Berg, 2002).

21. Curt Gutmann, "Boxen als Geschäft und als Sport," *Der Querschnitt* 8, no. 8 (1928): 560.

22. Quoted in Birk Meinhardt, *Boxen in Deutschland* (Hamburg: Rotbuch, 1996), 11.

23. Ibid., 72.

24. Erich Kästner, quoted in Peter Jelavich, *Berlin Cabaret*, 197–98.

25. Quoted in *Sport in Berlin: Vom Ritterturnier zum Stadtmarathon*, ed. Gertrud Pfister and Gerd Steins (Berlin: Verlag Forum für Sportgeschichte, 1987), 8.

26. Dr. Volkmar Iro, "Winke für mondaine Sommer-Reisen," *Sport im Bild* 32, no. 12, June 11, 1926): 522. Ruland, *Das war Berlin*, 185.

27. "Der Boxsport im Theater und im Kino," *Boxsport* 7, no. 338, Mar. 22, 1927, 2.

28. Bertolt Brecht, "Das Theater als Sport" (1920), repr. in Berg, *Der Kinnhaken*, 23–24. See also "Mehr guten Sport," his 1926 essay. To this end, he erected a stage in the form of a boxing ring on several occasions, as he did for the radio play *Hamlet* in 1930. Other dramatists expressed a similar desire to incorporate elements of sports spectatorship into theater, including Max Reinhardt, who wanted an *Arenabühne* (arena stage) and Erwin Piscator, who had Walter Gropius design for him a "total theater." See Anne Fleig, "'Siegesplätze über die Natur': Musils Kritik am Geist des modernen Wettkampfsports," in *Leibhaftige Moderne: Körper in Kunst und Massenmedien 1918 bis 1933* (Bielefeld: transcript Verlag, 2005), 92; and Franz Josef Görtz, "'Dichter, übt euch im Weitsprung': Sport und Literatur im 20. Jahrhundert," in *Schneller, Höher, Weiter: Eine Geschichte des Sports*, ed. Hans Sarkowicz, 348 (Frankfurt/M: Insel, 1996). For the specific reference to the *Hamlet* production, see Alfred Braun, *Achtung, Achtung, hier ist Berlin! Aus der Geschichte des Deutschen Rundfunks in Berlin 1923–1932* (Berlin: Haude & Spener, 1968), 47.

29. There were, in fact, several incarnations of "Martha Farra" in the 1920s, but they all performed more or less the same feats. See Wilfried Kugel, *Hanussen: Die wahre Geschichte des Hermann Steinschneider* (Düsseldorf: Grupello, 1998), 66.

30. Rumpelstilzchen, feuilleton from Mar. 5, 1925, in *Haste Worte?*, collected works, vol. 5, 1924/25 (Berlin: Brunnen, 1925), 221. His statement echoed some of the discourse on this side of the Atlantic in the 1920s, when writers like Grantland Rice spoke of women having to rescue men from a sinking ship, thanks to their

superior strength, honed in the sports arena. Max Schmeling also recalled seeing a performance by this woman, whom he referred to as "Frau Sandwiener." See Max Schmeling, *Erinnerungen*, (Frankfurt/M.: Ullstein, 1977), 41.

31. Illustration by Walter Trier, *Frechheit* 6, no. 11 (n.d.), cover. *Die Frechheit* also served as the monthly program book of the cabaret theater "Kabarett der Komiker."

32. Wedemeyer, *Starke Männer, starke Frauen*, 30. Fritz Giese, *Geist im Sport: Probleme und Forderungen* (Munich: Delphin, 1925), 81.

33. Ernst Hanfstaengl, *Unheard Witness* (New York: J. B. Lippincott, 1957), 64.

34. Rumpelstilzchen, feuilleton from June 8, 1921, in *Berliner Allerlei*, collected works, vol. 1 (Berlin: Verlag der Täglichen Rundschau, 1922), 242.

35. Rumpelstilzchen, feuilleton from Oct. 19, 1922, in *Und det jloobste?*, collected works, v. 3 (Berlin: Brunnen, 1923), 39.

36. Helga Bemmann, *Berliner Musenkinder—Memoiren: Eine heitere Chronik von 1900–1930* (Berlin/GDR: VEB Lied der Zeit Musikverlag, 1981), 160.

37. See Valeska Gert, *Ich bin eine Hexe: Kaleidoskop meines Lebens* (Reinbek bei Hamburg: Rowohlt, 1978), 57. Gert also re-creates "Boxkampf!" with the help of a younger dancer in the documentary film, *Nur zum Spaß, nur zum Spiel*, directed by Volker Schlöndorff. On Gert's importance to expressionist dance, see Gabriele Klein, "Weiblichkeit und Tanzkunst," in *Frauen-Räume: Körper und Identität im Sport*, ed. Sabine Kröner and Gertrud Pfister (Pfaffenweiler: Centaurus, 1992).

38. Hannah Höch, *Hannah Höch: Eine Lebenscollage*, Archiv-Edition, vol. 2 (1921–45), pt. 2, ed. Ralf Burmeister and Eckard Fuerlus, 181 (Berlin: Gerd Hatje, 1995). Jennifer Hargreaves, "Women's Boxing and Related Activities: Introducing Images and Meanings," *Body and Society* 3, no. 4, 1997, 45.

39. Ian Buruma, "Weimar Faces," *New York Review of Books* 53, no. 17, Nov. 2, 2006, 17. Throughout the 1920s, writers had discussed the idea of gender as role playing and masquerade, including Joan Rivière in a 1929 thesis on "womanliness as a masquerade." For a brief discussion of this, see Janet Ward, *Weimar Surfaces: Urban Visual Culture in 1920s Germany* (Berkeley: University of California Press, 2001), 88.

40. Judith Butler, *Gender Trouble: Feminism and the Subversion of Identity* (New York: Routledge, 1990, 1999), 175.

41. Judith Butler, *Bodies That Matter: On the Discursive Limits of "Sex"* (New York: Routledge, 1993), 237.

42. Oskar Neumann, "Der Meisterboxer," *Sport und Gesundheit*, no. 16, 1929, 256.

43. Max Schmeling enjoyed a 90 percent name recognition; Stresemann had 80 percent, Karl May 54 percent, and Henry Ford 49 percent. "Vom Sportleben unserer Vierzehnjährigen," *Die Leibesübungen*, June 20, 1930, 339.

44. *Simplicissimus* 35, no. 15, July 7, 1930.

45. Gustav Stresemann, quoted in "Außenminister Dr. Stresemann über den Sport," *Die Leibesübungen*, no. 5/6, Mar. 20, 1927, 151.

46. G. Bach, "Kampfgeist!," *Boxsport* 5, no. 226, Jan. 23, 1925, 2.

47. Ludwig Haymann, quoted ibid.

48. "Ist der Boxsport Ro [*sic*]," *Der Querschnitt*, no. 6 (Dec. 1921): 223.

49. Max Schmeling noted that Belling had told him of his personal interest in boxing at their first meeting. Max Schmeling, *Erinnerungen*, 95. Piscator even had his bedroom arranged to accommodate a punching ball and his morning boxing-

style workouts. For a picture, see Siegfried Giedion, *Befreites Wohnen* (Zürich: Orell Füssli, 1929), 26.

50. David Bathrick makes this point with regard to the deep interest of Bertolt Brecht and others in the sport of boxing. See "Max Schmeling on the Canvas: Boxing as an Icon of Weimar Culture," 113–36.

51. Alfred Flechtheim, quoted in ibid., 119.

52. Kurt Tucholsky, *Deutschland, Deutschland ueber Alles* (Reinbek bei Hamburg: Rowohlt Taschenbuch, 1929, 1973), 178.

53. Fritz Löbl, "Lernt Boxen!," *Sport und Sonne* 5, no. 14, Oct. 15, 1929, 526.

54. Kurt Jackmush, *Boxwoche* 1 (1923), quoted in Dieter Behrendt, "'Boxen mußte de, boxen, boxen,'" in *Arena der Leidenschaften: Der Berliner Sportpalast und seine Veranstaltungen, 1910–1973*, ed. Alfons Arenhövel (Berlin: W. Arenhövel, 1990), 84.

55. Karl Kaiser, "Junge, werde ein Mann!," *Sportgeist* 2, no. 4, Apr. 1931, 5.

56. Ludwig Will, "Der Vernichtungswille," *Boxsport* 6, no. 304, June 21, 1926, 6.

57. Rudolf Hartung, "Männliche Körpererziehung im Lichte der Bodeschen Ausdrucksgymnastik," *Die Leibesübungen*, no. 23, Dec. 5, 1927, 554.

58. Bertolt Brecht, "Die Todfeinde des Sportes" (orig. ca. 1928), in *Der Kinnhaken*, 99.

59. For a clear discussion of the process, see George Mosse, *The Image of Man: The Creation of Modern Masculinity* (New York: Oxford University Press, 1996).

60. Tony Jefferson, "Muscle, 'Hard Men,' and 'Iron' Mike Tyson: Reflections on Desire, Anxiety and the Embodiment of Masculinity," *Body and Society* 4, no. 1, 1998, 84.

61. Josef Keil, "Der Wert des Boxens für die Polizei," *Boxsport* 2, no. 70, Jan. 1922, 2.

62. Gustav Schäfer, *Boxen als Leibesübung, Kampfsport und Selbstverteidigung* (Oldenburg i. O.: Gerhard Stalling, 1925), 12. A recent article in the *New York Times* stated that a boxer's ability to take punches stemmed from a mixture of genetics, confidence, and stamina and suggested that no amount of training or "hardening" could improve it. In the words of one trainer, "Either you got chin [can take it], or you don't." See Geoffrey Gray, "A Glass Jaw Can Be a Matter of Heart," *New York Times*, Sept. 15, 2005, C24.

63. J. Müller-Mühlheim, *Der deutsche Tornado*, serialized in *Boxsport* 7, no. 341, Apr. 12, 1927, 25.

64. Paul Lerner, *Hysterical Men: War, Psychiatry, and the Politics of Trauma in Germany, 1890–1930* (Ithaca, NY: Cornell University, 2003), 250, 227.

65. Adolf Hitler, *Mein Kampf*, trans. Ralph Mannheim (Boston: Houghton Mifflin, 1962), 410; quoted in David Bathrick, "Max Schmeling on the Canvas," 129. Victor Klemperer used a boxing metaphor to describe Germany's military position in 1940 and to question Hitler's own ability to take it. On May 16, 1940, he wrote: "Hitler is like a boxer who must win in the first round; he cannot last two rounds." Klemperer, *I Will Bear Witness: A Diary of the Nazi Years, 1933–1941*, trans. Martin Chalmers (New York: Random House, 1998), 338.

66. Hans Natonek, "Bruder Boxer," *Berliner Börsen-Courier*, Mar. 4, 1927, repr. in *Glänzender Asphalt: Berlin im Feuilleton der Weimarer Republik*, ed. Christian Jäger and Erhard Schütz, 231 (Berlin: Fannei & Walz, 1994).

67. Kurt Doerry, "Das Sportgesicht," *Sport im Bild* 28, no. 3, Jan. 20, 1922, 86.

68. Rumpelstilzchen, *Mecker' nich!*, collected works, vol. 6, 1925/26 (Berlin: Brunnen, 1926), 346.

69. Max Schmeling, *–8 –9—aus* (Munich: Copress, 1956), 24.

70. Regarding surgical constructions of the "Schmiß," see Sander Gilman, *Making the Body Beautiful: A Cultural History of Aesthetic Surgery* (Princeton, NJ: Princeton University Press, 1999), 122–24.

71. For a discussion of this notion, see Judith Halberstam, *Female Masculinity* (Durham, NC: Duke University Press, 1998). Halberstam does not address boxing in Weimar Germany at all, but she does discuss women's boxing quite extensively in her book, and she reveals that she herself boxed.

72. Jenni Olson wrote this in the 'zine *Girljock* (summer 1992): 22–24; quoted in Halberstam, *Female Masculinity*, 273.

73. Kasimir Edschmid, *Sport um Gagaly*, (Berlin: Paul Zsolnay Verlag, 1928), 136.

74. Dr. Margarete Streicher, "Die Gestaltung des Frauenturnens in Österreich," speech at the *Erste öffentliche Tagung für die körperliche Erziehung der Frau*, March 23, 1925, Landesarchiv-Berlin, Helene-Lange-Archiv #3139-3140 (film #76-3084–76-3085), 127.

75. P. von Reznicek, *Auferstehung der Dame* (Stuttgart: Dieck and Co., 1928), 139.

76. A similar set of assumptions regarding the civilizing influence of female sports fans emerged recently in the context of Iranian soccer spectatorship. In April 2006, Iran's president Mahmud Ahmadinejad advocated lifting the ban on female spectators at soccer matches on the grounds that their very presence would make the men behave better. He quickly reversed himself, however, in the face of an uproar from religious leaders, and he rescinded his decision on May 8. See Elisabeth Kiderlen, "Warum die Iranerinnen jetzt Fußball gucken dürfen," *Die Zeit*, no. 25, June 14, 2006, 55; and Christof Siemes, "Die Gegenrevolution ist auffem Platz," *Die Zeit*, no. 26, June 22, 2006, 40. See also the 2006 Iranian film *Offside*, directed by Jafar Panahi and distributed by Sony Pictures Classics.

77. Dr. Erwin Petzall, "Die Frauen und der Faustkampf," *Boxsport* 5, no. 243, May 22, 1925, 9.

78. "Die Frauen und der Boxsport," *Boxsport* 5, no. 245, June 5, 1925, 6.

79. Rumpelstilzchen, feuilleton from Oct. 16, 1924 in *Haste Worte?*, 42–43.

80. "Wie Sie zusehen: Beobachtungen mit dem Rücken zum Ring," *Sport und Sonne*, 39–40. George Orwell made a similar comment in 1945, writing that "a boxing audience is always disgusting, and the behavior of the women, in particular, is such that the army, I believe, does not allow them to attend its contests." See his essay "The Sporting Spirit" (1945), http://orwell.ru/library/articles/spirit/English/e_spirit. Adrian Shubert notes the presence of an identical discourse in Spain with regard to women watching the bullfights. See Shubert, *Death and Money in the Afternoon: A History of the Spanish Bullfight* (New York: Oxford University Press, 1999), 109.

81. Mara Herberg, "Inge und der Boxkampf," *Sport im Bild* 32, no. 16, Aug. 6, 1926, 697.

82. Horst-Eberhard Richter, interviewed by Beate Lakotta and Katja Thimm, "Die Helden sind ratlos," *Der Spiegel* 40, Oct. 2, 2006, 150. Richter does not give a date for learning to box, but he states that he did so as a child, and he was born in 1923.

83. G. Bach, "Kampfgeist!," *Boxsport* 5, no. 226, Jan. 23, 1925, 2.

84. Martha Werth, *Frauenart und Leibesübungen* (Göttingen: n.p., 1921): 27.

85. Petzall, "Die Frauen und der Faustkampf," 9.

86. Frau Dr. Herrnfeld, discussion after the lectures at the conference "Die körperliche Erziehung der Frau im Hinblick auf die Berufsarbeit," Mar. 22, 1925. Landesarchiv-Berlin, Helene-Lange-Archiv #3139 (film #76-3084): 76.

87. Dr. Elsa Matz, "Die Frau und der sportliche Wettkampf," in *Tagungs-Bericht: Frauen-Turn-und Sporttagung zu Berlin, 12. bis 15. Juni 1929* (Berlin: Verlag der Fachbuchhandlung für Leibesübungen, 1929), 48.

88. Ada von Niendorf, "Der Frauensport und seine Wirklichkeit," *Garçonne. Junggesellin*, no. 8, 1931, 13.

89. Hans Ostwald, *Sittengeschichte der Inflation: Ein Kulturdokument aus den Jahren des Marksturzes* (Berlin: Neufeld und Henius, 1931), 74; excerpted and translated in *The Weimar Republic Sourcebook*, ed. Anton Kaes, Martin Jay, and Edward Dimendberg, 77 (Berkeley: University of California Press, 1994).

90. "Fünf Damenboxkämpfe und zwei Kämpfe zwischen Negern und Weißen," *Boxsport* 2, no. 65, Dec. 8, 1921, 7.

91. "... Boxkämpfe in Koblenz," *Boxsport* 2, no. 66/67, Dec. 21, 1921, 10.

92. Petzall, "Die Frauen und der Faustkampf," 6.

93. "Frankfurter Glossen: Erwähnungen allerlei Art zu den jüngsten vier Boxgroßkampftagen," *Boxsport* 2, no. 83, Apr. 21, 1922, 6.

94. *Sport im Bild* 28, no. 20, May 19, 1922, 822.

95. See Mel Gordon, *Voluptuous Panic: The Erotic World of Weimar Germany* (Venice, CA: Feral House, 2000).

96. Hargreaves, "Women's Boxing and Related Activities," 38.

97. "Vorstands-und Technische Ausschuß-Sitzung des Deutschen Reichsverbandes für Amateur-Boxen," *Boxsport* 2, no. 65, Dec. 8, 1921, 13.

98. *Boxsport* 5, no. 240, May 1, 1925, 7. More recently, the practice has resurfaced. Regina Halmich, for instance, boxed against Stefan Raab in what *Der Spiegel* described as a "Juxfight" (a jesting fight). For her troubles, Halmich took home 500,000 euros. Gerhard Pfeil, "Richtig schöne Schläge," *Der Spiegel* 20, May 14, 2007, 142–43.

99. J. Butler, *Bodies That Matter*, 109 (italics in original). In a similar maneuver in the United States, the California State Boxing Commission passed Rule 256 in 1940, which banned women from receiving licenses to referee, second, or manage in the ring when male boxers were involved. The commission only passed the measure after Belle Martell became the first woman licensed to referee boxing matches in California less than one month earlier. Cecilia Rasmussen, "1st Woman Boxing Referee Rolled With Punches," *Los Angeles Times*, May 21, 2006, B2.

100. "Abschied mit Kinnhaken," Stadtblatt, *Berliner Tageblatt*, Aug. 2, 1928, 1.

101. *Die Austernprinzessin*, directed by Ernst Lubitsch, written by Hanns Kräly and Ernst Lubitsch (Germany, 1919). Kräly and Lubitsch freely adapted the storyline from Leo Fall's 1907 operetta, *The Dollar Princess*. The film purports to take place in America but deals with specifically German (and European) problems, such as the declining financial fortunes of the aristocracy and the competition between women for marriageable men. The American setting, however, reflects the Weimar Republic's fascination with the New World as well as Lubitsch's own reputation as an "American director." See Thomas Elsaesser, *Weimar Cinema and After: Germany's Historical Imaginary* (New York: Routledge, 2000), 209.

102. H. Volckert-Lietz, "Die Mode als Kampfmittel," *Münchner Neueste Nachrichten*, no. 361, Aug. 27–28, 1921, 20; quoted in Irene Guenther, *Nazi Chic? Fashioning Women in the Third Reich* (New York: Berg, 2004), 63. Although the

United States faced no such "Frauenüberschuß" (surplus of women) after the First World War, a scene appeared in the 1924 American film *The Last Man on Earth*, directed by J. P. Blystone, that bore a remarkable resemblance to the one in *The Oyster Princess*. The American film presented an apocalyptic future in which a disease has killed all adult males, except for one. The U.S. government buys him and brings him to the Senate chambers, where two female senators box over the right to own him. For a brief synopsis, see *Sports Films: A Complete Reference*, compiled by Harvey Marc Zucker and Lawrence J. Babich (Jefferson, NC: McFarland, 1987), 106.

103. *East and West* (directed by Sidney Goldin, 1923), simultaneously released as *Ost und West*, with Yiddish intertitles as well. Picon, like Oswalda, cultivated a tomboyish persona, frequently cross-dressing in her films and giving famously physical, gymnastic performances. Picon went to Europe in the early 1920s, where she made at least two other films, in addition to *East and West*.

104. Claire Waldoff, "Wer schmeißt denn da mit Lehm," lyrics repr. in *Die Lieder der Claire Waldoff*, ed. Helga Bemmann (Berlin: arani-Verlag, 1983), 5.

105. "Eduard demonstriert Boxen," *Boxsport* 5, no. 240, May 1, 1925, 9.

106. Quoted in Rumpelstilzchen, feuilleton from June 8, 1921, in *Berliner Allerlei*, collected works, vol. 1 (Berlin: Verlag der Täglichen Rundschau, 1922), 242.

107. Max Schmeling, *Mein Leben—meine Kämpfe* (Leipzig: Grethlein, 1930), 41.

108. Joe Biewer, "Heinrich Müller: Wundersame Geschichte einer Entwicklung," *Das elegante Köln*, July 2, 1929, 4. The sociologist Loïc Wacquant describes boxers as proud of "being self-made men in the literal sense that they produce themselves through daily bodily work in the gym." See "Whores, Slaves and Stallions: Languages of Exploitation and Accommodation among Boxers," *Body and Society* 7, nos. 2/3, 2001, 188–89.

109. Mr. S., "Heraus aus dem Ballsaal—auf den Sportplatz!," *Die Freundschaft*, no. 25, 1920, 3.

110. Hermann Berghausen, letter to the editor, *Die Freundschaft*, no. 26 or 27, 1920),4.

111. Magnus Hirschfeld, *Berlins drittes Geschlecht* (1904), 54, quoted in Bernd Wedemeyer, *Starke Männer, starke Frauen*, 99.

112. See, to offer just two examples, its use in Hans Bötticher, "Bessere Fußarbeit," *Boxsport* 7, no. 338, Mar. 22, 1927, 1; and in Bertolt Brecht, "Gedenktafel für 12 Weltmeister," in *Die Gedichte von Bertolt Brecht in einem Band* (Frankfurt/M: Suhrkamp, 1993), 308.

113. H. von Wedderkop, "Hans Breitensträter," *Die Weltbühne* 17, no. 38 (Sept. 22, 1921): 296.

114. See Kai Marcel Sicks, "'Der Querschnitt' oder: Die Kunst des Sporttreibens," in *Leibhaftige Moderne: Körper in Kunst und Massenmedien 1918 bis 1933*, ed. Michael Cowan and Kai Marcel Sicks, 45 (Bielefeld: transcript Verlag, 2005).

115. Gustav Schäfer, *Boxen als Leibesübung*, 10.

116. R. W. Connell, "An Iron Man: The Body and some Contradictions of Hegemonic Masculinity," in *Sport, Men, and the Gender Order: Critical Feminist Perspectives*, ed. Michael A. Messner and Donald F. Sabo, 94 (Champaign, IL: Human Kinetics, 1990).

117. "Nachlese vom Prenzel-Davies-Kampf," *Boxsport* 2, no. 90, June 9, 1922, 2.

118. J. Müller-Mühlheim, *Der deutsche Tornado*, serialized in *Boxsport* 7, no. 341, Apr. 12, 1927, 25.

119. Walfried Lohmeyer, "Von der Psyche des Boxkampfes," *Boxsport* 2, no. 69, Jan. 12, 1922, 1.

120. Wacquant, "Whores, Slaves and Stallions," 188.

121. See Peter Gay, *Weimar Culture: The Outsider as Insider* (New York: Harper and Row, 1970).

122. For a history of the Miss Germany competition, see Veit Didczuneit and Dirk Külow, *Miss Germany: Die deutsche Schönheitskönigin* (Hamburg: S & L Medien Contor, 1998), 13. Hildegard Quandt was crowned the first "Miss Germany" in Berlin's Sportpalast on March 5, 1927.

123. Christiane Eisenberg, "Massensport in der Weimarer Republik. Ein statistischer Überblick," *Archiv für Sozialgeschichte* 33 (1993): 165.

124. "Was waren uns die Olympischen Spiele?" *Frankfurter Zeitung* 73, no. 601, Aug. 13, 1928, sports sec., 3.

125. Hannes Bork, *Der Deutsche Teufel* (serialized), *Boxsport* 5, no. 225, Jan. 16, 1925, 24.

126. Joe Biewer, "Heinrich Müller: Wundersame Geschichte einer Entwicklung," *Das elegante Köln*, July 2, 1929, 4.

127. "Springer und Werfer in Amsterdam," *Illustriertes Sportblatt: Sport-Spiegel des Berliner Tageblatts*, July 19, 1928, 2 (3. Beiblatt [supplement]).

128. "Schmelings zweite Heimkehr," *Sport und Gesundheit*, no. 41, 1929, 656.

129. "Da rollt der Dollar," *Boxwoche*, no. 279, Mar. 10, 1929, cover.

130. Max Schmeling, "Wie kamen Sie zu ihrem Schicksal?" *Das elegante Köln*, Dec. 1, 1929, 20.

131. "Wie Schmeling wahrer Weltmeister wurde," *B.Z. am Mittag*, July 4, 1931, 1. Schmeling had defeated Young Stribling in a technical knockout.

132. "Zwei Machthaber," *Ulk*, no. 48, 1929, 40. Walter Herzberg drew the caricatures.

133. The film in which he performed the daredevil stunts was titled *Der Held des Tages. Sensationsfilm in 7 Akten* [Hero of the day—a sensation film in 7 acts], directed by Rudi Bach (Berlin, Althoff, 1921). His later film bore the surprisingly similar title *Der Herr des Todes*, based on a novel by Karl Rosner, directed by Hans Steinhoff (Berlin: Maxim Film-Gesellschaft, n.d.).

134. Peterssen appeared under the pseudonym "Carl Brisson" in the 1928 film, directed by Alfred Hitchcock, whose German title was *Eines starken Mannes Liebe*. Both the review of this film in *Berliner Tageblatt*, July 15, 1928; in sec. "Lichtspiel-Rundschau," 7. Beiblatt [supplement]) and in *B.Z. am Mittag*, July 13, 1928, in sec. "Film-B.Z." mentioned the fact that Peterssen had a starring role, since most Berlin boxing fans would have remembered him from his frequent bouts at the Sportpalast in the early and mid-1920s.

135. Prenzel appeared in *Und es lockte der Ruf der sündigen Welt*, directed by Carl Boese (Germany: Greenbaum-Film, 1925). Some in the press would later lament that he had not made more films. In 1931, Prenzel's radio play-by-play for Schmeling's victorious fight against Young Stribling earned him rave reviews. *B.Z. am Mittag* exclaimed, "Prenzel, Prenzel, you really should, of course, still become an actor, a film actor, a sound film actor." "Ein 'Wiederhören' mit Prenzel," *B.Z. am Mittag*, July 4, 1931, 2.

136. Rumpelstilzchen, feuilleton from Oct. 18, 1923, in *Bei mir—Berlin!*, collected works, v. 4, 1923/24 (Berlin: Brunnen, 1924), 58.

137. Friedrich Jahn, "Von 'Hoffnungen' im Boxsport," *Boxsport*, no. 217, 1924, 2, quoted in Ulrike Schaper, "'Das Boxen ist ein Sport wahrer Männlichkeit': Geschlecht im Ring: Boxen und Männlichkeit in der Weimarer Republik," paper presented at the Conference *"Geschlechterkonkurrenzen,"* Feb. 2–4, 2006, and available at www.ruendal.de/aim/tagung06/pdfs/schaper/pdf, 8.

138. Photograph for Ullstein Verlag, 1909 (www.ullsteinbild.de, Bild Nr. 00973511), repr. in *Der Querschnitt* 13, no. 5 (Aug. 1933): 340.

139. *Steuermann Holk*, directed by Ludwig Wolff, 1920 (produced by Maxim-Film-Gesellschaft Ebner & Co., Berlin). The film itself has survived only as a short fragment, which includes this scene, now in the possession of the Bundesarchiv-Filmarchiv and screened in fall 2009 at the Silent Film Festival in Pordenone, Italy. I am indebted to Philipp Stiasny for calling this fragment to my attention and sending me a brief description of its content.

140. Hans Egon Holthusen recalled the statement, which appeared as a caption to a photograph of a seventeen-year-old girl in the newspaper. See "'…Joe, mach die Musik von damals nach!,'" in *Alltag in der Weimarer Republik: Erinnerungen an eine unruhige Zeit*, ed. Rudolf Pörtner, 444 (Düsseldorf: ECON, 1990).

141. Carla Verständig, "Rhythmik, Leibesübungen und freie Frau," *Die Leibesübungen*, no. 12, June 20, 1927, 281.

142. *Sport im Bild* 28, no. 11, Mar. 17, 1922, 409.

143. "Zwei Filmschönheiten beim lustigen Boxkampf," *Sport und Gesundheit*, no. 19, 1930, cover.

144. Franz Kirchberg, "Frauensport und Frauengymnastik an der Deutschen Hochschule für Leibesübungen," *Die Leibesübungen*, no. 9, Aug. 1923, 416.

145. *Blätter des Sportpalastes: Programm*, no. 1 (Berlin, Wintersportsaison 1925/26): 23.

146. The Brandenburg women's track and field club received coaching at the punching ball, as reported in "Aus den Trainingquartieren," *Deutsche Sportzeitung* 20, no. 2, Jan. 12, 1926, 2; and *Sport und Gesundheit* featured American swimmers engaged in a sparring match on another of its covers (no. 17, 1929), although it dismissed this as "a funny boxing match."

147. "Heute boxt die Frau," *Die Arena: Das Sport-Magazin*, no. 1, Oct. 1926, 15.

148. P. von Reznicek, *Auferstehung der Dame*, 53.

149. Paul Morgan, "Ihre Sorgen. Ein Dialog in 3 Tageszeiten," *Sport im Bild* 34, no. 9, Apr. 27, 1928, 562.

150. Max Leusch, "Boxen für alle! Lernt alle Boxen!," *Sport und Sonne*, no. 1, Jan. 1928, 46.

151. Gustav Schäfer, *Boxen als Leibesübung, Kampfsport und Selbstverteidigung* (Oldenburg i. O.: Gerhard Stalling, 1925), 10.

152. See Birgit Haustedt, *Die wilden Jahre in Berlin: Eine Klatsch- und Kulturgeschichte der Frauen* (Berlin: edition ebersbach, 2002), 108. The relationship between Franz and Helen Hessel and the Frenchman Henri Pierre Roch became the basis for the novel and film *Jules et Jim*.

153. Schmeling, *Erinnerungen*, 99.

154. Baum, *Es war alles ganz anders*, 376.

155. Ibid., 377.

156. Quoted in Birgit Haustedt, *Die wilden Jahre in Berlin: Eine Klatsch- und Kulturgeschichte der Frauen* (Berlin: Edition Ebersbach, 2002), 125.

157. Birgit Haustedt makes this point regarding Baum. See Haustedt, *Die wilden Jahre in Berlin*, 120.

158. Dr. Franz Kirchberg, "Frauensport und Frauengymnastik an der Deutsche Hochschule für Leibesübungen," *Die Leibesübungen*, no. 9. Aug. 1923. 419.

159. Baum, *Es war alles ganz anders*. 377.

160. Annemarie Kopp, "Emanzipation durch Sport" (1927), repr. in *Frau und Sport*, ed. Gertrud Pfister (Frankfurt/M: Fischer, 1980), 69.

161. Erik Ernst Schwabach, *Die Revolutionierung der Frau* (Leipzig: Der Neue Geistverlag, 1928), 87.

162. Quoted in Christiane Eisenberg, "Massensport in der Weimarer Republik. Ein Statistischer Überblick," *Archiv für Sozialgeschichte* 33 (1993): 165, n. 111.

163. See, for example, the 1923 photograph of such a demonstration in Berlin's Lustgarten, in front of a crowd of several hundred. *Sport im Bild* 29, no. 23. June 8, 1923. 722.

164. "Selbstverteidigung," *Der Weg der Frau*, no. 3. 1932, repr. in *Neue Frauen: Die Zwanziger Jahre*, ed. Kristine von Soden and Maruta Schmidt, 171 (Berlin [West]: Elefanten Press, 1988).

165. As with so many of the films of the Weimar period, copies of *Die fightende Dame* (The Fighting Lady) no longer exist, and the *Bundesarchiv Filmarchiv* in Berlin had only sketchy information regarding the film's background, production, and distribution. I have based my description of the film on the plot outline provided by J. Michler, "Boxen als Selbstschutz für Damen: Ein netter Film aus dem Leben," *Boxsport* 7, no. 346, May 17, 1927, 8.

166. "Rund um Dempsey!" *Boxsport*, June 12, 1925, 4.

167. See Bernd Wedemeyer. For the American context during the same period, see John F. Kasson, *Houdini, Tarzan, and the Perfect Man: The White Male Body and the Challenge of Modernity in America* (New York: Hill and Wang, 2001), 29.

168. See Rumpelstilzchen, *Berliner Allerlei*, collected works, vol. 1, 1921 (Berlin: Verlag der Täglichen Rundschau, 1922), 242, 189.

169. Jack Dempsey, interviewed by Djuna Barnes (1921), in *I Could Never Be Lonely Without a Husband: Interviews by Djuna Barnes*, ed. Alyce Barry (London: Virago, 1987), 284.

170. "Impressionen im Ring," *Sport im Bild* 28, no. 11 (Mar. 17, 1922), 391.

171. Petzall, "Die Frauen und der Faustkampf," 9.

172. Giese, *Geist im Sport*, 81.

173. Hassenberger, "Breitensträters Debut in Wien," *Boxsport*, July 26, 1922, 6.

174. H. von Wedderkop, "Hans Breitensträter," 298.

175. Rumpelstilzchen, feuilleton from Oct. 16, 1924, in *Haste Worte?*, 43.

176. Hans Breitensträter, "Soll ein Sportsmann heiraten?" in *Der Querschnitt* (1932), repr. in *Der Querschnitt: Facsimile Querschnitt*, 287–88.

177. Bernd Wedemeyer, "'Ein Ereignis für den ganzen Westen.' Körperkultur in Weimar zwischen Öffentlichkeit, Kunst und Kultur," in *Leibhaftige Moderne: Körper in Kunst und Massenmedien 1918 bis 1933*, ed. Michael Cowan and Kai Marcel Sicks, 187–99 (Bielefeld: transcript, 2005).

178. Schmeling, *Erinnerungen*, 85–86. For a good example of one of these books, see *Der männliche Körper*, ed. Dr. Emil Schaeffer, Schaubücher (coffee-table book) 31 (Zürich: Orell Füssli, 1931).

179. Erwin Mehl, review of *Männliche Körperbildung*, ed. Eugen Matthias and Fritz Giese, in *Die Leibesübungen*, no. 20, Oct. 20, 1926, 485.

180. The photograph of Schmeling appeared in *Sport und Sonne*, no. 8, Aug. 1927, 465; and again in *Sport und Sonne* 5, no. 6, June 1, 1929, 275. It appeared on the cover of *Boxsport* 7, no. 339, Mar. 29, 1927.

181. "Schmelings zweite Heimkehr," *Sport und Gesundheit*, no. 41, 1929, 656.

182. Magnus Hirschfeld, *Geschlechtskunde*, vol. 4 (Stuttgart: Julius Püttmann, 1930), 179.

183. For the example of Erich Brandl, see *Der Querschnitt* 5, no. 9 (1925): 816. For the triptych featuring Hartkopp, Scholz, and Müller, see *Der Querschnitt* 9, no. 5 (1929), repr. in *Der Querschnitt: Facsimile Querschnitt durch den Querschnitt 1921–1936*, ed. Wilmont Haacke and Alexander von Baeyer (Frankfurt/M: Ullstein, 1977), 146.

184. *Freundschaft und Freiheit: Ein Blatt für Männerrechte gegen Spießbürgermoral, Pfaffenherrschaft und Weiberwirtschaft*, no. 7. Mar. 17, 1921, 54.

185. *Freundschaft und Freiheit*, no. 3. Feb. 17, 1921, 54.

186. *Die Insel: Das Magazin der Einsamen* 5, no. 2, Feb. 1930, cover. The glorification of male fighters has always contained an element of homoeroticism. As Allen Guttmann writes, "The frenzy of the mostly male spectators at a boxing match must be more than the excitement occasioned by the demonstration of the manly art of self-defense." See Guttmann, *The Erotic in Sports* (New York: Columbia University Press, 1996), 146. For a discussion of the homoerotic appeal of today's sports stars, in general, see Mark Simpson, "How sports became the new gay porn," *Out*, July 2006, cover article. Simpson dubs this phenomenon "sporno."

187. "Frau Adi. Eine Sport-Groteske von Hanoff," *Sport im Bild* 28, no. 52. Dec. 29, 1922. 2051.

188. Herberg, "Inge und der Boxkampf," 697.

189. *Die Boxerbraut: Lustspiel in 5 Akten*, directed by Johannes Guter, written by Robert Liebmann (Germany, Universum-Film AG [Ufa], 1926). The film is difficult to find, although I managed to view a version with Russian intertitles. A four-page summary of the plot can be found in the Bundesarchiv-Filmarchiv, Berlin, File # 1886.

190. *Abwege*, directed by G. W. Pabst, 1928 (produced by Erda-Film GmbH for Ufa).

191. Janice Taylor, "Die Herren Athleten," trans. Hans Wagenseil, *Der Querschnitt* 12, no. 6 (June 1932): 193.

192. Schmeling, *Erinnerungen*, 140.

193. Review of *Liebe im Ring*, *Kinematograph*, no. 65 (1930), available in Bundesarchiv-Filmarchiv [Mappe #9906].

194. *Knockout*, directed by Karl Lamac and Hans Zerlett (Germany, 1934).

195. *Liebe im Ring*, directed by Reinhold Schünzel (Berlin: Terra-Film, 1931), censor cards available at Bundesarchiv-Filmarchiv, Berlin, microfiche #837, Prüf. #25333.

196. "Die Europameisterschaften der Amateure," *Boxsport* 5, no. 243, May 22, 1925, 17.

197. For a discussion of Räderscheidt's work, including this painting, see Janina Nentwig, "Akt und Sport: Anton Räderscheidt's 'hundertprozentige Frau,'" in *Leibhaftige Moderne: Körper in Kunst und Massenmedien 1918 bis 1933*, ed. Michael Cowan and Kai Marcel Sicks, 101 (Bielefeld: transcript Verlag, 2005).

198. Claire Waldoff, "Hannelore," lyrics by Willy Hagen; repr. in *Die Lieder der Claire Waldoff*, 43.

199. Friedrich Ostermoor, "Joe Edwards boxt mit der Polizei," *Die Arena: Das Sportmagazin*, no. 1, Oct. 1926, 14. An artist identified only as Eichberg did the illustrations.

200. *Sport und Sonne*, Jan. 1927, cover.

201. Marlice Hinz, "Reiseflirts, gnädige Frau?" *Sport im Bild* 34, no. 3, Feb. 3, 1928, 140.

202. *Sport und Spiel auf See*, brochure for the Hamburg-Amerika Line (Hapag), 1926, n.p.

203. Photograph taken from *Neue Frauen: Die zwanziger Jahre*, ed. Kristine von Soden and Maruta Schmidt, 140 (Berlin: Elefanten, 1988).

204. "Sportverniedlichung: boxende Filmdivagruppe," in Fritz Giese, *Geist im Sport. Probleme und Forderungen mit 81 Abbildungen* (Munich: Delphin, 1925), 70.

205. *Sport und Sonne* 5, no. 16, Nov. 15, 1929, 590.

206. Quoted in Ruland, *Das war Berlin*, 191.

207. *Sport im Bild* 36, no. 17, Aug. 26, 1930, 1270.

208. Karina, "Miss Kiki langweilt sich…," *Die Arena: Das Sportmagazin*, no. 3, Dec. 1926, 194–96.

209. Patrice Petro, *Joyless Streets: Women and Melodramatic Representation in Weimar Germany* (Princeton, NJ: Princeton University Press, 1989), 34.

210. J. Butler, *Bodies That Matter*, 237.

211. The planned exhibition on women's boxing matches, which was never realized, was published in *Das "Museum für Leibesübungen" zu Berlin 1924–1934: Dokumente und Materialien*, Sporthistorische Blätter 4 (Berlin: Sportmuseum Berlin, 1994), 75.

212. Petro, *Joyless Streets*, 34.

213. Walther von Hollander, "Frauensport, aber richtig!" *Die Koralle: Magazin für alle Freunde von Natur und Technik* 29, July 19, 1936, 961–63.

214. Gerhard Pfeil, "Richtig schöne Schläge," *Der Spiegel* 20, May 14, 2007, 143. On Susi Kentikian's German citizenship, see Nina Willborn, "Süße Susi filmt ihre Box-Woche," *Bild-Zeitung*, www.bild.de (Aug. 26, 2008).

Chapter 3

1. Werner Scheff, *Der Läufer von Marathon: Ein Sportsroman* (Berlin: Drei Masken, 1928), 335–36. In the film version of the story, released in 1933, Georg Cornelius lives. See the Zulassungskarten, Prüf-Nr. 33125, in the Bundesarchiv-Filmarchiv. Scheff also published the tennis novel *Das weiße Spiel* in 1928 (see chap. 1).

2. Ibid., 341–42. Scheff tapped into a larger European anxiety about the "yellow peril" that extended to sports. A committee for promoting youth sports in 1905, for instance, attributed Japan's recent military victory over Russia to its superior physical fitness and warned that Germany risked falling behind in this area. See Derek Linton, "Reforming the Urban Primary School in Wilhelmine Germany," *History of Education* 13, no. 3 (1984): 217. This belief in Asian athletes' purported superiority in running events seems to have waned markedly by the last half of the twentieth century. Liu Xiang, who won the gold medal in the 110-meter hurdles at the 2004 Olympics, actually saw his win as an important blow against the stereotype of *inferior* Asian runners: "I believe I achieved a modest miracle for the yellow-skinned Chinese people and the Asian people." Quoted in Evan Osnos, "The Boxing Rebellion," *New Yorker*, Feb. 4, 2008, 58–59.

3. George L. Mosse, *Nationalism and Sexuality: Respectability and Abnormal Sexuality in Modern Europe* (New York: Howard Fertig, 1985), 31.

4. Quoted in Horst Ueberhorst, "The Importance of the Historians' Quarrel and the Problem of Continuity for the German History of Sport," *Journal of Sport History* 17, no. 2 (1990): 238.

5. Arnold Hahn, "Entdeckung des weiblichen Körpers," *Das Tage-Buch* 6, no. 46, Nov. 14, 1925, 1720.

6. *Der Herr*, no. 2, 1932, 2. Quoted in Tina Dingel, "Der männliche Körper als Schaufensterpuppe? Herrenmode und Konstruktion eines 'adäquaten' Körpers," in *Leibhaftige Moderne: Körper in Kunst und Massenmedien 1918 bis 1933*, ed. Michael Cowan and Kai Marcel Sicks, 175 (Bielefeld: transcript Verlag, 2005).

7. Siegfried Kracauer (1927), describing the Weisenhof Siedlung in Stuttgart, quoted in Janet Ward, *Weimar Surfaces: Urban Visual Culture in 1920s Germany* (Berkeley: University of California Press, 2001), 62.

8. Willi Baumeister, *Hochsprung* (1928). For a good discussion of Baumeister's artistic focus on athletes, see Michael Mackenzie, "The Athlete as Machine: A Figure of Modernity in Weimar Germany," in Cowan and Sicks, *Leibhaftige Moderne*.

9. Gertrud Pfister, "Sport auf dem grünen Rasen: Fußball und Leichtathletik," in *Sport in Berlin: Vom Ritterturnier zum Stadtmarathon*, ed. Gertrud Pfister and Gerd Steins, 73 (Berlin: Forum für Sportgeschichte, 1987).

10. Otto Peltzer, *Umkämpftes Leben: Sportjahre zwischen Nurmi und Zatopek* (Berlin: Verlag der Nation, 1955), 10.

11. Christiane Eisenberg, *"English Sports" und deutsche Bürger: Eine Gesellschaftsgeschichte 1800–1939* (Paderborn: Ferdinand Schöningh, 1999), 250–61. Allen Guttmann lists seven characteristics of modern sports, including rationalization, quantification, the quest for records, and the specialization of roles, all of which apply to track and field and only in exceptional cases to *Turnen*. See Guttmann, *From Ritual to Record: The Nature of Modern Sports* (New York: Columbia University Press, 2004).

12. Georg Kaiser, "Man in the Tunnel" (1929), quoted in John Hoberman, *Sport and Ideology*, 8 (Austin: University of Texas Press, 1984).

13. Rumpelstilzchen mentioned it in his feuilleton from Sept. 26, 1929, in *Piept es?*, collected works, vol. 10, 1929/1930 (Berlin: Brunnen, 1930), 38.

14. SPD delegate Toni Pfülf, quoted in "Leibesübungen und Reichstag," *Der Leichtathlet* 2, no. 32, Aug, 10, 1925, 4.

15. Gideon Reuveni, "Sports and the Militarization of Jewish Society," in *Emancipation through Muscles: Jews and Sports in Europe*, ed. Michael Brenner and Gideon Reuveni, 48–49 (Lincoln: University of Nebraska Press, 2006).

16. Quoted in Barbara J. Keys, *Globalizing Sport: National Rivalry and International Community in the 1930s* (Cambridge, MA: Harvard University Press, 2006), 123 and 234, n.42. The Weimar Republic adopted the black, gold, and red flag originally popularized by the democratic-nationalist movement in the first half of the nineteenth century. For a track and field journal's report on the *Turnen* movement's decision, see "Zum Austritt der DT aus dem DRfL," *Der Leichtathlet* 2, no. 37, Sept. 16, 1925, 5.

17. Prof. Dr. Steffen, "Die Leichtathletik im Rahmen des Deutschen Turnfestes," *Die Leibesübungen*, no. 19/20, Oct. 30, 1923, 480.

18. Edmund Neuendorff, *Turnerjugend* 9, no. 9, May 7, 1927, 157; repr. in "Offener Brief an Edmund Neuendorff," *Der Leichtathlet* 4, no. 22, May 31, 1927, 5.

19. See Frank Becker, *Amerikanismus in Weimar: Sportsymbole und politische Kultur 1918–1933* (Wiesbaden: Deutscher-Universitäts-Verlag, 1993), esp. 30–31.

20. See Andrew D. Morris, *Marrow of the Nation: A History of Sport and Physical Culture in Republican China* (Berkeley: University of California Press, 2004).

21. For a discussion of Weimar Germany's fascination with America in the business context, see Mary Nolan, *Visions of Modernity: American Business and the Modernization of Germany* (New York: Oxford University Press, 1994).

22. Quoted in Raffael Scheck, *Mothers of the Nation: Right-Wing Women in Weimar Germany* (New York: Berg, 2004), 97.

23. See Winfried Joch, "Von Amateur zum Kleinunternehmer," in *Schneller, höher, weiter: Eine Geschichte des Sports*, ed. Hans Sarkowicz, 244 (Frankfurt/M: Insel, 1996).

24. W. H. Haës, "Die Amerikaner," *Der Leichtathlet* 2, no. 37, Sept. 16, 1925, 10.

25. Michael Mackenzie, "From Athens to Berlin: The 1936 Olympics and Leni Riefenstahl's *Olympia*," *Critical Inquiry* 29, no. 2 (winter 2003): 302–36.

26. Albert Conrad-Hansen, "Film und Leibesübungen: Einige Worte über die Bedeutung des Filmes für Turnen und Sport," *Die Leibesübungen*, no. 20, Oct. 20, 1926, 466.

27. Dr. Hans Loose, "Erlebtes und Geschautes anläßlich der Deutschen Meisterschaften in Leichtathletik," *Die Leibesübungen*, no. 18, Sept. 20, 1926, 429.

28. Richard Honisch, "Wirtschaft und Leibesübungen," *Die Leibesübungen* 3, no. 22, 1927, 532; quoted in Frank Becker, "Der Sportler als 'moderner Menschentyp.' Entwürfe für eine neue Körperlichkeit in der Weimarer Republik," in *Körper mit Geschichte: Der menschliche Körper als Ort der Selbst- und Weltdeutung*, ed. Clemens Wischermann and Stefan Haas, 239 (Stuttgart: Franz Steiner, 2000).

29. See Michael Hau, *The Cult of Health and Beauty in Germany: A Social History, 1890–1930* (Chicago: University of Chicago Press, 2003), 136.

30. Sebastian Haffner wrote this in 1939. See his *Geschichte eines Deutschen: Die Erinnerungen 1914–1933* (Munich: Deutscher Taschenbuch Verlag, 2004), 73–74.

31. Richard Harbott, "Der deutsche Sprinterkurs im Frankfurter Stadion," *Die Leibesübungen*, no. 13, July 5, 1926, 314.

32. John Hoberman, *Mortal Engines: The Science of Performance and the Dehumanization of Sport* (New York: Free Press, 1992), 5.

33. "Der Sportsmann als Versuchs-Kaninchen," *Berliner Illustrirte Zeitung* 40, no. 22, May 31, 1931, 885.

34. Dr. Otto Peltzer, "Wer ist der beste 400-m-Läufer der Welt," *Der Leichtathlet* 5, no. 45, Nov. 6, 1928, 6.

35. Hoberman, *Mortal Engines*, 134–48.

36. Fritz Giese, *Geist im Sport* (Munich: Delphin, 1925), 29.

37. Eugen Kißling, "Deutsche Gewichtheber gehen in Front," *Sport und Sonne*, no. 6, June 1928, 353. On physical bulk as a marker of wastefulness, see Maren Möhring, *Marmorleiber: Körperbildung in der deutschen Nacktkultur (1890–1930)* (Köln: Böhlau Verlag, 2004), 298.

38. Dr. Willy Meisl, "Die Leichtathletik," in *Die Olympischen Spiele in Amsterdam 1928*, ed. Deutscher Reichsausschuß für Leibesübungen, 49 (Leipzig: Verlag für Industrie und Kultur, 1928).

39. Rumpelstilzchen, feuilleton from July 3, 1924, in *Bei mir—Berlin!*, collected works, vol. 4, 1923/24 (Berlin: Brunnen, 1924), 343.

40. Käte Bruns, "Kampfsport der Frau?" *Sport und Gesundheit*, no. 8, 1929, 121.

41. "Athletik im Frauensport," *Sport und Sonne* 6, no. 10, Oct./Nov. 1930, 331. Interestingly, this same article was reprinted in a magazine for military sports, which tended to be more socially conservative. See "Athletik im Frauensport," *Sportgeist* 2, no. 7, July/Sept. 1931, 16.

42. Walter Ball, "Das Geheimnis der Leistungsfähigkeit in der Damenleichtathletik," *Damen-Sport und Damen-Turnen* 2, no. 12, June 1919, 135.

43. Janet Ward describes the general tendency in Weimar Germany to view "the body as surface." See Ward, *Weimar Surfaces*, 228.

44. Berliner Sport-Club, "Über modernen Frauensport," *Sport im Bild* 30, no. 9, May 9, 1924, 460.

45. H. Reinking, "Der Sport und seine Eingliederung in die körperliche Erziehung des weiblichen Geschlechts," in *Die körperliche Ertüchtigung der Frau* (Berlin: F.A. Herbig, 1925), 95.

46. Milly Reuter, "Athletisch oder graziös? Eine zeitgemäße Frauenfrage," *Sport im Bild* 32, no. 18, Sept. 3, 1926, 790.

47. Fritz Kniese, "Werde Schön: Schönheits- und Gesundheitstips in Wort und Bild," *Sport und Sonne*, no. 1, Jan. 1927, 36.

48. Poem quoted in Dr. Helmut Kost, "Sportfrau und Frauensport," *Die Leibesübungen*, no. 3, Feb. 5, 1930, 50. See also "Frauen-Turn-und Sporttagung in Berlin," *Der Leichtathlet* 6, no. 25, June 17, 1929, 14, which similarly emphasized the Teutonic woman's strength.

49. Werner Scheff, *Der Läufer von Marathon*, 20.

50. Advertisement for Carmol liniment, *Der Leichtathlet* 8, no. 28, July 21, 1931, 9.

51. Alexander Abraham, "Die Frau im Kampfsport," *Sport und Sonne*, no. 10, Oct. 1927, 582.

52. "Aesthetische Bewegungen in der Athletik: Kugelstoßen eine besonders gute Übung," *Sport und Sonne*, no. 8, Aug. 1927, 470.

53. Bruno Mahler, "Die Wurfübungen," *Die Leibesübungen*, no. 19, Oct. 5, 1930, 582–83.

54. Lisa Groß, "Die neuen deutschen Frauen-Rekorde," *Der Leichtathlet* 3, no. 48, Nov. 30, 1926, 22.

55. Heinrich Mann, "Sie reichen sich die Hände. Eine Zeitbetrachtung," *Uhu* 3, no. 4, January 1927. The illustration appeared on p. 47, the quotation on p. 50.

56. "Neues im Frauensport," *Der Leichtathlet* 6, no. 24, June 10, 1929, 13.

57. *Die Olympischen Spiele in Los Angeles 1932*, ed. Cigaretten-Bilderdienst Hamburg-Bahrenfeld (Hamburg-Bahrenfeld: H. F. und Ph. F. Reemtsma, 1932), 43.

58. Wolf Hart, "Auch die Damen die S.C.C. gewinnen," *Der Leichtathlet* 2, no. 23, June 8, 1925, 16; "Die Leistungen der Frauen," *Der Leichtathlet* 3, no. 34, Aug. 24, 1926, 13.

59. Karl Ritter von Halt, quoted in Walter Kühn, "Wohin führt der Weg? Eine kritische Betrachtung zur Frauensportbewegung," *Die Leibesübungen*, no. 8, Apr. 20, 1926, 193.

60. Rudolph Stratz, *Lill: Der Roman eines Sportmädchens* (Berlin: August Scherl, 1929), 60, 110, 125.

61. Rumpelstilzchen, feuilleton from June 16, 1927, in *Berliner Funken*, collected works, vol. 7, 1926/27 (Berlin: Brunnen, 1927), 339. Only Siegfried possessed

the skills and strength to defeat Brunhilde, which he secretly did on behalf of Gunther.

62. "Die moderne Amazone," *Sport und Gesundheit*, no. 40, 1930, cover.

63. Rudolf Hartung, "Männliche Körpererziehung im Lichte der Bodeschen Ausdrucksgymnastik," *Die Leibesübungen*, no. 23, Dec. 5, 1927, 555.

64. Carl Diem, "Zum neuen Jahre," *Die Leibesübungen*, no. 1, Jan. 15, 1925, 2.

65. Josef Waitzer, "Die Arbeit des Meisters," *Sport und Sonne*, no. 1, Jan. 1927, 10.

66. *Metropolis*, directed by Fritz Lang (Germany, Ufa, 1927).

67. "Ein Neger läuft 220 Yards in Weltrekordzeit," *Der Leichtathlet* 2, no. 18, May 4, 1925, 11.

68. *Die Olympischen Spiele in Los Angeles 1932*, 14.

69. Paul Landau, "Girlkultur: Von der Amerikanisierung Europas," *Westermanns Monatshefte* 141, no. 845, Jan. 1927, 565.

70. Heinz Cavalier, "Otto Peltzer," *Der Leichtathlet* 8, no. 26, July 7, 1931, 3.

71. Reinhold Simon, "Der Olympische Typ," *Sport und Gesundheit*, no. 12, 1929, 180. Jack Schuhmacher-Paris, "Der Speerwerfer und die Läufer," *Start und Ziel* 5, no. 3, Mar. 1, 1929, 73.

72. Philipp Winter, "Rekordsport und persönlicher Sport," *Die Leibesübungen*, no. 8, Apr. 20, 1930, 214.

73. Kost, "Sportfrau und Frauensport," 53.

74. The article in *Der Leichtathlet* responded specifically to a set of accusations leveled by Professor Baetzner in the journal *Medizinische Welt* (Mar. 28, 1931). *Der Leichtathlet* 8, no. 15/16, Apr. 15, 1931, 3.

75. Anson Rabinbach, *The Human Motor: Energy, Fatigue, and the Origins of Modernity* (New York: Basic Books, 1990).

76. H. Peukert (gymnastics teacher), "Der Sport und die Dame," *Garçonne: Junggesellin*, no. 26, 1931, 6.

77. A number of parallels between 1806 and 1918 reinforced this response, starting with France's repeat role as the victorious, occupying power. Furthermore, the Treaty of Versailles, like the earlier Peace of Tilsit, severely limited the size of the Prussian/German army to 42,000 in 1806 and 100,000 in 1918.

78. For a good discussion of the scandal and of "hardened masculinity," see Marcus Funck, "Ready for War? Conceptions of Military Manliness in the Prusso-German Officer Corps before the First World War," in *Home/Front: The Military, War and Gender in Twentieth-Century Germany*, ed. Karen Hagemann and Stefanie Schüler-Springorum, 43–67 (New York: Berg, 2002).

79. The Deutscher Reichsausschuß für Leibesübungen referred to track and field athletes and other sportsmen as a "freiwillige Kerntruppe." Hajo Bernett, *Leichtathletik im geschichtlichen Wandel* (Schorndorf: Karl Hoffmann, 1987), 121.

80. Max Brandt, "Der Militärsport," *Illustrierter Sport*, Apr. 29, 1919, 17.

81. Dr. Ostrop, "Hans Hoffmeister," *Der Leichtathlet* 2, no. 36, Sept. 9, 1925, 5; and Martin Brustmann, "Was bedeuten die Olympischen Spiele für die deutsche Jugend?," *Der Leichtathlet* 4, no. 5, Feb. 1, 1927, 9; "Olympia-Nachspiel in Köln," *Der Leichtathlet* 5, no. 33, Aug. 14, 1928, 22–23; "Athletik Meisterschaften. Corts läuft 10,4 Sek," *B.Z. am Mittag*, 1; Beilage zum Sport [sports supplement], July 16, 1928, 1–2; *Zur Olympiade 1928*, ed. *B.Z. am Mittag* (Berlin: Ullstein, 1928), 24.

82. Heinz Cavalier, "Seid Heimkämpfer," *Der Leichtathlet* 4, no. 16, Apr. 20, 1927, 6.

83. Cavalier, "Front und Heimat," *Der Leichtathlet* 5, no. 33, Aug. 14, 1928, 6.

84. Carl Diem, "Das neue Ziel," in *Der Sport am Scheideweg*, ed. Willy Meisl, 160 (Heidelberg: Iris, 1928).

85. F. P. Lang, "Neujahrswünsche: Die Deutsche Sportbehörde für Leichtathletik," *Der Leichtathlet* 6, no. 53, Dec. 23, 1929, 3–4.

86. Martin Wagner (1929), quoted in Henning Eichberg, "Disziplinierung und grüne Wellen: Zur Sozialökologie der Berliner Sportstätten," in *Selbstbeherrschte Körper*, ed. Wolfgang Dreßen, 27 (Berlin: Verlag sthetik und Kommunikation, 1986).

87. See Hajo Bernett, *Leichtathletik in historischen Bilddokumenten* (Munich: Copress, 1986), 118, 177–86, which includes pictures of some of these competitions.

88. "Hindernislauf," *Illustrierter Sport* 8, no. 38, Sept. 21, 1920, 722.

89. Karl Halt, "Der Zehnkampf," *Sport im Bild* 27, no. 19, May 13, 1921, 677.

90. A number of magazines published this photograph. See, for one, *Sport und Sonne*, no. 11, Nov. 1928, 645.

91. "Glossen zum 11. September. Peltzer sollte filmen," *Der Leichtathlet* 3, no. 38. Sept. 21, 1926, 5.

92. Otto Peltzer, *Umkämpftes Leben: Sportjahre zwischen Nurmi und Zatopek* (Berlin: Verlag der Nation, 1955), 44.

93. *Hamburger Echo*, Aug. 4, 1928, 2.

94. Rumpelstilzchen, feuilleton from May 31, 1923, in *Und det jloobste?*, collected works, vol. 3, 1922/23 (Berlin: Brunnen, 1923), 259.

95. Wilhelm Dörr, "Großer Vormarsch deutschen Sports," *Sport und Sonne*, no. 9, Sept. 1928, 523. See also the article "Borner schlägt Körnig," which referred to one top 5,000-meter U.S. runner explicitly as German-American and the others as simply "American." *Der Leichtathlet* 2, no. 26, June 29, 1925, 14.

96. The author of this piece, Dr. K. Carl, identified himself as "an experienced sports teacher and racial expert ["Rassenkenner"]." "Amerika führt weiter! Das deutsche Element in der amerikanischen Athletik," *Sport und Sonne* 6, no. 8, Aug./Sept 1930, 267.

97. Hans Borowik, "Erlebtes und Erlauschtes," *Der Leichtathlet* 8, no. 30, Aug. 4, 1931, 13.

98. *Die Olympischen Spiele in Los Angeles 1932*, 53.

99. "Urteile der Sportpresse," *Der Leichtathlet* 9, no. 34, Aug. 23, 1932, 9.

100. See Gertrud Pfister, "'Das Geschlecht läuft immer mit': Frauen und Langstreckenlauf im medizinischen Diskurs," in *Langlauf durch die olympische Geschichte: Festschrift Karl Lennartz*, vol. 1, ed. Jürgen Buschmann and Stephen Wassong (Cologne: Carl und Liselott Diem-Archiv, 2005).

101. For data on the birthrate, see Atina Grossmann, *Reforming Sex: The German Movement for Birth Control and Abortion Reform, 1920–1950* (New York: Oxford University Press, 1995), 3. On the debates surrounding the quality of children born in Germany, see also Paul Weindling, *Health, Race, and German Politics Between National Unification and Nazism, 1870–1945* (New York: Cambridge University Press, 1989); and Michael Hau, *Cult of Health and Beauty in Germany*, 56.

102. "Rückblick auf die Berliner Leichtathletikzeit 1919," *Illustrierter Sport* 7, no. 30, Nov. 18, 1919, 596.

103. "Peltzer läuft 400m. in 48,9 Sek.," *Der Leichtathlet* 2, no. 19, May 11, 1925, 13.

104. Ann Taylor Allen, "German Radical Feminism and Eugenics, 1900–1908," *German Studies Review* 11 (1988): 34.

105. Frl. Schöppe, "Aussprache nach den Vorträgen," Mar. 22, 1925, at the Erste Öffentliche Tagung für die körperliche Erziehung der Frau (Landesarchiv Berlin: Helene-Lange-Archiv 3139, BDF Film 76-308(4), 65).

106. Mr. Buchgeister, "Ueber Frauensport," *Der Leichtathlet* 3, no. 33, Aug. 17, 1926, 22.

107. Charlotte Deppe, "Die Mutter und der Sport," in *Tagungs-Bericht: Frauen-Turn- und Sporttagung zu Berlin, 12. bis 15. Juni 1929* (Berlin: Fachbuchhandlung für Leibesübungen, 1929), 69.

108. Hugo Sellheim, "Auswertung der Gymnastik der Frau für die ärztliche Praxis," *Medizinische Klinik* 27 (1931): 1740, quoted in Gertrud Pfister, "Vom Mädchenreigen zum Body-Building. Zur Entwicklung des Frauensports in Berlin," in Pfister and Steins, *Sport in Berlin*, 156.

109. Kost, "Sportfrau und Frauensport," 51.

110. Hermann Fromme, "Die körperliche Ertüchtigung des weiblichen Geschlechts," *Damen-Sport und Sport-Turnen* 2, no. 10, May 1919, 109.

111. Buchgeister, "Ueber Frauensport,", 22.

112. Dr. med. Hermine Huesler-Edenhuizen, "Erfahrungen und Wünsche einer Frauenärztin," in *Die körperliche Ertüchtigung der Frau: Neun Vorträge gehalten auf der Ersten öffentlichen Tagung für die körperliche Ertüchtigung der Frau* (Berlin: F.A. Herbig, 1925), 26.

113. Grete Gräber, "Die Ehe der Sportlerin," *Der Leichtathlet* 5, no. 51/52, Dec. 18, 1928, 27.

114. Hildegard Fritsch, "Mütter treibt Sport! Ratschläge zur Körperpflege für Mütter," *Sport und Sonne* 5, no. 12, Sept. 15, 1929, 473.

115. Helmut Buchholz, "Gründet Mädchen- und Frauen-Abteilungen," *Start und Ziel* 2, no. 2, Feb. 1, 1926, 34.

116. Hajo Bernett, *Leichtathletik in geschichtlichen Wandel*, (Schorndorf: Karl Hoffmann, 1987), 127. The sports club SC Charlottenburg instituted the *Paarlauf* at its very first postwar meet in May 1919. See "Eine neue Art des 'Paarlaufens' beim Sportfest des S.C. Charlottenburg," *Damen-Sport und Damen-Turnen* 2, no. 9, May 1919, 105. For a much later example of this same practice, see the report on a 1929 track meet in Saxony, by Rolf Drax, "Frauensport in Mitteldeutschland," *Der Leichtathlet* 6, no. 4, Jan. 22, 1929, 16.

117. Gertrud Pfister, "Vom Mädchenreigen zum Body-Building. Zur Entwicklung des Frauensports in Berlin," in *Sport in Berlin*, 139.

118. "Die lustige Gymkhana-Staffel," *Der Leichtathlet* 4, no. 24, June 14, 1927, 23.

119. Controversy has surrounded the women's 800 meters again more recently, when the South African runner Caster Semenya's gold-medal–winning performance at the 2009 world track and field championships prompted some to question her biological sex.

120. Given that the meet took place in Paris, one might have expected a particularly triumphant outburst of patriotic gloating by the home press, but the blandly straightforward headline "German Women in Paris," in Germany's leading track and field journal, struck a surprisingly unemotional note. "Deutsche Frauen in Paris," *Der Leichtathlet* 3, no. 40, Oct. 5, 1926. 14.

121. Bryan Field, "U.S. Girl Athletes Best at Sprinting," *New York Times*, June 20, 1928, 31.

122. "Frauenwettkämpfe in Göteborg," *Der Leichtathlet* 3, no. 36, Sept. 7, 1926, 23.

123. "Deutscher Frauensport marschiert!," *Sport und Sonne*, no. 8, Aug. 1927, 466.

124. "Frauen-Meisterschaften," *Sport und Sonne*, no. 8, Aug. 1927, 518. Lina Batschauer had captured the German championship in the 1,000 meters in 1926. The following year, the track and field association shortened the distance to 800 meters, in order to conform to the new Olympic distance, and Batschauer won that event also, at the 1927 championships.

125. "Die einzige Goldmedaille für Deutschland: Frau Radtkes Weltrekord," *Der Leichtathlet* 5, no. 32, Aug. 7, 1928. cover, 9. The press spelled her last name as both "Radke" and "Radtke." Based on recent biographies, I have settled on the former spelling.

126. *Vossische Zeitung*, no. 184, Aug. 3, 1928, 15.

127. *Berliner Tageblatt* 57, no. 363, Aug. 3, 1928, 1 (sports sec.). Along with Radke-Batschauer, two other German women also qualified for the final heat of eight competitors.

128. "Deutschlands Leicthathletik-Meister," *Illustriertes Sportblatt, 1. Beiblatt des Berliner Tageblatts*. July 16, 1928, 1.

129. Willy Meisl, "Die Leichtathletik," in *Die Olympischen Spiele in Amsterdam 1928*, 48.

130. Eugen Wagener, "Die erste Goldene auf der Aschenbahn," *B.Z. am Mittag*, Aug. 3, 1928, 1, sports sec.

131. Charlie Roellinghoff, "Siegreiche Amazonen!" *B.Z. am Mittag*, Aug. 4, 1928, 5.

132. Fred Hildenbrandt, "Die Olympischen Girls," *Berliner Tageblatt*, Aug. 9, 1928, 1, sports sec.

133. Advertisement for Kola Dallmann, *Berliner Tageblatt*, Aug. 22, 1928, 1, 3, Beiblatt [supplement].

134. Heinz Cavalier, "Amsterdamer Tagebuch," *Der Leichtathlet* 5, no. 33, Aug. 14, 1928, 11.

135. P. Schopf, "Die Mittelstrecke," *Der Leichtathlet* 5, no. 36, Sept. 4, 1928. 18.

136. Erich Harte, "Die Olympischen Spiele 1928 in Amsterdam," *Die Leibesübungen*, no. 21, Nov. 5, 1928, 525. When Harte noted that the International Women's Track and Field Association had decided to keep the 800 meters in its 1930 World Women's Games, he might have added that the association had sanctioned the race since 1922, without a problem.

137. Dr. Lina Müller-Passavant, "Der Kampfsport!" a response to an article in *Berliner Morgenpost*, by G. K., *Der Leichtathlet* 5, no. 47, Nov. 20, 1928. 19.

138. Milly Reuter, "Die Frau im Sport," in *Welt-Olympia 1928 in Wort und Bild*, ed. Josef Waitzer and Wilhelm Dörr, 97 (Berlin: Conzett und Huber, 1928). Reuter had finished fourth in the discus competition at the 1928 Games.

139. Dr. Fr. Messerli, "Die Wettkämpfe der Damen," in *Die Olympischen Spiele 1928. St. Moritz–Amsterdam*, ed. Julius Wagner, Fritz Klipstein, and Dr. Fr. Messerli, 65 (Zurich/Stuttgart: Julius Wagner, 1928).

140. Dr. Mallwitz, in response to a speech by the women's sports advocate Alice Prof, in *Tagungs-Bericht*, 17.

141. Dr. Hede Bergmann, in response to Dr. Franzmeyer, who responded to a paper by Dr. Elsa Matz, "Die Frau und der sportliche Wettkampf," in *Tagungs-Bericht*, 55.

142. "Prager Gedanken," *Start und Ziel* 6, 1930, 303–5; quoted in Gertrud Pfister, "Breaking Bounds: Alice Profé, Radical and Emancipationist," in *Freeing the Female Body: Inspirational Icons*, ed. J. A. Mangan and Fan Hong, 106 (Portland, OR: Frank Cass, 2001).

143. Gertrud Pfister, ed. *Frau und Sport* (Frankfurt/M: Fischer, 1980), 36.

144. Quoted in Hajo Bernett, *Leichtathletik in geschichtlichen Wandel* (Schorndorf: Karl Hoffmann, 1987), 176.

145. Walther von Hollander, "Frauensport—aber richtig!" *Die Koralle: Magazin für alle Freunde von Natur und Technik* 29, July 19, 1936, 961.

146. *New York Times*, Aug. 17, 1936, quoted in David Clay Large, *Nazi Games: The Olympics of 1936* (New York: W. W. Norton and Company, 2007), 290.

147. Bergmann emigrated to the United States in 1937, where she reigned as the national champion in the women's high jump in 1937 and 1938 and in the women's shot put in 1937. She returned to Germany for the first time in 2002, when her hometown of Laupheim renamed its sports stadium in her honor. See Ira Berkow, "Long Overdue, Germany Recognizes a Champion," *New York Times*, Oct. 28, 2002, D11.

148. Adolf Hitler, *Mein Kampf* (New York: Stackpole Sons, 1939 [orig. 1925]), 210.

149. Gregor Land, "Der Sport und die Langeweile," *Der Querschnitt* 13, no. 2 (Feb. 1933): 98.

150. Quoted in Keys, *Globalizing Sport*, 125.

Conclusion

1. Willy Meisl, "Vorschau in Vergangenheit," in *Der Sport am Scheidewege*, ed. Willy Meisl, 83 (Heidelberg: Iris, 1928).

2. Wolfgang Graeser, *Körpersinn: Gymnastik-Tanz-Sport* (1927), repr. in *Der Sport im Kreuzfeuer der Kritik: Kritische Texte aus 100 Jahren deutscher Sportgeschichte*, ed. Hajo Bernett, 133 (Schorndorf: Karl Hoffmann, 1982).

3. Hans Gragün, "Sport-Exhibitionismus," *Das Tage-Buch* 2, no. 2, Jan. 15, 1921, 47.

4. The tennis player Gottfried von Cramm and the middle-distance runner Otto Peltzer, to give just two of the most prominent examples, suffered persecution under the Nazi regime for having violated Paragraph 175, which banned all expressions of same-sex desire. Neither one had openly professed such desires during the Weimar Republic, despite that era's much-vaunted tolerance. Cramm married twice, and Peltzer cultivated a monastic image. See Manfred Herzer, "Die Strafakte Gottfried von Cramm, Berlin 1938," *Capri: Zeitschrift für schwule Geschichte* 4, no. 1 (June 1991): 3–14; and Manfred Herzer, "Dr. Otto Peltzer—Ein Pädophiler überlebt den Nazi-Terror," *Capri: Zeitschrift für schwule Geschichte*, no. 27 (Dec. 1999): 32–34.

5. Arthur Gütt, "Frau und Volksgesundheit," in *N.S. Frauenbuch*, ed. Ellen Semmelroth and Renate von Stieda, 129–30 (Munich, 1934), quoted in "Women, Men, and Unification: Gender Politics and the Abortion Struggle Since 1989," Jay Mushaaben, Sara Lenox, and Geoffrey Giles, in Konrad Jarausch, *After Unity*, 144 (Providence, RI: Berghahn, 1997).

6. Quoted in Irene Guenther, *Nazi Chic? Fashioning Women in the Third Reich* (New York: Berg, 2004), 122.

7. SS Obergruppenführer Jeckeln, "Ein Wort an die Frauen," *Frankfurter Zeitung*, June 1, 1937; quoted in Guenther, *Nazi Chic?*, 99. On the continuities

between Weimar and Nazi Germany with regard to women's sports, see also Gertrud Pfister, "Biologie als Schicksal: Zur Frauen-, Gesundheits- und Sportpolitik im Nationalsozialismus," in *Frauen-Räume: Körper und Identität im Sport,* ed. Sabine Kröner und Gertrud Pfister, 41–60 (Pfaffenweiler: Centaurus, 1992).

8. Christine Walther, *Siegertypen: Zur fotografischen Vermittlung eines gesellschaftlichen Selbstbildes um 1900* (Würzburg: Königshausen & Neumann, 2007), 137.

9. Quoted in Sander Gilman, *Making the Body Beautiful: A Cultural History of Aesthetic Surgery* (Princeton, NJ: Princeton University Press, 1999), 179.

10. See Thomas Alkemeyer, "Normbilder des Menschen: Der männliche Sportler-Körper in der Staatsästhetik des 'Dritten Reichs,'" *Sozial- und Zeitgeschichte des Sports* 6, no. 3 (Nov. 1992): 72–73.

11. Götz Aly, *Hitler's Beneficiaries: Plunder, Racial War, and the Nazi Welfare State,* trans. Jefferson Chase (New York: Henry Holt, 2006), 322.

12. The sports historian Gertrud Pfister makes these points on women's sports in "Cold War Diplomats in Tracksuits: The *Fräuleinwunder* of East German Sport," in *Militarism, Sport, Europe: War without Weapons,* ed. J. A. Mangan, 223–52 (Portland, OR: Frank Cass, 2003). For more on sports in the German Democratic Republic in general, see Molly Wilkinson Johnson, *Training Socialist Citizens: Sports and the State in East Germany* (Leiden: Brill, 2008). For a discussion of the GDR's use of performance-enhancing drugs, see Steven Ungerleider, *Faust's Gold: Inside the East German Doping Machine* (New York: St. Martin's Press, 2001).

13. Alice Schwarzer, "Panik im Patriarchat," interview in *Der Spiegel,* no. 22, May 29, 2006, 100.

14. Nadine, quoted in "Hitliste," *Berliner Zeitung,* special sec. "Zeitung in der Schule," May 7, 1999, 17.

15. For an example of the Levi's advertisement, see *Der Spiegel,* no. 39, 1998, 270–71. For a profile of Fikriye Selen near the peak of her celebrity, see Gerhard Pfeil, "Stabile Seitenlage," *Der Spiegel,* no. 14, Apr. 5, 1999, 242.

16. Quoted in Gerhard Pfeil, "Wasser in den Augen," *Der Spiegel,* no. 36, Sept. 8, 2005, 107. For another example of an immigrant seeking upward mobility in German society through boxing, see the interview with the Turkish boxer Oktay Urkal, "Paradies auf Erden," *Der Spiegel,* no. 30, 1996, 133.

17. Selena Roberts, "After Showing Some Skin, Haas Shows His Mettle," *New York Times,* Aug. 29, 2002, C17.

18. Jörg Kramer, "Der Lernfußballer," *Der Spiegel,* no. 21, May 19, 2008, 124.

Index

CPSIA information can be obtained at www.ICGtesting.com
Printed in the USA
BVOW08s2133281115

428542BV00003B/18/P